Turkish Immigrants in the European Union

In October 2005, Turkey officially started the first phase of the accession process towards European Union membership. Many analysts and politicians predict this process will be long and difficult; Turkish membership may not happen before 2014–15, if at all.

Amongst the many tough, contested issues that will mark the accession process will be immigration and integration. Opponents highlight that many Turkish immigrants, due to cultural differences, have failed to integrate into their host societies. Yet, there are also those who claim that Turkey is a dynamic society whose growing educated population could help address the dilemmas of shrinking and aging populations faced by most EU member countries. They also argue Turkey is economically growing, and democratic with a buoyant civil society which would assist integration.

This book is an analytical and empirically based contribution to the ongoing debate, addressing questions such as

- What are the demographic trends in Turkey compared to those of current EU member countries?
- What is the potential scope of immigration from Turkey to the EU?
- What will be the driving forces of immigration from Turkey under alternative scenarios?
- What can be predicted concerning the composition of this immigration?
- How will these trends affect Turkish immigrants in Europe?
- What is the integration problem of Turkish immigrants, what form does it take and what can be done about it?

This book was previously published as a special issue of *Turkish Studies*.

Refik Erzan is a Professor of Economics at Bogaziçi University

Kemal Kirişci is Jean Monnet Professor of European Integration at Bogaziçi University

Turkish Immigrants in the European Union

Determinants of Immigration and Integration

Edited by Refik Erzan and Kemal Kirişci

Routledge
Taylor & Francis Group

London and New York

First published 2008 by Routledge
2 Park Square, Milton Park, Abingdon, Oxon, OX14 4RN

Simultaneously published in the USA and Canada
by Routledge
270 Madison Ave, New York NY 10016

Routledge is an imprint of the Taylor & Francis Group, an informa business

Transferred to Digital Printing 2009

Typeset in Times by Genesis Typesetting Ltd, Rochester, Kent

British Library Cataloguing in Publication Data
A catalogue record for this book is available from the British Library

Library of Congress Cataloging in Publication Data

ISBN 10: 0-415-41401-6 (hbk)
ISBN 10: 0-415-49527-X (pbk)

ISBN 13: 978-0-415-41401-2 (hbk)
ISBN 13: 978-0-415-49527-1 (pbk)

Contents

Notes on Contributors

The editors:

Refik Erzan is a Professor at the Department of Economics, Boğaziçi University, Istanbul. He is also the Director of the Center for Economics and Econometrics and Deputy Director of the Center for European Studies. Erzan received his PhD in Economics from the University of Stockholm at the Institute for International Economic Studies. He served as an economist/consultant at UNCTAD and ILO in Geneva, and UNIDO in Vienna, and as a senior economist at the World Bank in Washington, DC. Erzan's field is international economics, particularly international trade. His policy-oriented research topics include European integration.

Kemal Kirişci is a Professor in the Department of Political Science and International Relations at Boğaziçi University, Istanbul. He holds a Jean Monnet Chair in European Integration and is also the director of the Center for European Studies at the university. He received his PhD at City University in London. His areas of research interest include European integration, asylum, border control and immigration issues in the European Union, EU–Turkish relations, Middle Eastern politics, ethnic conflicts, and refugee movements. He has previously taught at universities in Britain, Switzerland and the United States.

The contributors:

Gamze Avcı is a Research Fellow at the Department of Turkish Studies at Leiden University since 2003 and has served as Assistant Professor at Boğaziçi University, Istanbul (1997–2002). She specializes in Turkish immigration to Western Europe and Turkey's relations with the European Union. Her work has appeared in journals like *European Foreign Affairs Review*, *European Journal of Political Research*, and *European Journal of Migration and Law*.

Cem Behar is Professor of Economics and Vice-President in charge of Academic Affairs (Provost), at Boğaziçi University, Istanbul. He has a PhD in Economics and trained as an economist and demographer at the University of Paris-I (Panthéon-Sorbonne) and the Institut de Démographie de l'Université de Paris. Behar taught at the University of Paris (Paris-I), the University of Washington (Seattle) and the

Ecole des Hautes Etudes en Sciences Sociales (Paris). Areas of special interest are population dynamics and historical demography.

Dirk Jacobs is Associate Professor of Sociology at the (Francophone) Free University of Brussels (ULB) and at the (Flemish) KUBrussel. He is a member of the *Groupe d'études sur l'Ethnicité, le Racisme, les Migrations et l'Exclusion* (GERME) of the *Institut de Sociologie* at the *Université Libre de Bruxelles* (ULB).

Hubert Krieger is a research manager of the Living Conditions Unit at the European Foundation for the Improvement of Living and Working Conditions, which is an EU agency that provides information for policy making, specifically at EU level. He is currently working on new development projects on the interface between living and working conditions, on a new monitoring instrument on the quality of life in an enlarged Europe and mobility between EU member states and immigration to the EU from third countries. He is an expert on industrial relations, labor law, workers' participation, employment, work organization, financial participation, work–life balance and equal opportunities. He is the author of several books and articles. He holds a PhD in social policy and labor market economics from the University of Cologne and a MSc in European social policy from University College Dublin.

Bertrand Maître is a research analyst at the Economic and Social Research Institute, Dublin. He is a graduate of Economics in the University of La Sorbonne Paris-I in 1990. He is currently involved in a number of projects using a range of European and Irish data sets. His research interests include the distribution and packaging of household income and multidimensional approaches to poverty and social exclusion. He has published recently on these issues in the *European Sociological Review* and the *Journal of European Social Policy*.

Karen Phalet is a Research Fellow at ERCOMER (*European Research Center on Migration and Ethnic Relations*) and Associate Professor of Cross-Cultural Studies at Utrecht University, the Netherlands.

Veysel Özcan studied social sciences in Mannheim, Amsterdam and Berlin, where he received his Diploma (Masters) in 2002. He worked as a researcher at Humboldt University Berlin and the Social Science Centre Berlin. Currently he is an adviser on immigration and integration policy in the office of Cem Özdemir, member of the European Parliament.

Janina Söhn studied sociology at the Free University Berlin (Germany) and at the New School for Social Research (USA). Since 2003 she has been a researcher at the "Programme Intercultural Conflicts and Societal Integration" at the Social Science Research Centre Berlin (WZB). She has worked on issues of education, language and integration of immigrants as well as citizenship and naturalization.

Marc Swyngedouw is Professor of Political Sociology at the Catholic Universities of Leuven and Brussels, and an academic director of ISPO (*Institute for Social and Political Opinion Research*), Catholic University of Leuven (KULeuven).

Christiane Timmerman has a PhD in Social and Cultural Anthropology (KULeuven). She is coordinator of the research unit on Ethnic Minorities and Migration, the Research Policy Centre of Equal Opportunities and the Research Group on Poverty, Social Exclusion and the City (OASeS) at the University of Antwerp. She teaches anthropology and is co-chairwoman of the Antwerp Centre on Migration Studies (ACMS). She is also Director of Academic Affairs of the University Centre St Ignatius, Antwerp (UCSIA)

Johan Wets (PhD Social Sciences) is a senior research associate of the Higher Institute for Labor Studies of the University of Leuven. He is also Assistant Professor of Comparative Sociology of the Catholic University of Brussels. His research interests are migration dynamics, the link between migration and development, the integration of the migrant population in the host communities and other migration-related topics.

Introduction

REFİK ERZAN[*] & KEMAL KİRİŞCİ[**]

*Department of Economics, Boğaziçi University, Istanbul, Turkey, **Department of Political Science, Boğaziçi University, Istanbul, Turkey

Turkish immigration has long been important in European–Turkish relations. What started out as temporary labor migration in the early 1960s has culminated in a Turkish community of more than 3 million immigrants and their families in European countries, excluding those immigrants that became naturalized.[1] Most of these migrants reside in Germany, followed by France, Holland, Austria, Britain and Belgium.[2] Officially-sanctioned labor migration from Turkey to European countries came to a halt almost entirely in the mid-1970s. However, in the following decades, family reunification and formation, as well as asylum, continued to be used as channels of immigration. Turkish authorities estimate that around 60–70,000 Turkish nationals continue to migrate to European countries each year. In addition, there is also a certain level of illegal migration taking place from Turkey to Europe.

The presence of a large Turkish immigrant community and the prospect of Turkish immigration deeply mark the relations between the European Union and Turkey. This has become increasingly obvious over the last few years. A critical turning point was the decision of the European Council's Copenhagen summit in December 2002 to review Turkey's progress in meeting the Copenhagen political criteria and accordingly start accession negotiations "without delay." Subsequently, opponents of Turkish membership in Europe steadily increased the level of their objections to the idea of Turkish membership. The pitch of objections reached an especially high level during the run-up to the European Council summit in December 2004 and the Council of General Affairs and External Relations meeting in October 2005—when finally the decision was taken to start accession negotiations with Turkey. Opposition to Turkish membership has been partly based on a fear of a "flood" of Turkish nationals entering EU countries. Additionally, many have also pointed to the difficulties faced by Turkish immigrants to integrate themselves into their host societies. This "integration" problem has been used as evidence for how Turkey does not and cannot fit culturally into Europe.

Correspondence Address: Refik Erzan, Department of Economics, Center for Economics and Econometrics, Boğaziçi University, 34342 Bebek, Istanbul, Turkey. Email: erzan@boun.edu.tr; Kemal Kirişci, Department of Political Science, Director of the Center for European Studies, Boğaziçi University, 34342 Bebek, Istanbul, Turkey. Email: kirisci@boun.edu.tr

Opponents of Turkish membership allege that as membership will allow Turkish nationals to enjoy the right to "free movement of labor and persons" millions of Turks will migrate to EU countries in search of jobs. They argue that this will increase unemployment and worsen the cultural clash between Turks and local Europeans. They attribute the integration problems that many Turkish immigrants experience to fundamental cultural and religious differences. These differences are then employed to reinforce their broader argument that Turkey basically is not "European" and should not become a member of the European Union. Instead, they have argued that Turkey should be extended an undefined "privileged relationship" with the European Union. These have been powerful arguments that have resonated with public opinion in Europe. Although these arguments failed to prevent the start of accession negotiations they nevertheless left a deep imprint on the "Negotiation Framework for Turkey" adopted at the General Affairs Council on October 3, 2005.[3] This document, which will govern the accession negotiations, makes it amply clear that there will be long transitional periods before Turkish nationals will be able to enjoy the right to "free movement of labor" if and when membership takes place. Furthermore, the document envisages for individual EU members the possibility after accession to continue to restrict this right even after the transitional periods are over.

The issue of immigration and the integration of immigrants have acquired importance in the EU independently of Turkey. It was at the November 1999 Tampere Council meeting that an ambitious agenda to develop common EU policies on asylum and immigration was adopted.[4] It was in particular the issue of stopping and combating illegal migration into the EU that acquired particular attention and urgency in subsequent years. Simultaneously, the issue of the integration of migrants from third countries also attracted growing attention.[5] The European Commission went as far as adopting a *Handbook on Integration* to assist the individual efforts of member countries.[6] This was also a period of growing recognition of demographic trends in EU countries that pointed at their steadily ageing and falling population. Inevitably, this has led to calls that the EU will need to import labor at some point in the future. Nevertheless, most EU member countries remained reluctant to entertain the idea of encouraging labor immigration other than in the most restricted manner.

In November 2004, it was the turn of the Hague Council to adopt an ambitious program for a second generation of policies on immigration and integration issues.[7] This time, compared to Tampere, especially the issue of integration of third-country immigrants received greater attention. However, decision making in this area remained within the competence of member states, with the European Commission's role limited to preparing reports and studies. The Commission's report on managing economic migration is a case in point. The Commission soberly points out the need for immigrants in EU countries.[8] However, the issue of immigration continues to be hostage to the harsh realities of domestic politics in member countries.

Anti-immigration sentiments in many EU member countries play a central role in the resistance against Turkey's prospects of EU membership. Paradoxically, this is occurring at a time when there is also a growing recognition that given the ageing problem and demographic trends in Europe there will actually be a need in Europe for a member with a young and dynamic population.[9] This fear and concern of Turkish immigration is driven by many factors, of which an important one concerns the difficulties that a large proportion of Turkish immigrants have faced in respect to integrating themselves into their host societies. In Europe many do not hesitate to attribute this failure to integrate to profound "cultural" differences between Turkey and Europe. Clearly, the problem of integration that Turkish immigrants face is much more complicated than the rather simplistic manner in which the issue is often handled by European public opinion. Firstly, there are many Turkish immigrants who have indeed integrated and done quite well in their host societies.[10] Furthermore, integration is a two-way process. The absence of an environment sympathetic to addressing the challenges that immigrants face aggravates the problem of integration.[11] In the meantime, the issue of Turkish immigrants in Europe and the problem of their integration continues to cast a dark shadow on the "pre-accession" period and the politics surrounding accession negotiations.

The peculiarities of Turkish accession as well as developments within the EU suggest that issues related to immigration and integration will remain central to the future of EU–Turkish relations. It will constitute an important part of the official agenda, attract public interest as well as lead to growing academic interest. These are some of the questions that will be pertinent to the coming years of EU–Turkish relations: Will there be immigration from Turkey to EU member countries? What will drive immigration from Turkey? What will the composition of this immigration be? What are the demographic trends in Turkey compared to the ones in EU member countries? How will these trends impact on Turkish immigration and demand for immigrants in Europe? What is the integration problem of Turkish immigrants? What form does it take? What can be done?

Immigration and Integration Issues

"Immigration" remains a relatively easy term to define. Factors that drive immigration are also reasonably straightforward. Country of origin and host country demographics, economics, politics and social factors as well as the relationship between existing stocks and new flows play a critical role in determining the rate and composition of immigration. On the other hand, "integration" is a much more complicated term to define. Literature in this regard is much more ambiguous and inconclusive. What constitutes "integration" remains multidimensional and complex as well as nebulous.[12] This is also further complicated by the constant efforts to distinguish between "assimilation" and "integration" whereas the two terms appear to be more of a continuum. In turn, these issues are closely tied to definitions of citizenship and national identity in host countries.[13]

In the case of both "immigration" and "integration" over the last few years there has also been a growing recognition of the interaction between host and sending countries at the societal as well as governmental level. Unlike in the case of the nineteenth century, in recent decades immigrants have not simply ruptured their connections and ties to their home countries. In that sense, transnationalism has been an important and growing phenomenon complicating the integration picture.[14] Furthermore, it has also been recognized that the policies adopted by sending states are also very important in respect to the nature of immigration and the issue of integration. This inevitably points at the need for better appreciation of the manner in which host and sending country policies interact and impact on each other.

In a number of European countries and especially in Germany, for a long time there was a reluctance to accept immigration for what it is: immigration. Instead, a constant assumption that the migrants were "guest workers" who would one day return home prevailed. It is only over the last decade or so that serious thought has begun to be given to the "integration" of the "guest workers" of yesterday and "immigrants" of today. On the other hand, those countries whose political systems were more realistic about what they were facing, such as Holland, Belgium (partly), France, Denmark and Sweden, introduced diverse policies to manage the integration of immigrants. France is a special case in the sense that it aimed, at least theoretically, to assimilate immigrants, while the others adopted various shades of multicultural approaches. What is striking is that whatever the approach, whether be it the French assimilationist, the German exclusionary, the Dutch multicultural or the Scandinavian welfare-paternalistic approaches, they all seem to encounter the problems associated with weak integration on the part of immigrants in respect of employment, education, political participation and social integration.

Turkey itself, too, for a long time considered Turkish immigrants in Europe as "guest workers" and expected that they would one day return home. Turkish policies towards them were very much determined by these considerations. It is only recently that it has been recognized that many are there to stay. More recently, this has been reflected in Turkish governments' encouragement of Turkish immigrants to take up citizenship of the countries in which they reside. However, the notion that both the Turkish government and European civil society could be partners in the efforts to meet the challenges raised by the failure of the integration of Turkish immigrants is still at the early stages of consideration. The prospects of cooperation between Turkey and the European Union in respect of the integration of the current stock of Turkish immigrants will depend on the form that the future of EU–Turkish relations takes. A Turkey that is advancing towards EU membership, with the intensification of relationship between Turkish and European governments and civil society, is likely to be able to contribute to meeting the challenge of integration. The opposite is likely to happen if Turkey drifts away from its membership aspirations.

Another aspect of EU–Turkish relations is that the nature and composition of the Turkish immigrant stock in Europe is likely to change with EU membership. This could have important consequences in terms of both the challenge of integrating the existing stock but also in terms of ameliorating the negative public opinion in Europe towards Turkish membership. EU–Turkish relations have been transformed dramatically since the 1999 Helsinki European Council when Turkey was given candidate status for membership. Turkey has profoundly transformed itself economically and politically. Pre-accession will most probably accelerate this transformation, which will have important consequences in terms of immigration and integration issues.

Firstly, the developments in the Turkish economy and politics will have an impact on Turks' decision to migrate or not. This will also influence the type of immigrants that may move from Turkey to EU countries. The existing patterns of immigration characterized by family reunification and family formation, driven by the current Turkish immigrant stock in Europe, will be accompanied by a movement of labor and persons that is likely to be better educated and more professional. This will inevitably generate new social and political dynamics within the Turkish communities in Europe but also between them and the host societies. The patterns of education, socialization and participation in the politics of host societies are likely to change. This in turn will transform the social and political environment surrounding the issue of the integration of the existing stock as well as improve host society perceptions of Turkish immigrants and of Turkey.

Secondly, a Turkey that is becoming increasingly integrated in the European Union will less and less appear as the "other" in Europe. An important aspect of the integration problem of Turkish immigrants, closely associated with a sense of being treated differently and of alienation from mainstream society, would be solved through the process of becoming part of the host society. In a similar vein, the efforts to address the demographic challenges and the ageing problem that most European societies face will become relatively easier as the tendency to see Turks as the "other" becomes eroded.

Thirdly, it is also likely that if EU–Turkish relations progress smoothly Turks will increasingly be seen as partners in addressing the challenges associated with demographic decline. This sense of partnership should also help initiate the prospects of greater contacts between European and Turkish civil society. Civil society in Turkey, partly as a function of EU involvement, has grown and become more effective over the last couple of years. There are a number of influential non-governmental organizations that address the issues of "honor killings" and female education, for example. These non-governmental organizations could eventually cooperate with their counterparts in EU countries in addressing similar problems among Turkish immigrant communities. Furthermore, it is likely that as immigration and integration issues are increasingly handled at the EU level rather than just at the national level, addressing these challenges, with the support of European and Turkish civil society, may also become somewhat easier.

In the meantime, Turkish immigrants continue to face major difficulties in respect of integration. Turkish immigrants perform poorly in the new employment environment in which they find themselves, which has changed drastically since the 1960s and 1970s. A significant portion of the current "stock" of immigrants suffers from unemployment. The failure of labor integration is very closely linked to education: Turkish immigrant children by and large perform poorly compared to German children and immigrant children from many other countries. This, in turn, inevitably aggravates the difficulties in accessing the labor market and achieving broader integration into the host society.

Another important aspect of integration involves civic participation. Turkish immigrants—compared to other immigrants and sometimes even to the host society—appear to have a lively associational life. Until recently this associational life was centered around developments back in Turkey rather than being focused on the politics of host societies. This has generally been highlighted as a development complicating integration as immigrants remained politically isolated from local politics. However, more recently Turkish immigrant activists have noted that there is a fledgling associational life that is beginning to focus on the problems of immigrants as well as broader local issues of interest to the communities in which immigrants live. These activists have also reported that associations that do indeed take an interest in local politics and the integration problems of immigrants are increasingly taken seriously by local politicians and authorities in their respective host societies. This may open avenues of civic participation that can help cooperation between immigrants and their host communities. This in turn may facilitate the development of better integration policies.

Social integration, with its many facets, is another challenge. One very important facet has to do with the place and status of women in the Turkish immigrant communities. Gender relations within the Turkish immigrant community deeply impact on host society perceptions of Turkey as well as of Turkish immigrants. The relationship between integration and gender is multifaceted. The isolation of women from the rest of the society, especially among conservative Turkish immigrants, and the issue of arranged marriages, have serious consequences for integration. This manifests itself particularly through the impact it has on education and socialization of immigrant children. Furthermore, it provokes negative public perceptions of the Turkish immigrants themselves, further aggravating the problem of integration by complicating the relationship between the immigrants and the rest of society.

These challenges have been aggravated by host as well as sending country policies or the lack of policies towards immigration and integration. The existing stock of immigrants in a host country from a particular source has an overriding impact on the composition of new migrants and their behavior. In the absence of coordinated immigration and integration policies, this "network effect" tends to multiply the existing patterns and problems.

The Volume

We recognize that it would be too ambitious to address in one volume all aspects of the "immigration" and "integration" paradox from both a conceptual and a policy perspective. Nevertheless, in the context of evolving and intensifying EU–Turkish relations we believe that we can start to address at least some aspects of this complexity and where possible also raise some policy recommendations. Firstly, now that EU–Turkish relations are entering the pre-accession period, the need to address the relationship between potential future Turkish immigration and the old immigrant stock and the challenge of their integration is an issue that deserves systematic attention.

Secondly, taking stock of the integration problems facing Turkish immigrants and the challenges ahead at a time when the accession of Turkey is on the cards but Europe is entering a difficult period of "soul searching" seems to be a timely exercise. While Europe increasingly recognizes that the integration failure is also partly Europe's responsibility, in most of the key EU member states anti-immigrant feelings are on the rise. The picture is further complicated by a rising recognition that Europe is ageing and that immigration, though politically a terribly difficult issue, appears to be one of the options for addressing the demographic problems of Europe.

Thirdly, in light of these developments there is a window of opportunity in terms of synergies that could be created between immigration and integration policies for the receiving countries as well as for Turkey. Particularly, more liberal immigration policies would dilute the overriding impact of the existing stock of migrants on immigration and integration issues and open up new perspectives.

Fourthly, the EU itself seems to be a new factor. Until late 1990s, immigration-related issues were addressed at the national level. However, member states are increasingly recognizing the need to cooperate much more closely. Immigration and integration issues are far from being transferred to the EU decision-making level. Yet, as the Tampere and Hague Programmes suggest, there is growing pressure on the member states to involve the institutions of the EU. The EU itself could become a "tool" for encouraging the creation of synergies but also a more conducive environment for addressing and tackling the challenges associated with immigration and integration.

The contributions to this volume result from a project supported by the Open Society Institute Assistance Foundation focusing on immigration issues in EU–Turkish relations. The project was started in the autumn of 2003. It aimed to bring these issues to public attention in Turkey and to start a dialogue between Turkish and European academics. The project also aspired to provide research-based information and knowledge for those taking part in the larger debate on EU–Turkish relations. Three workshops and one conference were held during the course of 2004 at Boğaziçi University. Papers by academics, officials and members of civil society were presented and discussed. A majority of these papers can be found on the website of the Center for European Studies at Boğaziçi University (http://www.ces.boun.edu.tr).

The essays in this volume are divided into two parts. The first set deal with the issue of immigration from Turkey. Cem Behar in "Demographic Developments and Complementarities: Ageing, Labor and Migration" starts by challenging the view of those that see a complementarity between the population of Turkey and the demographic structures of the countries of the European Union. He argues that this notion of complementarity is devoid of any solid demographic foundation. The idea of a demographic "complementarity" between a "young" Turkey and an "older" Europe is considered to be the product either of wishful thinking or of an irrational fear of massive and uncontrollable immigration and of its effects on the labor market and unemployment. Young immigrants required to prevent the effects of an ageing population would have to make up an unrealistically large flow, while the immigrant population itself would be ageing in the host country. Behar, on the other hand, using basic demographic data, shows that managing migration will soon have to become a European priority—rather than, as the current EU policy amounts to, trying to prevent migration. Demographic differentials, he notes, will not disappear overnight and it is high time for Europe to consider the alternative of turning these temporary demographic differentials into an advantage and to make migration a socially and politically acceptable issue.

In light of the demographic imbalances between Europe and Turkey analyzed by the first study, Refik Erzan, Umut Kuzubaş and Nilüfer Yıldız in "Immigration Scenarios: Turkey–EU" directly address the question of the size of the Turkish immigration that might actually take place. The study estimates the eventual immigration from Turkey to the EU when Turkey becomes a full member. Alternative methods and growth scenarios are scrutinized in forecasting probable migration flows. The analyses are essentially based on the experience of countries that joined the EU. The estimation methods are those used in recent studies scrutinizing the membership consequences of the Central and East European countries. Special attention was paid to the experience of the southern "cohesion" countries—Greece, Portugal and Spain. Finally, forecasts are also made based primarily on the Turkish emigration record. The simulation results for net migration from Turkey to EU-15 in the period 2004–2030 is between 1 and 2 million, foreseeing a successful accession period with high growth and free labor mobility starting in 2015—a rather optimistic assumption exploring the upper limits of the immigration potential. On the other hand, if Turkey's membership process is endangered and high growth cannot be sustained, the authors estimate that a higher number of people may penetrate the EU despite the prevailing strict restrictions on labor mobility.

In "Migration Trends in an Enlarging European Union," Hubert Krieger and Bertrand Maître set out the broader picture in respect of immigration trends inside the European Union. The piece highlights that migration covers a wide range of important challenges as high unemployment in major receiving countries of the EU, the concern in regard to the social and cultural integration of migrants and the reduced social cohesion of receiving countries due to the lack of civic and political participation. Within this context, the focus of this contribution is on labor market issues of migration towards the old EU-15 from three regions: the NEW10, the two accession countries entering in 2007 (Romania/Bulgaria) and Turkey. The study addresses in particular two questions: i) What is the expected volume of migration into the "old" member states? ii) What is the structure of potential migrants from the NEW10, the two accession countries and from Turkey? While the Erzan *et al.* study pursues the econometric route, this study is based on *Eurobarometer* survey data collected for the European Commission in spring 2002.

The second set of contributions addresses the question of the integration of Turkish immigrants in a number of EU member countries. Integration policies in Europe diverge and converge in different ways. Yet it seems that in all receiving West European societies integration is incomplete or imperfect. Gamze Avcı in

"Comparing Integration Policies and Outcomes: Turks in the Netherlands and Germany" focuses on one of the largest immigration groups in both countries, namely the Turks and their cultural, social and economic incorporation. For that purpose, she overviews developments in patterns of political participation and organization, labor-market performance, housing issues, social welfare, educational achievements and language capabilities of Turks in these two countries. These specific "integration indicators" are traced alongside political and policy developments within the receiving society. Finally, Avcı concludes by identifying the policy strengths and weaknesses in the area of the integration of immigrants across the two countries and across time but also spot policy areas where the two countries could possibly learn from one another.

Johan Wets in "The Turkish Community in Austria and Belgium: The Challenge of Integration" brings a comparative perspective of Turkish immigrant communities in two relatively small members of the European Union. The study focuses primarily on the position of Turkish immigrants in the Austrian and Belgian labor markets and traces the outcome of diverging policies of labor incorporation in both countries. Wets notes that Turkish workers are almost exclusively blue-collar workers and that they are mostly found in the least favorable sectors of the economy. This outcome is partly attributed to the poor educational background of Turkish immigrants that has persisted through the generations.

Poor educational performance is one factor that is most conspicuously linked to the poor levels of integration of Turkish immigrants. Failure to succeed in educational institutions, high levels of drop-out and poor linguistic skills repeatedly come up as a common denominator of Turkish immigrants across European countries. The importance of education becomes particularly striking because those Turkish immigrants who have excelled in their respective host societies are also immigrants that have completed higher levels of education and have acquired full command of the local language. Veysel Özcan and Janina Söhn in "The Educational Attainment of Turkish Migrants in Germany" offer an in-depth analysis of the educational dimension of the failure of Turkish immigrants to integrate. In particular, they focus on the second generation of Turkish migrants in Germany, the vast majority of whom were either born in Germany or at least attended school there but have constantly failed to achieve levels comparable to native German students. At the same time, the Programme for International Student Assessment (PISA) has shown that the educational opportunities for persons in Germany, with or without a migration background, are highly unequal. Özcan and Söhn offer a detailed analysis of how this inequality impacts on the performance of Turkish immigrants and search for the structural causes of their poor educational performance.

A widespread complaint that many Europeans raise about Turkish immigrants is arranged marriages and violence against women. Many consider these problems are vivid signs of Turkish immigrants' failure to integrate into their host societies. Christiane Timmerman in "Gender Dynamics in the Context of Turkish Marriage Migration: The Case of Belgium" addresses the gender dimensions related to Turkish migration and their integration and participation in European society. In this study special attention is paid to the interrelations between Turkish immigration and marriage dynamics from a gender perspective. Timmerman examines the impact that existing gender relations within Turkey have on immigrants' ability to cope with the European environment. In particular she stresses how both Turkish nationalism and Islam reinforce patriarchy in Turkish immigrant families. Special attention is paid to Turkish immigrants in Belgium; however Timmerman demonstrates that the phenomenon is applicable to most Turkish immigrants in other European countries, too. Timmerman concludes that the institution of arranged marriages and the influence of patriarchy play an important role in perpetuating Turkish immigrants' integration problems.

In the last contribution to this volume the question of the political participation of Turkish immigrants is addressed. In general an active participation in the political system of the host country through membership of political parties, through holding elected office or through civil society activism is considered almost a *sine qua non* of integration into the host society. The Turkish experience is somewhat puzzling. Turks are reputed to have a very lively associational life. However, this does not necessarily manifest itself in greater levels of integration. Dirk Jacobs, Karen Phalet and Marc Swyngedouw in "Political Participation and Associational Life of Turkish Residents in the Capital of Europe" address this puzzlement. They note that data from several Western European cities show that Turkish immigrants in the European Union tend to have a strong associational life, dense social networks and an important sense of community. This, they say, should lead to increased political trust and political involvement. Yet this does not appear to be the case in the Belgian region of Brussels-Capital. The authors argue that this is due to the difference in political opportunity structures in these cities, in particular the divergent emphasis on the importance of ethnic association. An interesting pattern which is, however, similar for Turks living in major Western European cities like Amsterdam, Berlin and Brussels, is that those people who are active in local Turkish associational life tend also to be involved in cross-ethnic associations of the host society. Given this context, the study tries to shed further light on the structure of Turkish associational life in Brussels and the issue of political involvement of the Turkish community in the Belgian and European capital.

Notes

1. For an extensive analysis of the history of this immigration and the situation of Turkish immigrants in Europe see Nermin Abadan-Unat, *Bitmeyen Göç: Konuk İşçilikten Ulus-Ötesi Yurttaşlığa* (İstanbul: İstanbul Bilgi Üniversitesi Yayınları, 2002).
2. For most recent figures about Turkish immigrants in European countries see Ahmet İçduygu, "Turkey: The Demographic and Economic Dimension of Migration," in Philippe Fargues (ed.), *Mediterranean Migration 2005 Report* (Robert Schuman Center, European University Institute, Florence, 2005), pp. 335–6 and Table 1. This report is available from http://www.carim.org.
3. For the text of the "Negotiating Framework for Turkey" adopted in Luxembourg on October 3, 2005 and its analysis, see *İktisadi Kalkınma Vakfı E-Bülteni* October 7–14, 2005. This e-bulletin can be found at http://www.ikv.org.tr.

4. For an assessement of the implementation of the Tampere Agenda see Communication from the Commission, *First Annual Report on Migration and Integration*, Com (2004) 508 final, July 16, 2004.

5. For the growing importance of "integration" issues at the EU level see Helene Ruth, "Building a Momentum for the Integration of Third-Country Nationals in the European Union," *European Journal of Migration and Law*, Vol.7 (2005), pp.163–80. See also Rita Süssmuth and Werner Weidenfeld (eds.), *Managing Integration: The European Union's Responsibilities towards Immigrants* (Washington DC: Migration Policy Institute, 2005).

6. *Handbook on Integration for Policy Makers and Practitioners* (Brussels: European Commission, Directorate-General for Justice, Freedom and Security, November 2004).

7. For the details of the programme see Communication from the Commission, *The Hague Programme: Ten Priorities for the Next Five Years*, COM (2005) 184 Final, May 10, 2005.

8. *European Commission, Green Paper on an EU Approach to Managing Economic Migration*, Com (2004) 811 Final, January 11, 2005, pp.3–4.

9. Daniel Cohn Benditt, a member of the European Parliament and the Green Party in Germany, noted during a conference organized by his party in Istanbul that Turks should not be too bothered by efforts to restrict the free movement of Turkish labor because by the time Turkey becomes a member of the European Union it is quite likely that there will be countries in the EU that will actively seek Turkish labor. *Turkey in the EU: A Common Future?* October 19–21, 2004, Istanbul.

10. Both Nermin Abadan-Unat, *Bitmeyen Göç: Konuk İşçilikten Ulus-Ötesi Yurttaşlığa* (İstanbul: İstanbul Bilgi Üniversitesi Yayınları, 2002) and Ayhan Kaya and Ferhat Kentel, *Euro Turks: A Bridge or a Breach between Turkey and the European Union?* (Brussels: Centre for European Policy Studies, 2005) show that just as there are many unemployed and poorly-integrated Turkish immigrants in Europe there are also Turkish immigrants who have done well in their host countries, including Turkish businessmen that actually employ locals and other immigrants in their businesses.

11. The *Handbook on Integration* highlights both the importance of the "two-way" nature of integration as well as the importance of a host society environment conducive to integration.

12. See for example, Kathya Ziegler, "Integrating Integration?" *European Journal of Migration and Law*, Vol.7 (2005), p.120.

13. Stephen Castle and Mark J. Miller, *The Age of Migration: International Population Movement in the Modern World* (Basingstoke, Hampshire: Palgrave, 2003), pp.39–44.

14. See, for example, Jose Itzigsohn and Silvia Giorguli Saucedo, "Immigrant Incorporation and Sociocultural Transnationalism," *International Migration Review*, Vol.36, No.3 (Fall 2002), pp.766–98.

Demographic Developments and "Complementarities": Ageing, Labor and Migration

CEM BEHAR

Boğaziçi University, Istanbul, Turkey

Introduction

Among all Middle Eastern countries,[1] Turkey's fertility is the lowest and its population seems to be ageing the fastest. The changes in Turkey's general demographic outlook and its predictable evolution during the first half of the twenty-first century show that its population is fast approaching the end of its first demographic transition. Fertility is already near replacement level. The age structure of the population will, in the coming decades, progressively approach that of Western European countries and will, on the way, undergo a fundamental ageing process. This process seems quite irreversible. We shall try here to take a closer look at various aspects of this ageing process, with particular emphasis on the Turkish adult population, the future labor supply and migration potential.

A Demographic "Window of Opportunity"

As far as the potential working-age groups are concerned and, during a period extending over the first quarter of the twenty-first century, Turkey will be benefiting from a sort of "window of opportunity." This window of opportunity will be embedded in the age structure of its population for the coming two or three decades.[2]

Correspondence Address: Cem Behar, Boğaziçi University, 34342 Bebek, Istanbul. Email: behar@boun.ed.tr,

Cross-country statistical analyses of economic growth have shown that a drastic decline in fertility rates contributes to the growth rate of the GDP of a country as long as the size of the working-age population continues to increase. This is mainly due to the fact that a progressively ageing population imposes, at least for some period of time, a smaller "demographic burden" upon the economically active, and especially upon the younger segments of the working population.

Not only do these younger segments of the economically active population have a smaller number of elderly parents to support, they also have a lower fertility level, as compared to their parental cohort and, therefore, have a smaller number of dependent children. These groups will most probably benefit from intergenerational wealth and welfare transfers. In order to be felt on a macro-level, however, the positive effects of this very particular transitional age structure obviously also require a significant increase in the educational level of the economically active population, that is, a collective effort towards an improvement in the "quality" of the labor force.

This phenomenon has been observed and statistically analyzed for countries like Taiwan, South Korea and Singapore in the 1970s and 1980s, the so-called "Asian Tigers" that had large GDP growth rates in those decades. In countries and during periods where the size of the population in productive ages continues to grow while fertility is decreasing or is already quite low, and the population has not yet aged much, economic performances and employment can indeed significantly improve. However, as fertility will continue to decline in the course of the process of demographic transition, the demographic sources of the growth of the potential labor force and active population will gradually exhaust themselves. Then, the older age groups will begin to constitute an increasing percentage of the total population, and a greater "burden" upon the economically active.

This "window of opportunity" cannot continue forever, obviously, because it depends on the level of fertility, the pace of its decline and the subsequent changes in the age composition of the population. This important demographic basis of economic expansion disappears after some time (perhaps 20 or 25 years in the case of Turkey), when the rate of growth of the adult population rapidly drops and the older section of the non-active population begins to replace its younger segment. If Turkey manages to seize this opportunity, however, the country could experience a simultaneous increase in economic growth rates and in the volume of employment. In that case, Turkey will possibly have a much narrower demographic potential— and a much smaller number of candidates—for eventual immigration.

One way or another, the Turkish population will still continue to increase for some time yet, due to the momentum and growth potential provided by its still rela- tively "young" age structure. With the size of the population tending to stabilize during the second quarter of the twenty-first century, though, the structure of the Turkish population will also undergo rapid modification. The consequences of the structural changes are, as a matter of fact, much more important and far-reaching than those of a simple stabilization of the size of the Turkish population. We will take here a closer look at some of these structural changes, particularly insofar as they affect the overall ageing process of the Turkish population, and more specifically, the working-age groups.

The Turkish Population in the Twenty-first Century

Table 1 gives a broad picture of the evolution and progressive ageing of the Turkish population since the middle of the twentieth century, and follows it up to the middle of the twenty-first century. Table 2 concentrates on some of the basic demographic indicators for Turkey in the coming few decades. The United Nations 2000 and 2002 "Medium Variant" projection options have been used in both of the synoptic tables presented here (Tables 1 and 2).[3]

On the question of fertility rates the United Nations' "Middle Variant" population projections of 2002 share with the 1995 Turkish State Institute of Statistics' projections the fundamental assumption that the Turkish total fertility rate is to reach basic replacement level (that is, on average, 2.1 children per woman) by the year 2010 at the latest (or in the 2005–10 period), and is to remain constant thereafter.

Past experience in the European countries that have completed their transition process and in which fertility levels remain well below replacement levels, however, shows that this assumption is not necessarily realistic. The assumption made about post-2010 Turkish fertility is therefore neither based on any set of observations or real population data, nor on any consistent theory about "post-transitional" demographic dynamics. It was probably simply accepted for lack of anything better.

Table 1. Population by Major Age Groups, Turkey, 1950–2050 (%)

	0–14	15–64	65+	Total	Median Age
1950	38.3	58.4	3.3	100	20.1
1955	39.4	57.1	3.4	100	20.4
1960	41.2	55.2	3.5	100	20.3
1965	41.9	54.1	4.0	100	19.0
1970	41.8	53.8	4.4	100	19.1
1975	40.6	54.8	4.6	100	19.3
1980	39.1	56.1	4.7	100	19.8
1985	37.6	58.2	4.2	100	21.4
1990	35.0	60.7	4.3	100	22.2
1995	32.3	63.0	4.7	100	23.8
2000	29.6	64.9	5.5	100	25.6
2005	27.6	66.6	5.8	100	27.6
2025	21.9	68.4	9.7	100	33.2
2050	19.4	61.9	18.7	100	38.7

Sources: Censuses of Population for 1950–1990; SIS (1995) for 1995–2005 (Projection alternative 2M); United Nations (2001) for 2025 and 2050 (Medium Variant); United Nations (2001) for Median Age.

Table 2. Projected Basic Demographic Indicators, Turkey, 2000–2050

	2000	2010	2025	2040	2050
Total Population (thousands)	66,668	75,145	86,611	95,123	98,818
Average Yearly Population Growth (%)	1.32	1.00	0.75	0.51	0.34
Crude Birth Rate (per thousand)	20.1	17.0	15.1	13.8	13.4
Crude Death Rate (per thousand)	6.2	6.4	6.7	8.2	9.5
Total Fertility Rate	2.30	2.10	2.10	2.10	2.10
Infant Mortality Rate (per thousand)	39	28	18	12	11
Life Expectancy (Male + Female)	70.5	72.9	75.8	77.4	78.6

The 2002 revision of the UN Projections, however, has revised downwards these fertility assumptions and has reduced post-2015 Turkish fertility levels to 1.85. This is a below-replacement level that is closer to the present European fertility levels. It is therefore not to be excluded that, in the not too distant future, and after having reached a peak (estimated to be at around 95 to 100 million) in about three or four decades from now, the Turkish population may even begin to decline.

With the size of the Turkish population tending to stabilize during the first quarter of the twenty-first century, its age structure will undergo rapid change. The consequences of this structural change are, in fact, much more important than those of a mere stabilization in the size of the population. Table 3 gives the relative percentage sizes of major age groups in the coming half-century.

In the same period of time, the percentage of the Turkish population aged between 15 and 64 will fluctuate less than the other structural components. Its relative weight will gradually rise from 64.1 percent in the year 2000 to 66.9 percent in 2030 and slowly decline thereafter down to 63.6 percent of the total population in 2050, and certainly even to lower levels thereafter, thus marking the coming to an end of the demographic "window of opportunity."

Table 3. Structural Changes and Various Age-Groups in Turkey's Population, 2000–2050 (%)

Age Groups	2000	2005	2010	2015	2020	2025	2030	2035	2040	2045	2050
0–14	30.1	29.1	26.4	24.1	23.0	22.6	22.0	22.1	20.3	19.7	19.5
15–24	20.3	17.5	17.0	16.7	16.2	14.5	13.7	13.7	13.7	13.4	12.9
65+	5.8	6.2	6.5	7.2	8.29	9.5	11.1	12.4	14.4	16.4	17.9
80+	0.6	0.8	1.1	1.3	1.4	1.5	1.8	2.2	2.7	3.3	3.8
5–14	19.4	19.8	18.1	16.1	15.1	14.9	14.7	14.2	13.6	13.1	12.9
18–23	12.3	10.7	9.8	10.6	9.9	8.8	8.1	8.2	8.1	8.1	7.8

Demographic Evolution and Economic Resources

A brief look at the future evolution of the size and relative shares of various age groups, as shown in Table 3, will help underline the demographic background of some crucial socio-economic issues in Turkey.

Younger Age Groups

The size of the Turkish population under age 15 will remain the same for the next quarter of a century, at around 20 million. Since the total size of the population will continue to increase, albeit at a decreasing rate, the share of this younger age group will be in a steady decline. As fertility rates continue to decrease, the number of newborn (aged 0) joining the Turkish population every year will continue to fall at a low but steady rate and the bottom part of the age pyramid, its base, will gradually contract. The share of the 0–14 age group will decrease from its present share of 30.1 percent to 19.5 percent at the end of the projection period. Within a few decades the population of Turkey will cease, at all events, to be a so-called "young" population.[4]

The next age group, between the ages of 15 and 24, will follow suit, and the percentage of the Turkish population in the 15–24 age bracket will fall from 19.4 to 12.9 percent during the next few decades. The 15–24 age group is particularly critical, because it represents the potential pool of labor supply, the new entrants into the Turkish labor force. We shall return to it shortly.

The relative stabilization in the yearly number of births automatically means that the number of children starting school (age 6) will also stabilize. Compulsory education in Turkey is now eight years, and presently the schooling rate in primary education stands at about 97 percent. Table 3 shows that the proportion of this age group in the total population will fall from 19.4 to 12.9 percent, while the absolute numbers are either stable or slightly shrinking.

In other words, the demand for primary schooling will be more or less stable for the whole length of the projection period. The priority in primary education in Turkey is therefore no longer the ability to supply effective services to an increasing number of service demanders but simply to improve the quality of existing infrastructure and services, with the necessary geographical adjustments and relocation to take on board horizontal mobility and rural migration. As a consequence, national economic resources and public funds need no longer be strained in order to provide more schools and more classrooms. The changes in the demographic structure of the population are, in this instance, providing a window of opportunity for diverting economic resources and government funds towards both other needs and quality improvement in education. Besides, higher quality and more appropriate basic education would, in turn, boost labor productivity, mobility, and employment levels, thus enhancing the positive overall effects of the demographic window of opportunity.

With the Turkish decline in fertility, the same relative stabilization in numbers will also occur as far as the potential demand for higher education is concerned but with, of course, a lag of about ten years. The Turkish population in the 18–23 age group grew at a yearly rate of about 2 percent in the 1990s. The annual growth rate of this age group will approach zero towards the year 2020, and may become negative thereafter.

However, the rate of college and university enrollment in this age group is as yet relatively low in Turkey (21 percent in 2002, inclusive of non-resident education, *açık öğretim*), as compared to countries of the European Union. Therefore, the effective demand for higher education may yet continue to rise for some time to come. However, the number of higher education institutions in Turkey and their capacities, too, will reach a level of sufficiency in the foreseeable future. This issue, too, will soon cease to be a purely quantitative one and will primarily become centered on teaching standards and quality, inter-institutional competition and systemic flexibility.

On a more general level, it is a fact that the average number of years of schooling of the Turkish population is on a fast rising trend. Future educational policies in Turkey will require not only a shift of resources and investments from basic primary education towards college and university education, but also a change in general orientation. This will involve a movement from the traditional, purely formal and linear succession of educational levels (primary/high school/college, etc.) to more purpose-oriented, adaptable and flexible types and structures of educational services (adult education and training, "part-time" programs, etc.). These will be bound to increase both the mobility and flexibility of the Turkish labor force.

The Adult Population and Potential Labor Supply

The percentage of the Turkish population aged between 15 and 64 will fluctuate less than the other structural components. Its relative weight will gradually increase from 64.1 percent in the year 2000 to 66.9 percent in 2030 and slowly decline thereafter to reach 63.6 percent of the total population in 2050. This group is the "adult population." It includes the potentially active labor force, but also potential high school and university students between the ages of 15 and 25.

If we consider absolute numbers, the total size of this adult population will constantly increase until about the year 2035. This is to be expected because the overwhelming majority of those included in that age group were born at a time when Turkish fertility was not yet declining rapidly, and these individuals were part of large birth cohorts. Their relative share within the total population will be higher than that of younger people, because those included in this last group consist of relatively low numbers, due to decreasing fertility levels.

The Turkish population will increase by about 30 percent over the next three decades. However, in the same period the population between the ages of 15 and 64 will increase somewhat faster, by about 40 percent and will go from 42 million in the year 2000 to about 60–62 million at the end of the projection period. This means a potentially growing labor force and labor supply. As already pointed out above, this increase may constitute the basis for the demographic "window of opportunity" enhancing labor productivity, mobility and flexibility. The relative weight of the 15 to 64 age group will tend to decrease towards the end of the projection period, that is to say, after 2025, due to the increase in the share of the elderly population.

Within this adult population, those in the 15 to 24 age bracket have particular importance. This subgroup represents the new entrants into the labor force and its youngest segment, and the numerical evolution of this age group does provide a view on the possible future structure of the Turkish labor market. As also shown in Table 3, the volume of this age group will remain relatively stable during the whole of the projection period. Its proportion of the whole of the Turkish population will, at the same time, decline from 20.3 to 12.9 percent.

However, we must keep in mind that this age group is the prioritized targeted group of Turkish national education policies, and therefore the age group that will certainly benefit most from the continuous rise in schooling rates. The general schooling rate at the secondary education level (corresponding to, approximately, the 15–18 age group) was equal to 59.4 percent in 1999/2000.[5] In conjunction with a projected rise in compulsory schooling from 8 to 11 years, Turkey plans to raise the proportion enrolled in secondary education progressively to 100 percent in the course of the next decade.

This means that, from the year 2010 onwards, and everything else being equal, a smaller and smaller percentage of the Turkish population in the 15 to 24 age group will be effectively entering the labor market and looking for work every year. The number of first-job seekers will be on a declining trend and, as already pointed out above, the pool of potential candidates for immigration will possibly be much smaller.

The Elderly

The age group that will, in the next few decades, most certainly grow at an unprecedented rate, in both absolute and relative terms, is the group above age 65. That the Turkish population is an ageing population is undisputable. Besides, compared to its neighbors in the West Asian region (according to the United Nations geographical classification) Turkey is the country where fertility levels have declined the fastest in the past few decades. The Turkish population will undergo an ageing process of a speed unprecedented in the region.

Turkey's population is expected to rise by somewhat more than 40 percent during our projection period. During the same period, the population aged 65 and over will more than double. The share of the elderly population within the total will thereby rise from 5.8 percent in the year 2000 to 9.5 in 2025 and 17.9 percent in 2050. As fertility continues to fall, and present generations age and are replaced with new and comparatively smaller birth cohorts, the ageing process will gain momentum in the second part of the projection period. It is estimated that the number of those aged 65 and over that stands at around 3.6 million in the year 2000 will reach about 17 million in 2050.

In about 25 years from now Turkey will no longer have a "young" population, whatever meaning we choose to assign to this expression. Indeed, the median age of the Turkish population, that is, the age that divides the population in two equal segments, will gradually rise from 24.9 in the year 2000 to 33.2 in 2025 and finally to 38.7 in 2050.

To give a more vivid picture of the ageing process worldwide, and to ensure comparability, the United Nations[6] has devised an ageing index. This index is defined as the number of persons 60 (or 65) years old or over per person under age 15 in the same population. This index is on a fast rising trend in Turkey and will increase from 0.192 in the year 2000 to 0.422 in 2025 and to 0.919 in the year 2050. The same index will, according to UN data computed on a regional basis, increase from 106 to 215 per 100 in Europe between 2000 and 2050. All European countries will, by 2030, have an ageing index of at least 100. That is, they will all have more people aged 65 and over than children and youths under age 15. By then, the Turkish demographic structure will have truly integrated into the European Union.

The ageing of its population is a type of demographic problem that Turkey will have to learn to come to grips with. In contrast to its past policies imbued with a demographic outlook geared on constant growth and a permanently "young" population structure, Turkey must therefore now begin to imagine a set of new future policies relative to issues such as health, housing, education, social security, etc. in order to address the needs of a demographic structure of a totally new kind. The ageing process as a whole, by diminishing the relative weight of potential migrants within the population, will have some mitigating effect on the Turkish migration potential, but this effect can be felt only in the long run, when ageing has already become effective.

The European Horizon of Population Decline

European demographers have sounded warning bells for at least the last 30 years to the effect that the population ageing process might eventually bring with it the possibility of declining population size in industrialized nations. The combination of ageing and absolute decline results from a history of below-replacement fertility plus a continuous increase in life expectancy. In the absence of major demographic catastrophes (wars, large-scale epidemics, etc.), absolute population decline is a natural and unavoidable consequence of the population ageing process. The issue of an absolute population decline in European countries and in Japan has, however, only very recently attracted the attention of public opinion at large. The means of trying to reverse this trend have been studied, but no hard and fast answer to the problem has yet emerged.

In these countries, fertility has not stabilized around a replacement level of two children per woman, as was generally expected in the 1970s and 1980s. European fertility levels seem to have fallen permanently much below this critical level. Their "post-transitional" developments have kept their fertility much below replacement levels. Besides, a new postwar "baby boom" seems, as things stand now, rather improbable.

Some European governments (France, Italy, Germany, Sweden and some Eastern European countries) have employed various means to affect fertility levels, including direct and indirect financial benefits and incentives, but these have met with very modest levels of success. The likely impact of migration as a counterbalance to ageing has also been examined. For the time being, the conclusion was that inflows of migrants will not be able to prevent future population declines (indeed, the migrant population undergoes the same ageing process as the host population), unless the migration flows are of a very large magnitude, on the scale of millions annually. This seems to be socially unfeasible and politically unsustainable.

As stated in the report of the United Nations Expert Group on Policy Responses to Population Ageing and Population Decline:

> In the short term, immigration can slow down the process of population ageing and prevent population decline. The volumes of immigrants that would be necessary to prevent population decline are relatively small in demographic terms. However, even in the short term, these levels of immigration are often considered politically and socially unacceptable for European countries.[7]

Therefore, replacement migration does not appear, for the moment, to be, in itself, whether in the medium or in the long run, a viable solution to the problem of population decline for European nations. "Immigration can only slow down the ageing process a little," stresses the United Nations Expert Group, and concludes that "Demographically speaking, an increase in fertility is the only way to stop population ageing in the long term ... a return of fertility to near replacement levels is the only way to stop a decline in total population."[8]

As rightly stressed by the same United Nations Expert Group, however,

> even a sharp upturn in fertility would not have a significant impact before at least 25 or 30 years, owing to the population momentum resulting from the current age structure. Thus, *population ageing is unavoidable*, and all countries will have to face the consequences and find ways to cope with them.[9]

Many European countries are already beginning to envisage seriously the possibility of a long-run path of population decline. Overall population decline is not, for the time being, a problem that should preoccupy the great majority of the less developed countries, though. It should be kept in mind, however, that a continuation of the demographic ageing process on its present trend will, given the mechanics of population replacement, inevitably bring the possibility of an absolute demographic decline to the forefront. The population decline issue may become an important one in the second half of the twenty-first century for many of the presently less developed countries. And Turkey is a case in point. Table 4 gives a broad idea of Turkish and European population perspectives.

Table 4.   Total Population (thousands)

	EU15	EU25	TR
2000	377,333	452,077	68,281
2010	383,219	456,633	77,966
2025	383,941	454,424	88,995

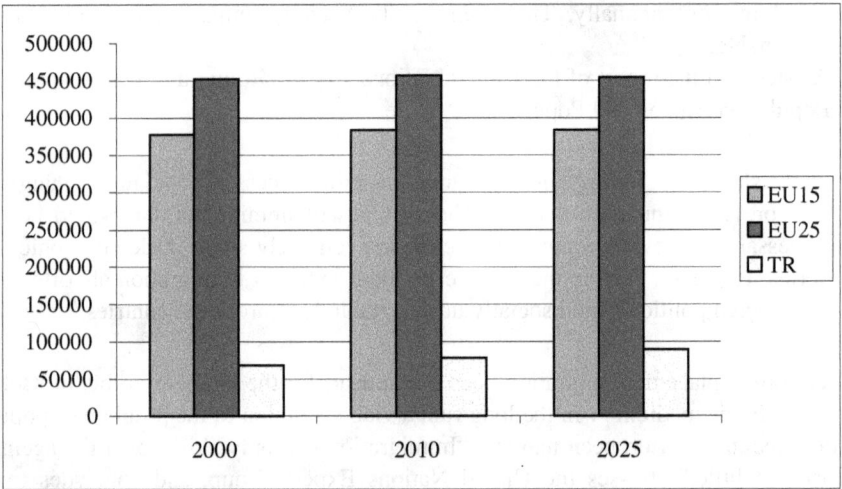

Source: UN, World Population Prospects (2002).

Demographic "Complementarity" and Migration Potential

In that sense, the frequently voiced thesis of a necessary (and either positive or nega-tive) *complementarity* between the population of Turkey and the demographic struc-tures of the countries of the European Union is totally devoid of any solid demographic foundation. The idea of a demographic "complementarity" between a "young" Turkey and an "older" Europe is either the product of wishful thinking (on the Turkish side), or of an irrational fear of a massive and uncontrollable immigration and of its effects on the labor market and unemployment (on the European side).

First of all, demographers have shown with certainty that, with regard to the ageing process of European populations, immigration cannot be a durable solution. It can only slow down the ageing process just a little bit and, in the long run, the cumulative number of young immigrants required to prevent ageing would result in a total population with a very large proportion of people of immigrant origin. Besides, the immigrant population itself will be ageing fast in the host country. Replacement migration, clearly, is not a panacea for the ills of ageing, nor will it constitute a compensation for demographic decline.

Besides, and on the basis of recent social and economic experiences, replacement migration as a solution to declining or ageing population has not been deemed politically and socially feasible by most European governments, as well as by international organizations such as the United Nations, the Organization for Economic Cooperation and Development, the Council of Europe, and others.

To give just one numerical example, a recent study by the Population Division of the United Nations tries to estimate the yearly number of migrants that would be necessary for the European population to remain constant over the next half-century.[10] In one of the scenarios put forward in this study, close to one million (949,000, to be precise) net yearly migrants appear to be necessary, from now (2005) to the year 2050, in order to stop the European population from decreasing further. This figure appears to be, for the time being, politically and socially unsustainable. And even if this figure were to be attained, the size of the 15–64 age group (that is, the population of working age) in Europe would still continue to decline. If the adult population, that is, the 15–64 age group is to remain constant, net migration to Europe would have to reach a yearly figure of 1.588 million during the whole of the 2000–2050 period. Germany and Italy alone would need about half that figure in order to keep their adult population from decreasing.

The idea of compensating and "complementing" the European population decline by Turkish migration is therefore simply outrageously unrealistic and meaningless from a strictly demographic point of view. The various European fears and phobias are, by the same token, totally unfounded. This is a conclusion dictated by the European demographic structures themselves. Migration in itself will never offset ageing. Besides, not only will Europe never consider having recourse to such a large contingent of migrants, but the sheer size of the numbers involved in the above scenarios of compensation makes all potential Turkish migration numerically insignificant.

It is also worth remembering that the magnitude of migration from the southern accession countries such as Greece, Spain and Portugal, contrary to all expectations, was negligible even after the end of their pre-integration transition period. Furthermore, a slow trend in the opposite direction might also have taken place. And potential immigration from those ten countries which joined the EU on May 1, 2004 has been estimated to be only around 1.1 million permanent immigrants and about twice as many temporary immigrants. Some other studies come up with very different numbers (a range of 700,000 to 2,600,000 migrants between 2005 and 2015). For Turkey, a figure of a total of 2.7 million permanent migrants is sometimes given, but this figure has, according to this author, no solid foundation.

Starting from 2005, but particularly so after 2010, the post-World War II baby boom generations in Europe will be retiring. The new entrants into the labor force, that is, the new generations born 40 years after the baby boom, will be much smaller in number than those leaving the labor force. Projections have shown that, by the year 2050, and unless a very drastic and highly improbable rise in fertility occurs, Europe will have a smaller total labor force than in 1950.[11] Between 2010 and 2050 the working age population will decrease in absolute terms by some 26 to 35 percent. This fall will obviously not be homogenous across the board. It may well be that some professions and occupations will soon be deserted, with a rise in the demand for labor in specific sectors where supply is insufficient.

The first collective reaction of the European Union to the ageing issue came about only in 2001. The 2001 Stockholm European Council agreed that half of the EU population in the 55–64 age group should be in employment by 2010.[12] The 2002 Barcelona Council also set precise targets concerning the elder portion of the working age population. The target is that "a progressive increase of about 5 years in the effective average age at which people stop working in the EU should be sought by the year 2010." The concept involved in this concerted action is that of "active ageing." Increasing the Labor Force Participation rate of women is also one of the prime objectives of the same policy.

The 2003 Report on the Social Situation in the EU stresses that "maintaining labour supply will increasingly depend on raising the activity and employment of women and older workers."[13] *Europe has chosen, first and foremost, to try to tap its own labor potential before having recourse to outside sources, that is, immigration.* The European Commission thinks that:

> it is of great importance that most Member States have considerable labour reserves among women and older workers. If existing barriers to participation are removed, these labour reserves could be used to counteract the impact of ageing on the size of the workforce.[14]

Immigration is therefore considered only as a *solution of last resort*, and recourse to it is left to the time when "labour reserves among the existing population are fully engaged." The Commission is well aware, however, that the increase in Labor Force Participation rates and the so-called policy of "active ageing" can only provide temporary relief. It nevertheless carefully avoids putting forward any policy proposal concerning migration. The only remark in this latest report on the European social situation concerns not the perspective or the numbers of immigrants, but the possibility of their successful integration.

Obviously the positive social and economic effects of immigration hinge on the ability of member states to secure the full integration of newcomers and their dependants into employment and the wider social fabric of European societies.

Conclusion: Perspectives, Scenarios and the Issue of "Migration Management"

Immigration in Turkey–EU relations is, obviously, both a matter of perception by public opinion at large, and a real and delicate social and economic issue. Current policies, as we know, are primarily oriented toward preventing undesirable migration, while trying to define better and to implement a realistic policy of integration.

Instead, basic demographic data show us that managing migration, instead of simply preventing it, should soon become a European priority. Demographic differentials and both push and pull factors will not disappear overnight and it is high time for Europe to consider the alternative of turning these temporary demographic differentials into an advantage and to make migration a socially and politically manageable issue. The impossibility of effectively implementing a zero migration policy is now widely recognized throughout Europe. There is a quite recent move, both by governments and by European intergovernmental organizations, towards acceptance that migration is a generally positive phenomenon and that the purpose of migration management should be to ensure an all round positive outcome. Besides, a migration management strategy requires a comprehensive approach to the labor market as a whole, takes in the complete spectrum and deals with both legal and illegal movements.[15]

To return to the case of Turkey, we may now try to briefly assess the eventual demographic impact of various Turkey–EU migration scenarios over the next quarter of a century by Erzan, Kuzubaş and Yıldız.[16] These Turkish labor migration scenarios are the only set of detailed country-specific simulations known to this author, and they have been put together here with working-age population projections for the EU25 in order to evaluate the possible demographic impact of Turkish labor migration.

The scenarios are based on data drawn from three sets of different basic reference groups: 1) Immigration from all Europe for the period 1967–2001; 2) Southern European countries (Spain, Portugal and Greece) for the same period; and 3) Turkey's own experience for 1967–2001. Within each of these three sets, two sub-scenarios were elaborated, according to, in the first two reference groups, whether free movement of Turkish labor within Europe would be possible or not by the year 2015, and, in the case of the third reference group, whether Turkey itself would be experiencing "high" or "low" economic growth between 2004 and 2030. So, a total of six Turkey–EU migration scenarios have been calculated. The net effect of the ageing of the Turkish population itself on the number of potential migrants has also been incorporated.

Table 5 puts together some of these results and relates them to the working-age population of the EU25 as projected by the UN. We have taken the 15–64 age group in Europe, as it is given in the UN (2002) population projections, as a proxy for the European working-age population.[17] The Turkish labor migration figures (that is, "changes in the Turkish migrant stock") are cumulative figures (centered around 2010 and 2025).

Table 5. Turkish Labor Migration to the EU Forecasts (cumulative figure) and European Working-Age Population in 2010 and 2025 (thousands)

		2010	%	2025	%
15–64 Age Group (EU 25)		307,087		288,103	
Net Change in the Turkish Migrant Stock	Lowest Scenario	320	0.104	960	0.333
Net Change in the Turkish Migrant Stock	Highest Scenario	760	0.247	2734	0.949

The total Turkish migration figures in the lowest and highest scenarios are to be compared to the range of permanent immigrants to the EU15 as expected to come from the ten countries that acceded in May 2004. This figure is expected to range from 700,000 to 2.6 million between 2005 and 2015, that is, more or less the same level as the projected Turkish figures given in Table 5. The total population in 2004 of the ten new accession countries (74.1 million) is also comparable to that of Turkey at the same date (71.3 million).

At all events, and whichever scenario eventually becomes a reality during the coming quarter of a century, it appears that the strictly quantitative demographic impact of Turkish labor migration to the EU will not exceed 1 percent of the total European labor force, even in the case of the most pessimistic scenario. In the more optimistic—and certainly more likely—scenarios, this impact will be minimal and will probably not even be felt. Indeed, the experience of Southern European countries shows that a successful accession period greatly reduces and even eliminates migration pressures.

A key issue in the debate on the effects of migration on European labor markets hinges upon the question of whether migration creates a short or long run segmentation within these markets or has an overall substitution effect. Although studies show that the segmentation hypothesis seems to be more relevant, substitution between nationals and migrants is also seen as possible.[18] Given the fact that a zero migration policy has not been and cannot be successfully implemented by the EU countries, managing migration in order to ensure that benefits accrue to all the parties involved will become the critical labor market policy in the coming decades.

Acknowledgment

The Assistance of Tuğçe Bulut is gratefully acknowledged.

Notes

1. That is, the "Western Asian" region, according to the United Nations geographical classification.
2. TUSIAD (Turkish Industrialists' and Businessmen's Association), *Turkey's Window of Opportunity—Demographic Transition Process and its Consequences* (Istanbul, TUSIAD, March 1999).
3. United Nations, Department of Social and Economic Affairs, *World Population Prospects—The 2000 Revision*, Volume I: Comprehensive Tables (New York: United Nations, 2001), pp.442 ff.
4. See United Nations, Department of Economic and Social Affairs, Population Division, *World Population Ageing: 1950–2050* (New York: United Nations, 2002).
5. State Planning Organization (SPO), *Long-Term Strategy and Eighth Five Year Development Plan, 2001–2005* (Ankara: SPO, 2001), p.87.
6. United Nations (2002), p.41.
7. United Nations, Department of Economic and Social Affairs Population Division, *Population Newsletter*, Vol.70 (December 2000), p.2.
8. Ibid.
9. Ibid., p.3 (author's emphasis).
10. "Replacement Migration: Is it a Solution to Declining and Ageing Populations", in Population Division, UN Department of Economic and Social Affairs, *Population Newsletter*, Vol.69 (June 2000), pp.1–5.

11. Aidan Punch and David Pierce (eds.), *Europe's Population and Labour Market beyond 2000* (Strasbourg: Council of Europe Publications, 2000), pp.23–27.

12. Commission of the European Communities, "Increasing the Employment of Older Workers and Delaying the Exit from the Labour Market", Brussels, March 3, 2004.

13. European Commission, *The Social Situation in the European Union—2003* (Brussels: EC, 2004), pp.8–9.

14. Ibid., p.9.

15. John Salt, James Clarke and Philippe Wanner, *International Labour Migration*, Population Studies, No.44 (Strasbourg: Council of Europe Publishing, 2004); John Salt, *Current Trends in Migration in Europe*, Strasbourg, Council of Europe Publications, January 2005.

16. Refik Erzan, Umut Kuzubaş and Nilüfer Yıldız, "Immigration Scenarios: Turkey–EU," Paper presented at the Conference on "Immigration Issues in EU–Turkish Relations: Determinants of Immigration and Integration," Boğaziçi University, Istanbul, October 8–9, 2004 (in this volume).17.United Nations, *World Population Prospects—The 2002 Revision* (New York, UN, 2003).

18. See John Salt, James Clarke and Philippe Wanner, *International Labour Migration*, Population Studies, 44 (Strasbourg: Council of Europe Publishing, 2004), especially pp.85–94.

Immigration Scenarios: Turkey–EU

REFİK ERZAN[*], UMUT KUZUBAŞ & NİLÜFER YILDIZ
*Department of Economics, Boğaziçi University, Istanbul, Turkey

Introduction

The purpose of the study is to estimate the eventual immigration from Turkey to the EU when Turkey becomes a full member and restrictions on labor mobility are removed. Alternative methods and scenarios are scrutinized in forecasting probable magnitudes for the period 2004 to 2030. The analyses are essentially based on the experience of countries that have joined the EU. The estimation methods are those used in recent studies that analyze the consequences of the membership of Central and East European countries. Special attention was paid to the experience of the southern "cohesion" countries—Greece, Portugal and Spain. Finally, forecasts were also made based primarily on the Turkish emigration record.

The number of Turkish immigrants in EU15 exceeds three million—about three-quarters residing in Germany (Figure 1). Occasionally, sensational news articles on the daunting level of potential migrants from Turkey catch the headlines in the EU media. Careless interpretation of casual opinion polls can put the number up to 25 percent of a population of about 70 million. Figures that emerge from serious research are a fraction of that. The survey of this literature undertaken by the 2004 "Impact Study"[1] of the EU Commission has reported that forecasts of immigration from Turkey to the EU-15 until 2030 range between 0.5 and 4.4 million, assuming free mobility of labor in about a dozen years from now. The Impact Study also underlines that to arrive at the higher end estimates (about 4 million) the studies have to stretch the data and the methodology.

Analytical studies follow two alternative methods in making immigration forecasts. The first one is statistical inferences based on scientifically designed surveys.[2]

Correspondence Address: Refik Erzan, Department of Economics, Center for Economics and Econometrics, Boğaziçi University, 34342 Bebek, Istanbul, Turkey. Email: erzan@boun.edu.tr

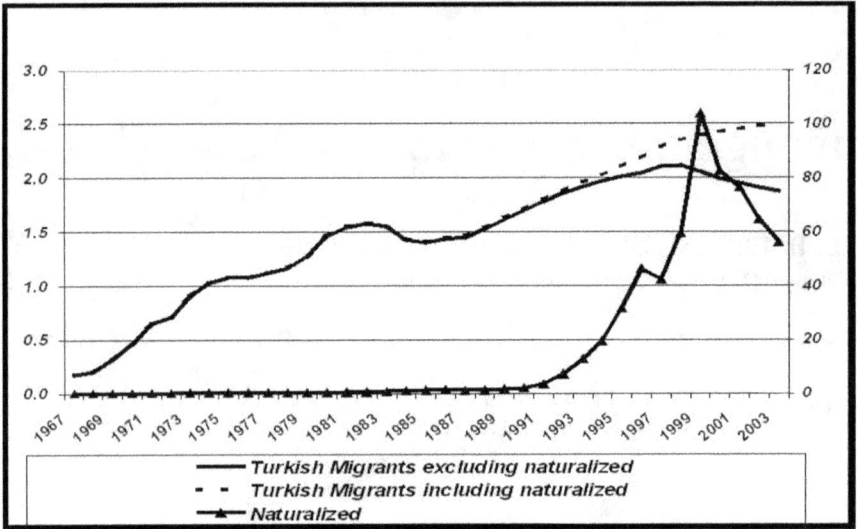

Figure 1.   Turkish migrants in Germany. *Note:* Left scale migrant stock (in millions), right scale annual naturalization (in thousands). *Source:* Federal German Statistical Office.

The second one is econometric methods. The latter draws on the pre- and post-EU membership experiences of emigration countries. Quantifiable determinants of immigration—pull and push factors—are identified and their joint impact on immigration is estimated. These estimates are then used to forecast eventual migration from future members.

Our simulation results for net migration from Turkey to the EU-15 in the period 2004–30 is between 1 and 2.1 million, foreseeing a successful accession period with high growth and free labor mobility starting 2015—a rather optimistic assumption to explore the upper bound of the immigration potential. On the other hand, if Turkey's membership process is endangered and high growth cannot be sustained, 2.7 million people may be penetrating the EU-15 despite the prevailing strict restrictions on labor mobility.

Reference Group: Immigration from All Europe, 1967–2001

At the first stage of analysis, we followed the method of the EU Commission report by Alvarez-Plata, Brücker and Siliverstovs[3] used in estimating potential migration from Central and Eastern Europe.[4] Using an econometric model, the study estimates migrant stocks in Germany originating from 19 source countries (Austria, Belgium, Denmark, Finland, France, Greece, Holland, Iceland, Ireland, Italy, Luxembourg, Norway, Portugal, Sweden, Switzerland, Spain, Turkey, UK, and (former) Yugoslavia). Germany was chosen as the host country because of the size of its migrant communities and the availability of robust time series data going back to 1967.

Table 1.   Regression Results—"All Europe" Sample, 1967–2001

Independent Variables	Coefficients	SE	P-value
M(−1)	1.23	0.019	0.000
M(−2)	−0.37	0.018	0.000
$Ln(W_f/W_h)$	0.05	0.006	0.000
$Ln(W_h)$	0.07	0.006	0.000
$Ln(e_f)$	0.34	0.033	0.000
$Ln(e_h)$	−0.10	0.008	0.000
FREE	0.01	0.001	0.000
GUEST	0.11	0.003	0.000
INTERVENTION	0.15	0.033	0.000
INSURGENCY	0.10	0.019	0.000
Adjusted R^2 = 0.99			

We used the specification that yielded the best overall result in the EU Commission study.[5] As explanatory variables; income level in the country of origin (w_{ht}) captures the cost of migration, employment rates (e_{ft}),(e_{ht}), the probability of finding jobs, and income differences between the home and host countries (w_{ft}/w_{ht}), the material return to migration. To these, the lagged migrant stocks ($m_{fh,t-1}$),($m_{fh,t-2}$) were added to measure the impact of "networking" among immigrants.

Introduction of free labor mobility among EU members was captured by the FREE dummy variable while GUEST denoted the 1967–73 period when "guest worker" agreements were operational. To correct for the jumps in immigration due to refugees and asylum seekers, WAR in (former) Yugoslavia and INTERVEN- TION (1980 military) and INSURGENCY (1990–94 terror) in Turkey were used. Table 1 gives the estimation results for the 1967–2001 period, indicating the coefficients of the explanatory factors and their significance levels.[6]

It was observed that all the estimated coefficients were significant and the overall explanatory power of the model (the fit) was very high. However, the small values of the coefficients indicated that income and employment rate differences did not have powerful effects in determining inter-European migration during the period under consideration.[7]

Migration Forecasts for Turkey, 2004–30

The coefficients obtained from the estimations for migration into Germany from the "all Europe" sample of 19 source countries (including Turkey) for the 1967–2001 period were used to make simulations for emigration from Turkey. Following similar studies, German per capita GDP was assumed to grow 2 percent annually and the employment rate would stay at the 1991–2001 average level. Income and employment projections for Turkey were adopted from our ongoing study scrutiniz- ing alternative growth scenarios for Turkey, analyzing demographic developments,

Table 2.   High Growth Scenario for Turkey, 2005–30 (annual values)

Urban GDP Growth	0.065
Urban Productivity Growth	0.03
Rural GDP Growth	0.02
Unemployment—2015	*Urban* 0.13
	Average 0.09
Unemployment—2030	*Urban* 0.05
	Average 0.04

urban and rural growth and productivity, internal migration (urbanization) and unemployment.[8] The main scenario used here foresees a successful EU accession with sustained high growth and gradually declining unemployment (Table 2). UN population projections were adopted in all computations.

Under these assumptions, projections were made for immigration from Turkey to Germany.[9] According to the latest available data covering the EU-15 area, Germany hosted 76 percent of all immigrants in the EU originating from Turkey.[10] Using this share as a benchmark, immigration estimates for Germany were inflated to represent the total for the EU-15 area.[11]

Two scenarios were simulated with these parameters. Both assumed that restrictions on labor mobility would be largely abolished in 2015. This rather optimistic assumption was adopted to arrive at an upper limit for immigration numbers.

The first simulation emulates for Turkey the actual experience of EU countries with free movement of labor (using the FREE dummy). This involves a considerable integration of these economies during the accession periods.

The second simulation emulates—repeats—for Turkey the experience of these countries (including Turkey) with guest worker agreements until 1973 (using the GUEST dummy). The purpose of simulating this *inferior* scenario is, again, to explore an upper bound for the migration potential.

When the actual membership-cum-free labor mobility experience of the EU countries—an experience that Turkey has yet to live through—was taken as the benchmark, immigration forecasts from Turkey exhibited a rather smooth curve (Figure 2). The small hike of 2015 transformed into a declining flow. Total net migration barely reached 1.1 million by 2030 (Table 3).

Instead of relying on the actual experience of the EU members with free labor mobility, when we emulated (and repeated) the guest worker episodes for Turkey in 2015, we observed a jump in migration, reaching moderate levels around 2020 (Figure 3). Even under this *inferior* scenario, the total immigration projection to EU-15 from Turkey until 2030 was not drastic, about 1.8 million (Table 3). This inferior scenario depicts an accession process not properly utilized for structural adjustment and integration.

The authentic free movement of labor scenario (the first scenario) incorporated the *socio-economic* improvements in the accession countries. These improvements

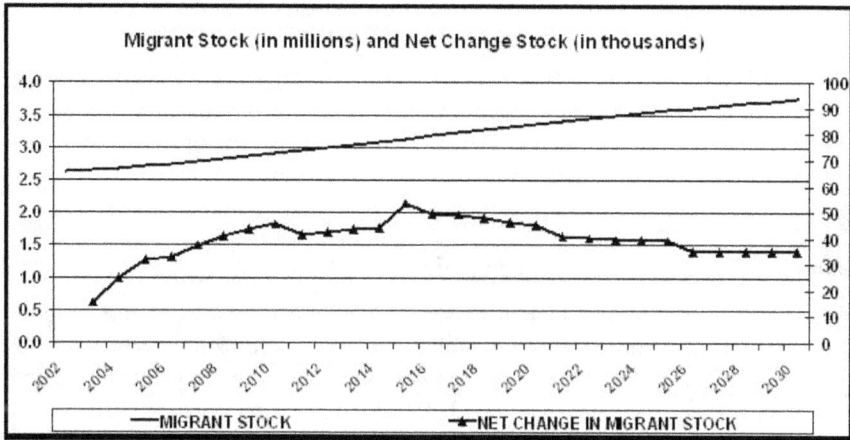

Figure 2. Simulation of free movement of labor.

relieved the migration pressures. Restrictions on labor became much less binding; hence, as they were removed, there was no major rush.

It should be emphasized that socio-economic improvements were not simply higher incomes and more jobs. Otherwise the coefficients for these basic economic variables would have been much larger in the estimations. The improvements in accession countries covered dimensions such as social security, health, education and regional disparities.

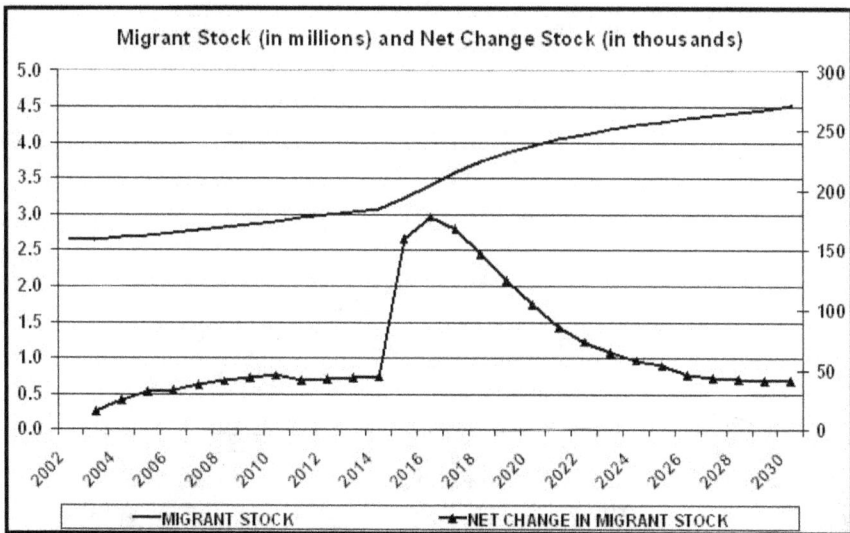

Figure 3. Simulation of guest worker scenario.

Table 3.   Comparison of the Two Scenarios—Reference Group: All Europe

Net Change in the Turkish Migrant Stock	2004–15	2015–30	Total
Scenario FREE	460,000	613,000	1,073,000
Scenario GUEST	564,000	1,274,000	1,838,000

Reference Group: Spain, Portugal and Greece, 1967–2001

We have verified the methodological accuracy of our estimations reported above (Tables 1 and 3) by comparing them with the findings of research conducted for the EU Commission on Central and Eastern Europe. We have also exchanged notes with these researchers at the October 2004 Istanbul conference where this paper was originally presented. Nevertheless, to test for sensitivity of the sample selection, we repeated our parameter estimations by excluding rich countries such as Austria and Denmark. We confined our sample to the southern "cohesion" countries—Greece, Portugal and Spain (and Turkey)—which had characteristics resembling Turkey at the time of their accession.

Figure 4 depicts the immigration episodes from these countries and Turkey to Germany. To adjust for differences in country sizes, the net immigration figures were given as percentages of their respective populations. There were major flows from all these countries during the guest worker agreements. As restrictions on labor mobility were lifted, the decreasing Spanish migrant stock continued its tendency. In Greece and Portugal there was a modest hike in the number of migrants but it leveled out shortly after. In the more recent years, the stock was declining, indicating reverse net migration.

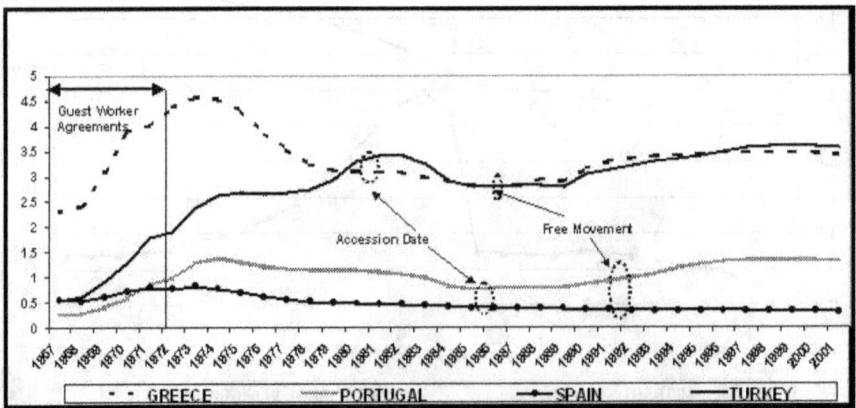

Figure 4.   Migrants in Germany as percentage of source country population.

Table 4. Comparison of the Two Scenarios—Reference Group: Southern Europe

Net Change in the Turkish Migrant Stock	2004–15	2015–30	Total
Scenario FREE	320,000	640,000	960,000
Scenario GUEST	440,000	1,480,000	1,920,000

Migration Forecasts for Turkey Based on Southern Europe, 2004–30

Estimates for the "determinants" of migration were obtained using similar specification as with "all Europe" for the period 1967–2001. Using these parameters, again, the *two simulation* exercises were repeated—the *FREE* and *GUEST* scenarios. In both simulations, Turkey was assumed to be on its baseline high growth path (Table 2). 2015 was retained as the regime switching date. Computations for Germany were adjusted for the EU-15 in the same way as in the previous exercises.

The picture that emerged closely resembled that of the "all Europe" sample. When the free labor mobility experience of Greece, Portugal and Spain was emulated for Turkey, a small hike occurred in migration that stabilized promptly at a low level. In this scenario, total net migration forecast until 2030 was not exceeding 1 million (Table 4).

The experiment using the Southern Europe sample but mimicking the guest worker syndrome led to a major jump that normalized in due course. The total net migration estimate approached 2 million, doubling the previous forecast based on the actual membership experience of these countries. Nevertheless, even this inflated figure was considerably below sensational projections.

Turkey's Own Experience as the Only Reference, 1967–2001

How to inflate the migration forecasts further? "Turkey is not any other South European Country," "unlike Greece, Portugal and Spain, Turkey has a nomadic tradition." If these prejudices are taken for granted, Turkey's own experience would be the only benchmark.

The model was estimated for the period 1967–2001 for immigration from only Turkey to Germany. The coefficients of the explanatory variables denoting income and employment differences were again significant. So were the INTERVENTION and INSURGENCY dummies. The absolute values of the income and employment parameters were considerably greater than those obtained in estimations with the "all Europe" and "Southern Europe" samples. This was expected since Turkey has not yet had the socio-economic transition that the current EU members have accomplished during their accession periods.

Using the parameters obtained from these estimations, migration projections were made for the 2004–30 period, and they were adjusted upward for EU-15. Obviously, these parameter estimates and projections, unlike the previous ones, did not contain any information on actual EU membership or free labor mobility experience. The only labor mobility Turkey had in accordance with an agreement was the guest worker episode of the 1960s until 1973.

High Growth, EU Membership and Free Movement of Labor: Forecast 2004–30

In our first simulation with the Turkish record as the only benchmark, we retained our baseline high growth scenario as depicted in Table 2. Following a successful accession period, Turkey becomes an EU member and free labor mobility is introduced in 2015. Given that Turkey's only experience with a labor arrangement was the guest worker episode, free movement of labor could only be introduced in the forecast as the repetition of this experience.

The resulting projection exhibited a major jump in migration that moderated gradually. The forecast for total net migration until 2030 reached 2.1 million. This somewhat exceeded the higher scenario based on the South European experience (Table 5).

Suspended EU Accession, Lower Growth and No Free Mobility of Labor: Forecast 2004–30

Our last simulation depicts a scenario where Turkey's EU accession is suspended. High growth cannot be sustained and unemployment climbs. More specifically, the urban GDP grows at 4 percent annually with 1.5 percent productivity increase and rural GDP stagnates. Unemployment approaches 20 percent.[12]

In this scenario, the prevailing EU visa regulations are retained. This obviously curtails major jumps in migration. However, the slow pace in income growth and the deterioration in the labor market increase migration pressures considerably. An increasing number of the potential migrants penetrate the EU. The forecast for total net migration until 2030 in this scenario exceeded 2.7 million. The result is a warning that if the membership perspective is lost, the EU may end up having more immigrants from Turkey despite strict restrictions on labor mobility. This paradoxical scenario is indeed realistic for three reasons.

Firstly, Turkey's growth record clearly shows that very high rates can be achieved but cannot be sustained without political stability and inflow of foreign savings. Without the EU anchor provided by the membership perspective, a growth performance that can cope with unemployment is not feasible.

Table 5. Comparison of the Two Scenarios—Reference: Only the Turkish Experience

Net Change in the Turkish Migrant Stock	2004–15	2015–30	Total
High Growth—Membership—Free Movement of Labor	246,000	1,888,000	2,134,000
Lower Growth—No Membership—No Free Movement of Labor	760,000	1,974,000	2,734,000

Secondly, unlike successful accession scenarios, not only would growth in Turkey be slower and unemployment higher, but also sensitivity of migration to income and unemployment differences would be greater.[13]

Thirdly, the prevailing restrictive visa system of the EU and the absence of labor mobility provisions cannot stop immigration. The EU currently receives about 70,000 (gross) migrants from Turkey, annually. (Because of return migration, net migration is about half of this gross inflow figure.[14]) Most of them come from family unification and family formation. In the presence of a very large Turkish migrant community in the EU of about 3 million (with major trade, investment, tourism and educational links), all conceivable tight-door policies short of totalitarian rules would be porous. A relative deterioration in Turkey would certainly increase this inflow considerably and reduce return migration.

Finally, it should be noted that the eventuality of political turmoil was not incorporated in the projections. With the lost EU perspective and climbing unemployment, this is more than a slim possibility. Estimations based on past records show that political and security problems lead to waves of migration.[15] Add that to the 2.7 million forecast!

Impact of the Ageing of the Turkish Population on Migration

In this study, as the estimations were based on past population structures, the impact of the changes in the age composition of Turkish population was not specifically taken into consideration.[16] However, the propensity to migrate differs considerably among age groups and the very young Turkish population is bound to age.

A regional survey conducted in Turkey by Hacettepe University, Ankara, jointly with the Netherlands Interdisciplinary Demographic Institute (NIDI) and Eurostat[17] revealed that the tendency of people aged 55 and above to migrate was extremely low.[18] Hubert Krieger's study based on Eurobarometer surveys corroborated these results. Turkish population is ageing. According to the UN projections, the share of people aged 55 and above in Turkey will nearly double by 2030 (Figure 5). When this demographic development was crudely incorporated in our projections, it was found that total migration forecasts to 2030 had to be scaled down by about 300,000.

Conclusion

As Turkey becomes an EU member and enjoys free movement of labor, the net inflow of migrants will be in the direction of the EU-15 in the foreseeable future. The projections for potential Turkish migration based on the experiences of various groups of countries differed (Table 6). However, the figures involved were by no means sensational, despite the fact that we wishfully assumed that free movement of labor would be introduced as early as 2015.

In the debate about Turkish EU membership and free movement of labor it is often overlooked that the EU cannot exercise a zero migration policy even if permanent safeguards were used. Even under the currently prevailing strict regime, there

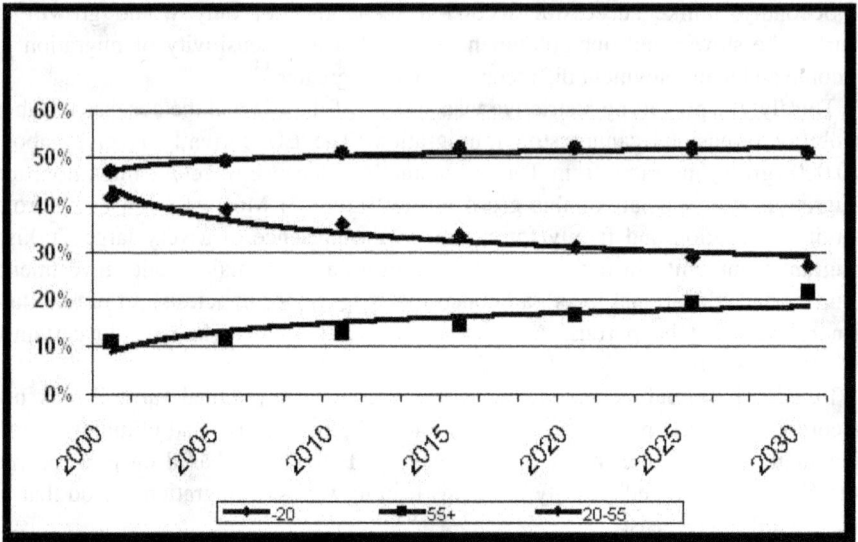

Figure 5.   Share of age groups in total population

Table 6.   Summary: Migration Forecasts from Turkey to EU-15

Reference Group: "All Europe"

High Growth—Membership—Free Movement of Labor	2004–15	2015–30	Total
Scenario FREE	460,000	613,000	1,073,000
Scenario GUEST	564,000	1,274,000	1,838,000

Reference Group: Greece, Portugal, Spain and Turkey

High Growth—Membership—Free Movement of Labor	2004–15	2015–30	Total
Scenario FREE	320,000	640,000	960,000
Scenario GUEST	440,000	1,480,000	1,920,000

Reference Group: Only the Turkish Experience

	2004–15	2015–30	Total
High Growth—Membership—Free Movement of Labor	246,000	1,888,000	2,134,000
LOWER Growth—NO Membership—NO Free Movement of Labor	760,000	1,974,000	2,734,000

is an annual net migration from Turkey to the EU-15 in the order of 35,000 people. Any slowdown or suspension in Turkey's accession process is likely to lead to lower growth and higher unemployment in Turkey. Moreover, the reform process might slow down or be partially reversed. The consequence of such a combination would be a drastically higher number of potential migrants, a considerable proportion of whom would be finding their way into the EU—as experience has shown irrespective of legal restriction. It is thus possible that if Turkey loses the membership perspective, the EU may end up having more immigrants than under a free movement of labor regime with a prosperous EU-member Turkey. Moreover, the composition of this migration would be less conducive for the EU labor markets and for integration in the host societies.

The experiences of Greece, Portugal and Spain indicate that a successful accession period with high growth and effective implementation of the reforms reduces and gradually eliminates the migration pressures. There is no *a priori* reason why Turkey would not go through a similar experience.

Acknowledgments

An earlier version of this study was presented at the conference "Immigration Issues in EU–Turkish Relations: Determinants of Immigration and Integration," Boğaziçi University, Istanbul, October 8–9, 2004. It is based on the findings of the "twin projects"—employment and immigration, at Boğaziçi University, Center for Economics and Econometrics (http://www.cee.boun.edu.tr) and Center for European Studies (http://www.ces.boun.edu.tr), sponsored by Open Society Institute Assistance Foundation (OSIAF). The authors are grateful to Nalan Baştürk, Guneş Ertürk and Engin Evrenos for important contributions to the research.

Notes

1. Commission of the European Communities, "Issues Arising from Turkey's Membership Perspective" [COM (2004) 656 final]. The studies surveyed include Harry Flam, *Turkey and the EU: Politics and Economics of Accession* (Stockholm: Institute for International Economic Studies, 2003); and A.M. Lejour, R.A. De Mooij and C.H. Capel, *Assessing the Economic Implications of Turkish Accession to the EU*, CPB, Document No. 56 (The Hague: Netherlands Bureau for Economic Policy Analysis, 2004).
2. See Hubert Krieger and Bertrand Maitre, *Migration Trends in an Enlarging European Union*, in this volume.
3. Patricia Alvarez-Plata, Herbert Brücker and Boris Siliverstovs, *Potential Migration from Central and Eastern Europe into the EU-15—An Update* (Berlin: DIW, 2003).
4. See also Tito Boeri and Herbert Brücker, *The Impact of Eastern Enlargement on Employment and Labour Markets in the EU Member States* (Brussels: European Commission, 2001).
5. $$m_{fht} = \alpha_h + \beta_1 m_{fh,t-1} + \beta_2 m_{fh,t-2} + \beta_3 \ln(w_{ft} / w_{ht}) + \beta_4 \ln(w_{ht}) + \beta_5 \ln(e_{ft}) + \beta_6 \ln(e_{ht}) + u_{fht}$$

   m_{fht}: The share of migrants from country h residing in country f (Germany) as a percentage of home population

   w: Wage (income, proxied by GDP-PPP per capita)

   e: Employment rate (1-unemployment rate)

h, f, t: Home, foreign country and year, respectively.

Population data from World Development Indicators (2003), migrant stock data from the Federal German Statistical Office, per capita GDP from Maddison (2002) and Groningen Growth and Development Center, employment rates, from OECD Economic Outlook.

6. The model is estimated using SUR. This method was chosen because of its superior performance with large databases in the EU Commission study. Common slopes were assumed for all countries but intercepts were allowed to be country specific.

7. As the estimation is semi-logarithmic, a coefficient with an absolute value of 1 implies that a change in this variable would affect the dependent variable at the same rate of change. Values smaller than 1 imply smaller impacts.

8. See "Growth, Employment and Active Policies," Boğaziçi University, June 2004, http://www.cee.boun.edu.tr.

9. The iterations include the decline in unemployment in Turkey (about 1 percentage point) resulting from migration to the EU.

10. The migrant stock data used in the simulations do not cover those who were naturalized in Germany. Data on naturalization of EU citizens were not available for Germany. Therefore naturalized immigrants could not be included in the estimations covering all European source countries. (Data on naturalized immigrants originating from Turkey were available.) Although naturalization entailed considerable numbers in the last decade, it did not affect the immigration projections significantly.

11. This assumes that all other EU-15 countries that host immigrants have the same "pull" effect as Germany.

12. In this lower growth scenario, average (urban + rural) unemployment reaches 17% in 2015 and 22% in 2030. Migration to the EU reduces these figures to 16% and 19%, respectively.

13. Coefficients for income and employment differences have considerably higher values in the estimations with the "Turkish experience only" compared with that of the "all Europe" and "South European" samples. The reason is lesser convergence of the Turkish socio-economic system.

14. We have cross-checked stock and flow data (OECD, SOPEMI) for current Turkish migrant inflow to EU-15. Due to missing data, we do not have exact figures. We infer that the gross inflow can be 60,000 to 90,000 and the gross outflow 30,000 to 40,000.

15. As reported in the first section of the study, in the estimations covering 1967–2001, dummy variables INTERVENTION (1980) and INSURGENCY (1990–94) were highly significant and improved the fit considerably.

16. The estimations based on 1967–2001 data do implicitly incorporate the ageing experienced in the sample countries. However, the projections implicitly assume the same average population structure as in the past.

17. H. Öztaş-Ayhan, B. Akadlı-Ergöçmen, A. Hancıoğlu, A. İçduygu, İ. Koç, A. Toros, A. Sinan-Türkyılmaz, T. Ünalan, S. Üner and E. Kurtuluş-Yiğit, *Push and Pull Factors of International Migration: Country Report—Turkey*, Eurostat Working Papers: 3/2000/E/no.8 (Luxembourg: Hacettepe University, Ankara and the Netherlands Interdisciplinary Demographic Institute (NIDI), 2002).

18. The regional coverage of this study was not representative for Turkey as a whole. Therefore, the age configuration of propensity to migrate was not formally incorporated in our projections.

Migration Trends in an Enlarging European Union

HUBERT KRIEGER* & BERTRAND MAÎTRE**

*European Foundation for the Improvement of Living and Working Conditions, **Economic and Social Research Institute, Dublin, Ireland

Introduction

Migration is a serious policy concern for the European Union. It covers a wide range of important challenges as high unemployment in major receiving countries, concerns with regard to social and cultural integration of migrants, and the reduced social cohesion of receiving countries due to the lack of civic and political participation of even second and third generation migrants. However, migration may open up important opportunities, such as the reduction of the predicted long-term gap in labor supply in Europe due to demographic ageing, and the contribution to the improved financial sustainability of the pension systems of the receiving countries. These concerns are raised in relation to mobility inside an enlarged EU of 25 member states, but in particular regarding migration from "third" countries outside the Union.

Recent discussions on migration issues in Europe have been fueled by five issues: firstly, by the enlargement of the EU in May 2004 by ten new member states from

Correspondence Address: Hubert Krieger, European Foundation for the Improvement of Living and Working Conditions, Wyattville Road, Loughlinstown, Dublin 18, Ireland. Email: hkr@eurofound.eu.int

Central, Eastern and Southern Europe, secondly by the imminent enlargement by two additional countries from Eastern Europe in 2007 (Bulgaria and Romania), thirdly by the long-term prospect of Turkish EU membership with a possible accession after 2015, fourthly by the large numbers of illegal migrants who enter or try to enter the European Union, in particular on its eastern and southern boarders, and fifthly by the substantial numbers of asylum seekers in the EU.

For some politicians and for a significant part of the electorate in the former EU member states (EU15), a major concern is an expected "flood" of economic migrants from the new member states (NEW10) and the future accession countries. Concerns are based on a large income gap of around 60 percent between the Central and Eastern European countries and the "old" member states. In the case of Bulgaria, Romania and Turkey this GDP per capita gap may increase to over 70 percent. This income gap is significantly larger than in the previous southern enlargement of the EU.

In most member states the likelihood of increased inward migration from new and future member countries has become an important issue for the internal political debate. Strong headlines in the tabloid press, like "tidal wave of migrants ahead" or "hundreds of thousands of Roma invading Europe," influence public opinion. In some political circles, EU enlargement is mainly discussed in regard to its possible impact on the governance of the EU (overstretching) and on the redistribution of structural funds.

Economic concerns are related to a further increase of already high internal unemployment rates as result of a crowding out of local blue-collar workers in manufacturing and unqualified white-collar workers in the service sector by better qualified but also cheaper employees from new member states. Negative impacts on wages through "social dumping" of migrant workers are voiced in some trade union quarters. Social fears are raised in regard to a possible abuse of the existing non-contributory social welfare provisions ("welfare tourism") and increased competition for cheap housing in inner-city areas. Other concerns expressed are about increased crime levels and negative effects for the social cohesion of increasingly heterogeneous societies.

In the new member states and the future accession countries, the possible labor market effects are seen as double-edged. Countries with high levels of unemployment and low economic growth rates may benefit from the migration of low-skilled and unqualified workers by reducing labor supply and leaving fewer people without jobs. Also, the remittance payments of migrant workers have a positive impact on income, consumption and aggregated internal demand. If countries, however, face emigration of more highly qualified and younger people, this may erode their long-term competitive position. It is agreed that such a "brain and youth drain" may have negative repercussions on the developmental process.[1]

As a reaction to this lively internal debate, nearly all "old" member states—with the exception of Ireland, the UK and Sweden—have decided to use transitional arrangements for workers from new member states, providing a phased access to their national labor markets. But even the UK and Ireland have restricted access to non-contributory social welfare benefits during the first two years for migrants from the NEW10. This has caused in return a negative reaction in the NEW10, where many citizens felt they were being treated as "second class" Europeans.

The situation in regard to Turkey is even more contentious. Some fear an overstretching of the EU, some stress the cultural incompatibility between a Christian-based EU25 and a Muslim-based Turkish society and some fear the political influence of Turkey as the second largest member state after Germany in an EU of 28 members. Of even greater importance are traditional labor market and social issues, with some commentators predicting more than 3 million potential Turkish migrants.

Within this context, the focus of this piece is on labor market issues of migration towards the old EU15 from three regions: the NEW10, the two accession countries (AC2) entering in 2007 (Romania/Bulgaria) and Turkey.

The discussion covers in particular two questions:

- What is the expected volume of migration into the "old" member states?
- What is the structure of potential migrants from the NEW10, the two accession countries and from Turkey?

This study is based on Eurobarometer data collected for the European Commission, which was conducted in early spring 2002. It includes: Bulgaria, Cyprus, Czech Republic, Estonia, Hungary, Latvia, Lithuania, Malta, Poland, Romania, Slovakia, Slovenia and Turkey. In Cyprus, the survey only covers citizens living in the southern part of the island. An identical set of questions was posed to representative samples of the population aged 15 years and over in each country. The regular sample in these Eurobarometer surveys is 1,000 persons per country, except Malta and Cyprus (500). For this study, a 2,000 sample was used in Poland and Turkey to achieve better coverage. In each of the 13 candidate countries, national institutes associated with and coordinated by the Gallup Organization in Hungary carried out the survey.

Construction of Potential to Migrate

How is the potential to migrate defined and measured? The study measures the attitudes towards migration into the EU on two different levels: (1) general intention to migrate and (2) firm intention to migrate.

(1) The general intention to migrate reflects a basic attitude towards migration to the EU. The questionnaire includes a direct question: "Do you intend to go to live and work—for a few months or for several years—in a current European Union country in the next five years?" In order to control the validity of the answers to this question and to construct the indicator on the general intention to migrate, positive answers to this question are combined with the results of questions which measure the intention of regional mobility in the next five

years by moving to any place outside the same city, town or village. In this respect, one filter question and one follow-up question were asked: "Do you intend to move in the next five years?" and if the answer was positive the follow-up question: "In the next five years, do you intend to move to another city, town or village within the same region; to another region within the same country; to another country in Europe and to live in a country outside Europe?" Not only for logical reasons, but also from a common-sense point of view, it has to be assumed that anybody who intends to migrate into the EU also has a basic intention of regional mobility in the next five years.[2] Respondents answering positively to the combined indicator can be regarded as having over-come their "natural inertia" against migration and have a general intention to migrate into the EU.

(2) The firm intention to migrate to the EU provides a second measurement within the present study, which should provide the highest degree of probability to predict actual migration behavior by capturing, at least partly, the intensity of the intention to migrate. It has been measured with the help of four variables—two of which have already been used to measure the "general intention." In addition, these answers are controlled by a third indicator of "target regional mobility into the EU15" and by a fourth indicator, which measures the willing-ness to live in a country with a foreign language. The question was "How willing would you be to live in another European country, where the language is different from your mother tongue?" To accept explicitly the challenges that come with migrating to a country with another language provides an indicator of "medium level" strength of the seriousness to migrate. The response catego-ries vary from "very much," to "some extent," "not much" and "not at all." The indicator of a firm intention to migrate includes only those respondents who answered "very much" to this question. Similar to approaches by other scholars, the present study aims to capture the strength of the intention to migrate by using a four-dimensional scale.

Potential to Migrate into the EU15 and Comparison with Results from Other Studies

What is the potential to migrate to the EU15? As this study discusses migration in a broader quality of life context, the intention to migrate is calculated for the whole population from 15 years of age onwards.

According to the first column in Table 1, less than 5 percent (4.6 percent) of the citizens in all 13 countries have a general intention to move in the next five years. This is reduced to just below 1 percent (0.9 percent) for the firm intention to move from the 13 countries into the EU15. That means that only 20 percent of the popula-tion with a general intention to migrate has to be regarded as a "hard core" group, where a higher probability of actual migration can be predicted.

The highest general intention to migrate is shown in Turkey, with 6.2 percent, and in Bulgaria/Romania with 5 percent. Bulgaria itself reaches levels similar to

Table 1.   Potential to Migrate (%)

Country	General Intention	Firm Intention
Poland	3.7	1.0
Turkey	6.2	0.3
AC2 (Bulgaria/Romania)	5.0	2.0
NEW10	3.1	0.8
ALL 13	4.6	0.9

Turkey. The people in the NEW10 are more immobile at 3.1 percent. Within this grouping, the Maltese are most immobile with 1.3 percent. Hungary/Czech Republic/Slovakia have only a slightly higher general migration potential (2.4 percent). The conclusion for European Union migration policy is that all larger groups of potential migrants are outside the ten new member states. The highest percentages in the group of new member states are in Poland and the three Baltic countries with around 3.5 percent, which is a significantly lower migration potential than the AC2 and Turkey.[3]

The second indicator covers the firm intention to migrate. In three country clusters around 1 percent of the population has a firm intention to migrate into the EU: Poland, the NEW10 and ALL13. In regard to this indicator Bulgaria/Romania (AC2) also remains the top supply group for potential migrants, according to a firm intention to migrate by 2 percent of its population. The highest country result is in Bulgaria, with 2.5 percent and the lowest in Malta with 0.1 percent.

Turkey is a surprise in absolute and relative terms. The Turkish respondents topped the list of all 13 countries as far as the general intention is concerned and are nearly at the bottom of the list concerning a firm intention. Also in absolute terms it is incredible that only 0.3 percent of the Turkish population have a firm intention to migrate over the next five years.

What does this mean in absolute terms for the Turkish migration potential over five years under the condition of free mobility? Assuming a Turkish population stock of all inhabitants of 15 years and older of nearly 48.9 million in 2003, this would lead to a predicted migration potential of 3.03 million for the general intention and 0.15 million for the firm intention. Using a more realistic third indicator, the "basic intention to migrate," which was developed in the report on the migration potential by Krieger,[4] one would predict a minimum migration potential of around 400,000 Turkish citizens over five years in the EU15. The independent Commission for Turkey[5] led by Martti Ahtisaari comes to similar results as far as the upper limit is concerned. It estimates the Turkish long-term migration potential of 2.7 million. However, it leaves open two important questions: what is the basis for these figures and, secondly, what is its definition of the "long-term"? In order to control the results of both studies, it would be necessary to compare them with recent Turkish studies using a similar method. According to Turkish sources such studies are unfortunately not available.

Micro Studies

To what extent do these results concur with other micro and macro studies? Altogether four overview studies on the micro level are available covering Central and Eastern European countries in different combinations, though excluding Malta, Cyprus and Turkey. In 1998, the International Organization for Migration (IOM)[6] conducted a survey in 11 Central and Eastern European countries with a sample size of approximately 1,000 respondents per country. It covered seven candidate countries (Bulgaria, Romania, Slovenia, Hungary, Poland, Czech Republic and Slovakia). In a first step it identified the willingness to move to another country according to the length of the intended stay, ranging from a "few weeks," a "few months," a "few years" to staying "for the rest of one's life."[7]

As the results for the first two dimensions are relatively similar, we will cover only one of them, "very short-term" migration. In this respect, the countries show an extremely wide range of results, from 13 percent in Bulgaria to 56 percent in Slovakia. The low result for Bulgaria may be explained by its relative distance to Western European labor markets, which may have a prohibitive effect on short-term migration. Looking at the other extreme of intended stay, 7 percent of the respondents in Bulgaria and Slovenia opt for permanent migration. It is surprising that the Bulgarian propensity to migrate is only a third of the Romanian (21 percent).

The overall result of between 10 percent and 14 percent of respondents with an intention of permanent migration in Slovakia, Czech Republic and Poland seems extremely high, not to mention the 21 percent in Romania.[8] One aspect which may explain these extremely high figures is the coding of the available responses. The IOM study includes in the migration potential everyone who is "very likely" and "likely" to migrate. One can expect significantly lower figures by including only the respondents with a "very likely" intention. In addition, all indicators are taken at face value and the authors make no use of possible control variables, which are provided by other variables in the survey, e.g. a list of concrete activities.

As mentioned before, eight activities were measured, ranging from information gathering to selling property for migration and applying for a work permit. The analysis of these indicators allows an identification of the strength of the intention to migrate. The results show a strong variation between the seven countries. Obtaining relevant information for migration varies between 8 percent and 38 percent; Applying for a job has a range from 4 percent to 28 percent and the selling of property ranges from 0 percent to 11 percent. Looking at the results shows a constant pattern of extremely high values for Poland. It is difficult to believe that 11 percent of all Polish potential migrants sold property before migrating. The results for the other countries seem much more reliable. What is missing, however, is any attempt to create a more complex measurement instrument by combining different indicators.

A four-country study (Poland, Hungary, Czech Republic and Slovakia) was conducted by Fassmann and Hintermann (F/H) in 1996 and was published in 1997.[9]

It is based on a quota sample and includes 4,392 cases. The study measures three levels of intended migration. The general migration potential (level I) shows great differences between the countries: Slovakia with 30 percent, Hungary and the Czech Republic with 20 percent and Poland with nearly 17 percent. Accordingly, the Slovaks are twice as likely to migrate as the Poles. In comparison to the present study the results of F/H are, on average, around 10 times higher, with a range between 5 and 14 times (Slovakia). They also show a significant shift in relative order: In the present study Poland has the highest migration potential and Slovakia the third highest. In the F/H study it is the other way round. It is difficult to judge whether these large differences are due to the different methodology, the different quality of data or due to measuring different points of time.

Calculating the probable potential for migration halves the percentage in three countries and reduces it for Poland by two-thirds to 6 percent. The Slovaks keep the leading position with nearly 18 percent. The strongest indicator is the "real" potential for migration (level III). Here, Hungary has the lowest value with 0.7 percent, Poland is second lowest with 1.3 percent and the Czechs and Slovaks follow with 2.2 percent. As far as the three countries are concerned the step from the level II to level III indicator reduces the potential to migrate to less than one-ninth. For Poland it is only a reduction of one-fifth.

Comparing the firm intention to migrate reveals much lower differences between this study and the F/H study, as the results of the latter are between 0.3 and 1.4 percentage points higher than the present study. Both studies confirm the lowest propensity for migration in Hungary. They differ, however, as far as the country with the highest propensity is concerned. Despite some differences, the results of both studies point in the same direction and question seriously the gist of the magnitude of the IOM results.

To conclude: in comparison to other studies the present report may underestimate the potential to migrate due to its more rigorous operationalization and its lack of distinction between different forms of migration, leading to an under-representation of short-term migrants in the sample. In addition, all survey-based projections have in common the systematical underestimation of illegal migration, which represents a significant share of East–West migration.

Macro Studies

The last part of the empirical analysis in this section compares the estimates of the potential to migrate based on the Eurobarometer survey from 2002 with the results of an econometric study of the European Commission on *The Impact of Eastern Enlargement on Employment and Labour Markets in the EU and Member States*, which was conducted at nearly the same time.[10] Comparability is not easy as the studies use different methodologies. The present study is based on individual survey data, with all its advantages and disadvantages, to predict actual migration behavior. It predicts the possible increase in migration stock in the "old" EU member states within the next five years, i.e. by the end of 2006. Its key dependent variables are various estimated migration rates in the country of origin as a percentage of the population 15 years and older.

The European Commission study uses a macroeconomic approach in order to estimate annual migration flows between 2002 and 2030.[11] Unlike the present study, the Commission only includes eight new member states (NEW8) and two accession countries (AC2), leaving out the three southern Mediterranean countries Malta, Cyprus and Turkey. The coefficients for the estimation of the migration potential are based on time series data of the migration flows to Germany in the period 1967 to 1998. Its key dependent variable is the annual change in the ratio of the stock of migrants to the population in the receiving country. The theoretical assumptions are based on the human capital paradigm of migration. As independent variables the model uses the following sets of indicators: the difference of per capita purchasing power parity, the employment rate in the home and host countries, a lagged ratio of the stock of migrants to the home population and other institutional variables. In addition, the model is estimated with the help of country-specific effects to control for culture, policy, language, distance, etc.[12] For the dynamic analysis two additional basic assumptions are made as far as the baseline projection is concerned: that the GDP gap between old and new member states converges by two percentage points per year; and that the unemployment rates are stable.

Based on these assumptions the study estimates an increase of the stock of migrants from 1.16 million in 2002 to 3.9 million in 2030. The annual flow figures decrease from 340,000 in 2002 to below 3,000 in 2030.

Due to the different methodologies the two studies can only be compared on the basis of estimated changes in the stock figures in ten countries between 2002 and 2006. For this comparison the following calculations have to be made for the Commission study: the stock of migrants is predicted to be 1.16 million in 2002 and 2.25 million in 2006.[13] This results in a predicted increase of 1.1 million migrants in the time span 2002 to 2006 for the ten countries.

In order to make the present study comparable it has to provide results for the two dependent variables for the ten countries included in the Commission's study. The results are as follows:

- General inclination NEW8 and AC2: 3.7 percent
- Firm intention NEW8 and AC2: 1.2 percent

In the next step it has to calculate the population in the NEW8/AC2 for the age groups 15 years and older. The total population of the ten countries on January 1, 2001 was 102 million.[14] Subtracting the population under 15 years of age of around 19.5 million provides a total number of 82.5 million inhabitants in the ten countries of 15 years of age and older. Multiplying this basic figure with the three coefficients provides the following band of a predicted increase in the migration stock up to the end 2006 in absolute numbers:

- General inclination: 3.05 million
- Firm intention: 1 million (precisely 990,000)

The result of the comparison is that both methods lead to similar results predicting an increase in the total number of migrants from the ten Eastern European Countries of between 1 and 1.1 million people for the narrow band in the years up to the end of 2006 in the old member states of the EU.[15]

Why no "Tidal Wave" of Migrants?

Four main basic arguments are usually developed, which may explain the low probability of a significant inflow of migrants from the three country groupings into the EU:

- Firstly it is argued that a significant proportion of the overall potential of migrants from these countries has already arrived in the existing EU member states in recent years, i.e. before 2002. The available figures show that this had led to only a small increase in the population of the "older" member states. In 1998, the 15 EU member states hosted less than 900,000 citizens of the Central and Eastern European countries.[16]
- Secondly, the demographic situation in the 13 countries is similar to the demographic situation in the EU. Fertility in most of these countries is even lower than in the EU (with the exception of Turkey) and mortality has dramatically increased, with the consequence of a decreasing population trend in the next 30 to 40 years. Consequently, everything being equal, the employment chances for younger and better educated people will increase in the NEW10 and AC2. Based on this trend Fassmann and Muenz predict a decrease of the potential for migration.[17]
- Thirdly, transfer of resources for economic development, increased international trade and massive inward investment will accompany the accession process of the new and the future member states. This will accelerate the economic development process and will give the new member states a positive growth differential in relation to the "old" member states.
- In addition, contrary to the predictions of economic theory, European employees have taken only little advantage of the free movement within a common labor market. Straubhaar provides an explanation and notes: "To an important degree, trade has replaced the economic demand for migration in the EU."[18]

Socio-Economic Factors of Migration

This section discusses several important socio-economic variables in regard to their interrelationship with intended migration to the EU. All indicators are used in various concepts as proxies explaining migration behavior. Competing explanatory models of migration often use the same indicators. The intention of this section is to provide a descriptive analysis of the main socio-economic characteristics of those respondents who express a willingness to migrate. This provides some additional insights in the conceptual debate, e.g. on the increasing feminization of migration and the importance of individual unemployment as a driver for migration.

A second objective of the section is more political. The heterogeneity of the group of potential migrants has to be taken into account in designing relevant labor market and social policy measures in order to cope with the consequence of regional mobility. For policy makers it is important to know if the majority of migrants have higher or lower levels of education, are younger or older, and are unemployed or are in stable employment. "It is therefore important that policies are designed according to the opportunities and constraints specific to different groups … as well as according to specific groups' trans-national spheres of action."[19]

In the discussion of the effects of socio-economic factors we will distinguish in this section between NEW9 and Poland as we have enough cases to provide a specific analysis for Poland due to over-sampling. The same holds true for Turkey. All analysis is based on the general intention to migrate and not on the firm intention, as we would not have sufficient cases to make firm statistical conclusions.

Age

There is wide consensus in migration literature of a strong influence of age on migration.[20] Younger cohorts are regarded as more mobile, whereas beyond the age of 40 there is a significant drop of intended migration. From an economic point of view, two main explanations are given. Younger cohorts usually have better labor market prospects in the receiving country, in particular when they are prepared to take up lower-paid jobs mainly in the service sector. They often increase their labor market chances in the receiving countries by accepting work beneath their actual level of qualification, thus providing local employers with a lower wage rate combined with higher productivity. The second economic argument comes from human capital theory, which suggests a better return on investment in migration with decreasing age. Older workers have a lower economic incentive to migrate, as the amortization period for their investment is shorter.[21]

Figure 1 focuses on the people willing to migrate as a percentage of a specific age group. For NEW9 and ALL13 one out of ten of the youngest age cohort wants to

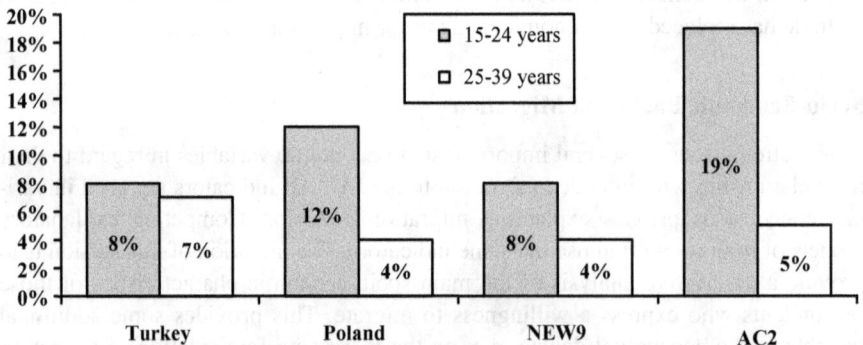

Figure 1.   Intention to migrate by age.

migrate into the EU. The highest tendency to migrate is shown in AC2, where nearly one in five wants to migrate. Poland reaches 12 percent and Turkey has a share of around 8 percent in the youngest age group. Overall, this has the potential of a massive "youth drain" from these countries.

As far as the second youngest cohort (25–39) is concerned, between 4 and 5 percent in NEW9, Poland and AC2 want to migrate. The highest percentage is in Turkey, where 7 percent of the 25–39 year old age group have a general intention to migrate to the EU. In this respect Turkey has a slightly higher age profile than the other three country groupings.

Gender

Traditionally, the largest proportion of migrants has been male. Younger men were sent out to look for work to finance the remaining family through remittance payments back home, whereas younger women stayed at home taking over family responsibilities. If female migration occurred it was family-linked and was seen in policy terms as a secondary type of migration. Kofman *et al.*[22] estimate that previously 65 percent of all female permanent migration into the EU was family-linked.

According to several authors[23] this common assertion is challenged with the feminization of international migration in Europe. One hypothesis is that the increasing level of education of women in many countries, the frequent loss of employment due to economic transformation, the search for new employment opportunities and a changing role model, which challenges the traditional male breadwinner model, has triggered a reverse trend. This is, however, based on the assumption that higher educational attainment and changed labor market conditions in the sending countries goes hand in hand with a higher propensity to migrate. In addition, female migration could be increased by better labor market opportunities for women in specific segments of the expanding service sector, e.g. in health, care and household-related services of the receiving countries.

The hypothesis of a "feminization" of migration is supported by a state-of-the-art overview by Nyberg-Soerensen *et al.*[24] They observe new groups of migrants emerging, which include young single women or female family breadwinners. An increasing number of women move independently rather than under the authority of older relatives or integrated into a family strategy. Migration takes place more and more within female networks which are separated from those of men. The group of female migrants differs in regard to their socio-economic background. Nyberg-Soerensen *et al.* identify four groups: (1) women from rural backgrounds migrating on their own or as part of family reunification; (2) low-skilled women from urban backgrounds migrating due to divorce, increasing poverty and deprivation levels; (3) more highly educated women motivated by the lack of appropriate job opportunities in the country of origin; and (4) women fleeing civil unrest in their home countries.[25]

Figure 2 shows the percentage of men and women with a general intention to migrate as part of the whole population of 15 years of age and older. In Poland and

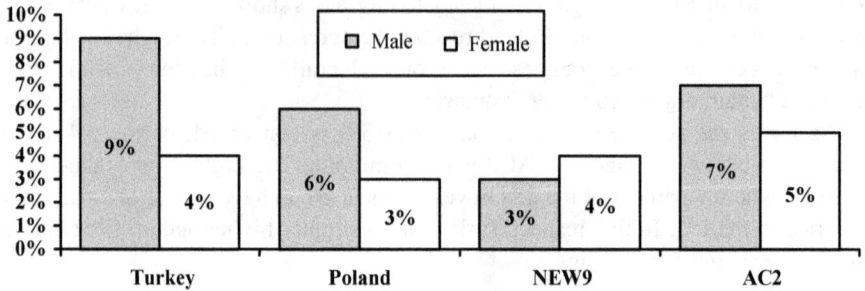

Figure 2.   Intention to migrate by gender.

the AC2 between 6 and 7 percent of all men want to migrate, in the NEW9 this is reduced to 3 percent. Turkey, with 9 percent, has the highest proportion of a male population which is mobile.[26]

As far as women are concerned, the country differences are less pronounced. Between 3 percent (Poland) and 5 percent (AC2) of the female population are mobile. The highest absolute share is in Romania and Bulgaria with 5 percent. However, the NEW9 are the only country grouping where we have a slightly higher percentage of women (4 percent) than men (3 percent) with a general intention to migrate. The situation in Turkey is completely the opposite: Here the proportion of men (9 percent) is more than double that of women (4 percent) with an intention to migrate.

Education

High educational attainment is regarded as a positive factor influencing migration. According to human capital theory, higher levels of education offer increased income returns on specific segments of the labor market. It is also argued that higher levels of education provide a greater ability to collect and process information, which lowers the risk and therefore increases the propensity for migration. Bauer and Zimmermann develop the opposite hypothesis based on an analysis of several international studies of migration.[27] They find an insignificant or even negative correlation between levels of education and propensity to migrate. This can be explained by the prevalence of low-skilled labor markets for migrants in the destination countries, which makes migration less beneficial for high-skilled individuals.

Some observers see the migration of students as a form of migration of young and qualified labor. In several receiving countries it has proven easier to switch from student to worker status than to migrate as a fully qualified employee.[28]

The empirical analysis of the bivariate effect of education shows important variations between the countries. As far as tertiary education is concerned more than 15 percent of the Turkish respondents want to migrate. The other three country groupings, with 3 to 4 percent, are significantly lower. Thus, as far as the general intention to migrate is concerned Turkey faces a serious threat of a brain drain in the years to come.

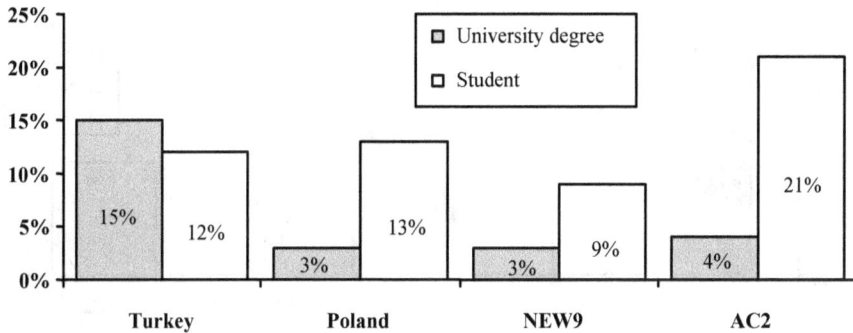

Figure 3.   Intention to migrate by education.

More serious for most country groupings is the potential loss within the student population. The AC2 are in danger of losing 1 in 5 of all students in the following five years, Poland has a figure of 13 percent and Turkey of 12 percent. The lowest are the NEW9 with just under 10 percent. Altogether, this represents the prospect of a serious combined "brain and youth drain" for all countries,[29] leading to the risk of reduced economic growth and negative developmental consequences as described by Myrdal,[30] Wallerstein[31] and by Olesen.[32]

Unemployment

Labor market theory emphasizes income differentials as the strongest and employ-ment differentials as the second strongest factors influencing migration—some scholars reverse the order.[33] As income and employment differentials cannot be measured within the remit of this contribution, we will concentrate on the behavior of the unemployed. In some countries with a high unemployment rate, the unem-ployed are more mobile than employed people. A counter-argument is developed based on socio-economic concepts, which stress the importance of a minimum of resources to provide the capability for migration as a realistic option. Both hypothe-ses suggest some cross-pressure on the intention to migrate for the unemployed, who may face the necessity but lack the resources for migration. The combined hypothesis would lead to a migration threshold: below the threshold one is too poor to migrate and above one is too comfortable.[34]

Economic concepts, focusing on search and information costs, predict that the unemployed have lower opportunity costs during the search process and less constrained time budgets for preparatory search and information behavior related to migration. This would suggest a higher propensity for migration by the unemployed in comparison to employed people with higher opportunity costs.

The share of potential migrants among the unemployed also shows large varia-tions between the four country groupings. In Turkey, 12 percent of the unemployed want to migrate. Also the unemployed in Bulgaria/Romania and Poland have a higher propensity for regional mobility (6/7 percent). The lowest mobility among

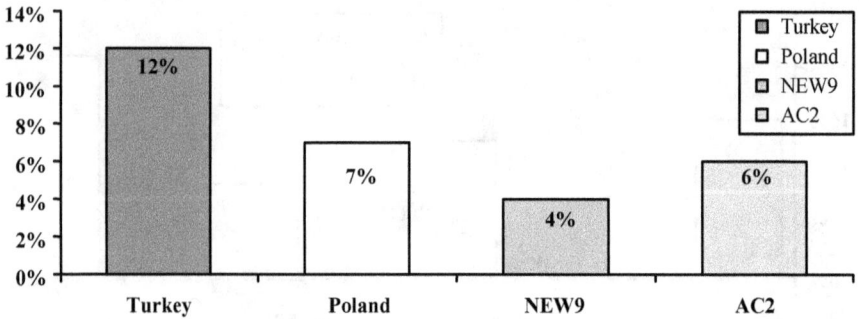

Figure 4.   Intention to migrate by the unemployed.

the unemployed is in the group of new Mediterranean and Central European member states (4 percent). These are countries with better current and future labor market conditions. Immobility may, under those conditions, be a more rational option for the unemployed.

Location

There is a longstanding debate on whether migration comes mainly from rural areas of the sending countries or to a higher extent from urban areas and larger towns. Again the four country groupings show some important structural variation on the same lines, as we have observed in the previous section. Turkey is the only country grouping in which we find a higher rural migration rate than an urban rate. Accordingly, in Turkey 7 percent of the respondents in rural areas and only 5 percent in cities have a general intention to migrate.

The situation in Poland and the NEW9 is different. Here the location-specific migration rate is double in cities compared to rural areas. The AC2 are in the middle with only a slightly higher propensity to migrate in urban areas.

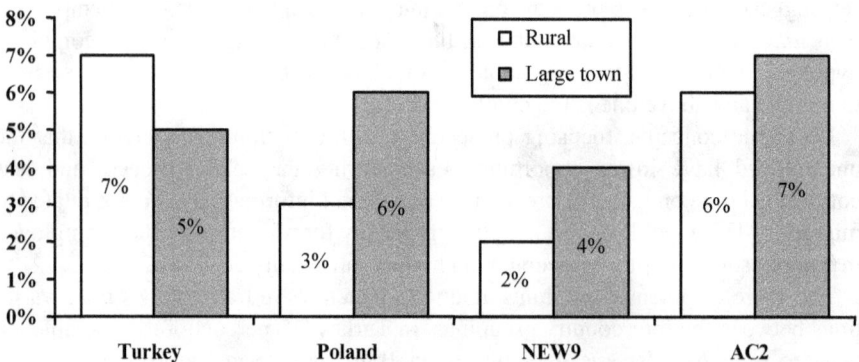

Figure 5.   Intention to migrate by location.

Summary

The bivariate analysis confirms the particular migration pattern of Turkey in comparison to the other country groupings. Potential Turkish migrants have a stronger rural background, are more often in the lowest income quartile and have a relatively high mobility rate within the unemployed. The combination of all three dimensions indicates additional challenging problems of labor market integration in the receiving countries. But there is also another structural feature of Turkish migrants, as they present the relatively highest proportion of migrants with a university degree and a significant proportion of migrants who are still studying. This part of the Turkish migration potential provides a lesser challenge for a successful economic integration.

The structure of potential migrants in the AC2 also has a particular feature. Migrants represent an exceptionally high percentage of students, singles and very young people in comparison to the other three country groupings. From a labor market perspective, potential migrants from the AC2 are probably the most promising group for successful integration in the receiving countries. At the same time, the stronger brain and youth drain creates a particular challenge for the future economic and social development of Bulgaria and Romania.

The NEW9 countries have their most specific feature in the relatively high percentage of female migrants. In addition, they have a similar profile to the AC2 but have a significantly lower level of intention to migrate.

Poland is in the middle between Turkey on one side and the AC2 and NEW9 on the other. It shares with Turkey the higher mobility rate of the unemployed and of men. Poland has more in common with NEW9 and AC2 in regard to the importance of youth, being a student and single and belonging to the highest income quartile.

However, the results of this bivariate are only of limited importance. They have to be tested in the final step of our analysis within a multivariate analysis.

Multivariate Analysis

Following the analysis of the influence of economic and socio-structural factors on the intention to migrate through a bivariate statistical analysis, this section provides a multivariate analysis using a logistic regression of odds ratios for four regional groupings or countries: Turkey, Poland, NEW9 and AC2. In preparation it is necessary to define, for each variable, a reference dimension, which takes over the function as a comparator for the odds of the other dimensions. An odds ratio above the value of 1 indicates a positive influence whereas an odds ratio with a value smaller than 1 indicates a negative relationship. All odds ratios are tested for their significance level. According to professional standards only results higher than a significance level of 95 percent are deemed statistically significant.

Components of the Models

The dependent variable that is used is the general intention to migrate. The study has identified the following set of important explanatory factors:

(1) *Gender.*   Gender is likely to have an impact on the general intention for migration. The model compares male to female (reference dimension).

(2) *Age group.*   The study distinguishes four age groups: 15–24, 25–39, 40–54 and 55+. It compares the first two categories and the last one to the age group of 40–54 years (reference dimension).

(3) *Marital status.*   The study identifies three categories: married/cohabiting, single and widowed/separated/divorced (reference group).

(4) *Employment status.*   The study distinguishes four categories: employed, unemployed, student and other inactive (reference group).

(5) *Education.*   The study makes the following distinction: Those who finished education at the age of 15, between 16 to 19 years, 20 years and older and those still studying. Respondents in the first category have been used as reference group.

(6) *Position in income distribution.*   Individuals are categorized by their position in regard to equivalent household income quartiles. The statistical model compares the other three lower quartiles to the top income quartile (reference group).

(7) *Location.*   Respondents are also classified according to their place of residence. The model used in the analysis compares a location in a large town to a location in a rural area or in a small or medium-size town (reference group).

(8) *Ownership of house or apartment.*   The survey provides a variety of information in regard to the housing situation of the respondent. The various categories have been summarized in two dimensions: tenant of a house or apartment and owner (reference group).

(9) *Social capital.*   The survey provides information on the degree of active involvement in a number of political, social, cultural, religious and other voluntary organizations. Based on an additive index, three levels of social capital have been identified. The statistical model compares medium and high level of social capital with low level of social capital, which functions as the reference group.

Main Results

The logistic regression of the general intention to migrate supports the observations in previous sections of different causal patterns in the four country groupings. This result reaffirms the strong influence of country-specific effects, which are increasingly considered in econometric models of migration.[35]

Overall, the statistical model for *Poland* includes only four significant causal relationships controlled for interaction effects with other variables in the model (see Table 2). None of these are surprising based on the bivariate analysis. Men in Poland are more likely to migrate than women. In this respect the Polish results do not support concepts predicting an increasing feminization of migration. The youngest age group, between 15 and 24 years of age, has also a significantly higher propensity to migrate than other age groups. It has in comparison to gender a

Table 2. Logistic Regression of the Odds of General Intention to Migrate for Poland and Turkey

	Turkey	Poland
Gender		
Female	Ref.	Ref.
Male	1.500 (NS)	2.625 **
Age		
40 – 54	Ref.	Ref.
15 – 24	1.305 (NS)	5.092 **
25 – 39	2.016 *	2.559 (NS)
55+	0.849 (NS)	0.0024 (NS)
Marital Status		
Others	Ref.	Ref.
Married/cohab.	1.057 (NS)	0.445 (NS)
Single	1.276 (NS)	0.811 (NS)
Employment Status		
Inactive	Ref.	Ref.
Employed	1.167 (NS)	2.211 (NS)
Unemployed	3.474 **	11.483 *
Student	3.813 **	9.326 *
Education		
Term. 15 years	Ref.	Ref.
Term. 16–19 years	1.625 (NS)	1.076 (NS)
Term. 20+ years	2.737 **	1.285 (NS)
Income		
Highest quartile	Ref.	Ref.
Lowest quartile	1.187 (NS)	0.428 (NS)
Second low. quart.	0.688 (NS)	0.821 (NS)
Third low. quart.	0.594 (NS)	0.491 (NS)
Location		
Rural + med. Town	Ref.	Ref.
Large city	1.072 (NS)	1.513 (NS)
House Ownership		
Owner	Ref.	Ref.
Tenant	1.659*	0.962 (NS)
Social Capital		
Low	Ref.	Ref.
Medium	1.966 **	0.627 (NS)
High	1.503 (NS)	0.879 (NS)

(*) p. ≤ 0.05; (**) p. ≤ 0.01; (***) p. ≤ 0.001

significantly higher independent effect on the probability to migrate. Not surprisingly, following the bivariate analysis, being a student has an even stronger effect on labor market mobility than gender and age.

These results are in line with the predictions based on human capital concepts and mainstream empirical research in Europe. Lastly, the unemployed are more strongly motivated to migrate than employed or inactive groups on the labor market. Uncertain employment prospects seem to be an important push factor.

To summarize: the Polish results show a certain polarization between one group of migrants being more strongly affected by push factors of unemployment and reduced chances on the national labor market (male employees) and another group reacting to pull factors of opportunities for the young and student population in the target countries.

Turkish results present a similar pattern. The bivariate analysis for Turkey had identified the following factors influencing migration:

- Male
- Single
- Age groups 15–24 and 25–39
- Better educated with tertiary degree
- Unemployed
- High income
- Living in rented accommodation

Are those results confirmed by the multivariate analysis? Unemployment and being a student are not only relevant factors in Poland but also in Turkey. In addition, the Turkish results reflect a polarization of the group of potential migrants. Also in Turkey students and better-educated people have a propensity to migrate. Different to Poles, Turks living in rented accommodation have a higher propensity to migrate and the age profile of potential migrants is older than in Poland. Turks seem to migrate at a stage in life when the family is already established. However, all in all, the structural patterns in Poland and Turkey are quite similar.

Table 3 contains the results for the NEW9 and for AC2. The new member states (NEW9) have a more consistent profile of potential migrants than Turkey and Poland. The multivariate analysis confirms the independent and significant influence of two factors, namely belonging to a younger age group (between 15 and 24 and between 25 and 39) and being a student. That means the migration pattern in the NEW9 seems to be more strongly influenced by pull factors than by push factors. In addition, it is worthwhile to notice that the multivariate analysis does not confirm an independent and statistically significant influence of gender on the intention to migrate.

In comparison to the other three statistical models, the results explaining the structure of migration from the new accession countries *Bulgaria and Romania* are more closely related to the structure in the NEW9 than to the structural pattern in Poland and Turkey. The model for the AC2 contains only two significant factors: young age (15–24) and medium and high social capital. In this way the results

Table 3. Logistic Regression of the Odds of General Intention to Migrate for the NEW9 and the AC2

	NEW9	AC2
Gender		
Female	Ref.	Ref.
Male	0.512 (NS)	1.310 (NS)
Age		
40–54	Ref.	Ref.
15–24	7.291 **	4.143 **
25–39	3.541 *	1.539 (NS)
55+	0.406 (NS)	0.035 (NS)
Marital Status		
Others	Ref.	Ref.
Married/cohab.	0.443 (NS)	0.690 (NS)
Single	0.649 (NS)	0.992 (NS)
Employment Status		
Inactive	Ref.	Ref.
Employed	7.091 (NS)	0.940 (NS)
Unemployed	13.156 (NS)	0.986 (NS)
Student	43.272 *	1.424 (NS)
Education		
Term. 15 years	Ref.	Ref.
Term. 16–19 years	0.645 (NS)	0.609 (NS)
Term. 20+ years	1.070 (NS)	0.406 (NS)
Income		
Highest quartile	Ref.	Ref.
Lowest quartile	0.778 (NS)	1.559 (NS)
Second low. quart.	0.750 (NS)	0.428 (NS)
Third low. quart.	0.751 (NS)	0.712 (NS)
Location		
Rural + med. Town	Ref.	Ref.
Large city	1.086 (NS)	1.584 (NS)
House Ownership		
Owner	Ref.	Ref.
Tenant	1.704 (NS)	1.634 (NS)
Social Capital		
Low	Ref.	Ref.
Medium	0.859 (NS)	3.164 **
High	1.249 (NS)	22.124***

(*) $p \leq 0.05$; (**) $p \leq 0.01$; (***) $p \leq 0.001$

confirm that higher degrees of social capital are more a facilitating factor than a barrier to migration. However, it is worth noting that none of the economic factors have a significant influence on the decision to migrate in AC2 despite the difficult overall economic conditions.

What do we learn in a comparative perspective from the results? In Table 4 we have tried to summarize the multivariate analysis of the four country groupings. First of all, it is remarkable that none of the various dimensions of the nine influence factors analyzed in the models has a significant influence in the four country groupings. Structurally, being young in the pre-family phase and being a student seems to be the most consistent predictor for the intention to migrate as it is relevant in three country groupings. As a dimension, age seems to have the strongest influence not only in the pre-family phase but also to a lesser extent in the family phase of the age group between 25 and 39 (mentioned twice).

Unemployment is only important in two country groupings, whereas income differentials in the sending countries seemed to be insignificant. Overall, material conditions in the sending countries seem to be of less importance than often predicted. Of some importance are social capabilities in the sending countries reflected in the degree of social capital, which seems to be, in comparative terms, as important as unemployment. Gender and the trend for a feminization of labor migration cannot be confirmed by these data. Only in Poland is gender important, but it confirms the traditional pattern of male-led migration.

Table 4.   Overview of the Results on Logistic Regression (X significant effect)

	Turkey	Poland	NEW9	AC2
Age				
15–24		X	X	X
25–39	X		X	
Employment Status				
Unemployed	X	X		
Student	X	X	X	
Education				
Tertiary	X			
Gender				
Male		X		
Social Capital				
Medium	X			X
High				X
House Ownership				
Tenant	X			

Notes

1. For more detail see Commission of the European Communities, *Communication from the Commission to the Council and the European Parliament—Integrating Migration Issues in the European Union's Relation with Third Countries*, COM (2002) 703 final (Brussels: CEC, 2002), p.15.
2. The dimension "within the same city, town or village" has not been included.
3. The more detailed figures can be found in the report by Hubert Krieger, *Migration Trends in an Enlarged Europe* (Dublin: European Foundation for the Improvement of Living and Working Conditions, 2004).
4. Ibid.
5. Commission for Turkey, *Turkey in Europe: More than a Promise* (Brussels: British Council Brussels, 2004).
6. IOM, *Migration Potential in Central and Eastern Europe* (Geneva: International Organization for Migration, 1999).
7. This means it covers not only migration to the EU.
8. According to the authors of the IOM (1999) study these results show "little permanent migration" and confirm only a "certain amount of long-term migration" (p.23). However, compared with other available studies these results seem extremely high.
9. H. Fassmann and C. Hintermann, *Migrationspotential Osteuropa—Struktur und Motivationen potentieller Migranten aus Polen, der Slowakei, Tschechien und Ungarn*, ISR Forschungsbericht Heft 15 (Vienna: Verlag der Oesterrechischen Akademie der Wissenschaften, 1997).
10. Commission of the European Communities, *The Impact of Eastern Enlargement on Employment and Labour Markets in the EU and the Member States* (Brussels: European Commission's Director General for Employment and Social Affairs, 2001). A more recent study by the same authors comes to very similar results. Commission of the European Communities and DIW, *Potential Migration from Central and Eastern Europe into the EU15—An Update* (Brussels and Berlin: DIW and European Commission's Director General for Employment and Social Affairs, 2003). Different predictions are reported for example in two earlier studies: S. Ardittis (ed.), *The Politics of East–West Migration* (Houndmills, Basingstoke, Hampshire and London: The Macmillan Press, 1994) and R.E. Baldwin, *Towards an Integrated Europe* (London: Centre for Economic Policy Research, 1994).
11. A critique of this kind of methodological approach can be found for example in H. Fassmann and R. Muenz, "EU Enlargement and Future East–West Migration," in IOM (ed.), *New Challenges for Migration Policy in Central and Eastern Europe* (Geneva: International Organization for Migration, 2002), pp.61f.
12. For more detail see: Commission of the European Communities (2001), p.96.
13. The following calculation was used based on Tables 7.10 and 7.11 in Commission of the European Communities (2001), pp.104–5: 1.99 million (stock 2005) plus 0.25 million (flow: 2006) adds up to 2.24 million end of 2006.
14. For more detail see: Eurostat, *Population Statistics* (Luxembourg: Office of Official Publications, 2002).
15. As far as the high level of projection is concerned a precise comparison cannot be made, as the Commission of the European Communities study (2001) gives no precise figures. Estimates based on Figure 7.6 (p.106) would suggest not more than a 10% increase leading by the end of 2006 to around 1.2 million migrants from the CC-10. This compares to a wider estimate by the Foundation of between 3 million and 1.5 million.
16. For more detail see Commission of the European Communities (2001).
17. Fassmann and Muenz (2002).
18. T. Straubhaar, "East–West Migration: Will it be a Problem?" *Intereconomics*, Vol.36, No.4 (2001), p.170; H. Hille and T. Straubhaar, "The Impact of EU Enlargement on Migration Movements and Economic Integration: Results of Recent Studies," in *OECD Migration Policies and EU Enlargement. The Case of Central and Eastern Europe* (Paris: OECD, 2001), pp.79–100; OECD, *Migration Policies and EU Enlargement. The Case of Central and Eastern Europe* (Paris: OECD, 2001).

19. N. Nyberg-Soerensen, N. Van Hear and P. Engberg-Pedersen, *The Migration–Development Nexus: Evidence and Policy Options. State of the Art Overview,* CDR Working Paper 02 (Copenhagen: Centre for Developmental Research, March 6, 2002), p.5.

20. More detail can be found in: Fassmann and Hintermann (1997); F. Kalter, *Wohnortwechsel in Deutschland* (Opladen: Leske und Budrich, 1997); T. Bauer and K. Zimmermann, *Assessment of Possible Migration Pressure and its Labour Market Impact Following EU Enlargement to Central and Eastern Europe,* IZA Research Report No.3 (Bonn: IZA, 1999); Pricewaterhouse Coopers, *Labor Migration in CEE* (http://www.pwcglobal.com/cz/eng/about/press-rm/2001).

21. Bauer and Zimmermann (1999), p.15.

22. E. Kofman, A. Phizacklea, P. Raghuram and R. Sales, *Gender and International Migration in Europe: Employment, Welfare and Politics* (London: Routledge, 2000), p.3.

23. Kofman *et al.* (2000); F. Anthias and G. Lazaridis (eds.), *Gender and Migration in Southern Europe: Women on the Move* (Oxford: Berg Publishers, 2000); E. Kofman, "Women Migrants in the European Union," Paper presented at the joint OECD and European Commission conference on "The Economic and Social Aspects of Migration," Brussels, January 21–22, 2003.

24. See Nyberg-Soerensen *et al.* (2002), pp.4–5.

25. Even though this typology is devised for less developed countries, it can be readily transposed on women from the candidate countries. However, due to the small number of cases, it is not possible to provide a more detailed breakdown for different groups of women on the basis of various country groupings.

26. At the other extreme are Hungary and Malta, where only 1% of the male population wants to migrate.

27. Bauer and Zimmermann (1999).

28. See for example, SOPEMI, *Trends in international Migration* (Paris: OECD, 2001) and Kofman (2003).

29. More detail regarding the expected brain drain can be found in W. Carrington and E. Detragiache, *How Big is the Brain Drain?*, IMF Working Papers, Research Department (Washington, DC: International Monetary Funds, 1998).

30. G. Myrdal, *An International Economy* (New York: Harper and Row, 1956).

31. I. Wallerstein, *The Modern World System: Capitalist Agriculture and the Origins of the European World Economy in the Sixteenth Century* (New York: Academic Press, 1974).

32. H. Olesen, *Migration, Return and Development: An Institutional Perspective*, CDR Expert Working Paper (Copenhagen: Centre for Developmental Research, 2002). The author, however, also analyzed the potential of return migration, combined with a possible "brain gain" for the originally sending countries (pp.9–12).

33. See, for example, B. Alecke, P. Huber and G. Untiedt, "What a Difference a Constant Makes. How Predictable are International Migration Flows?" in OECD (ed.), *Migration Policies and EU Enlargement. The Case of Central and Eastern Europe* (Paris: OECD, 2001).

34. See for example Olesen (2002), p.14.

35. A good example is the study of the European Commission on migration (2001), p.96.

Comparing Integration Policies and Outcomes: Turks in the Netherlands and Germany

GAMZE AVCI

Department of Turkish Studies, Leiden University, The Netherlands

Introduction

The presence of Turkish migrants in Western Europe has been the focus of many studies in different areas of research. Regardless of the areas examined, the focal point is how (dis)similar Turkish migrants are when compared to the natives in the various host countries. Although there are some policy initiatives at the European level, country-level differentiations remain meaningful since European governments have maintained their own national integration policies so far. The choice of comparing the Netherlands and Germany is interesting for two reasons. Firstly, the two countries are very similar when it comes to the Turkish communities they host. Secondly, the two countries were always considered to be very different policy-wise. The Netherlands was considered much more progressive and open than Germany, which insisted it was not an immigration country and which pursued limited integration policies. For many, Germany was the "black sheep" whereas the Netherlands was the *"Musterknabe"* (exemplary kid) in the immigration literature.

An important turning point came when, in 2004, a Dutch Parliamentary report declared that the Netherlands' 30-year experiment in trying to create a tolerant, multi-cultural society had failed and led to ethnic ghettos and sink or "black" schools.[1] This came at a time when the consensus on the success of the "multicultural" society and "integration" was already a highly contested phenomenon in the Netherlands.[2] The

Correspondence Address: Gamze Avcı, Department of Turkish Studies, Postbus 9515, 2300 RA Leiden, The Netherlands. Email: g.avci@let.leidenuniv.nl

discussion continues amidst continuous policy changes, which for many seem like a return to the so-called assimilation model. Daily reports appear in the newspapers on topics such as criminal immigrant youth, headscarves in schools, new, too-large mosques, Islamic schools and ghettoization in cities. Politicians continuously present new proposals.[3] In the Netherlands, the discussion on the immigration issue focuses on what is thought to be wrong and what should be changed. The policies of the past are criticized and a continuous toughening of laws is the general trend. In the academic realm, the response has been similar and some are even arguing that in the Netherlands "Good Intentions Sometimes Make Bad Policy."[4]

Given that Germany and the Netherlands had different approaches to immigration in the postwar period with a similar flow of migration into their respective countries, it is interesting to review the experience of both. It is important to note, however, that the policies cover a period of over 40 years and a large range of areas, thus it is rather difficult to judge *overall* policy success or failure as well as good or bad policy *as a whole*. For that reason, the paper will discuss and compare some selected fundamental indicators of integration after reviewing the policy developments in the two countries in the recent past.[5] The indicators chosen are classic key indicators of integration, such as labor market participation and education, but also more controversial ones such as naturalization and dual citizenship, political participation, use of homeland-originated media and levels of intermarriage. Finally, given the similarities in outcome despite the application of diverging approaches, the paper will look at what may possibly explain the constraints of policy in both countries. It will be argued that the second group of indicators operates in a more "transnational" context, i.e. there are strong links across borders to the country of origin. With existing "national" models of integration some of these latter indicators are perceived as particularly problematic and are targeted by both receiving countries in their new wave of integration policies.

Postwar Migration and Policy

Germany

Turks are the largest group of foreigners living in Germany. At the end of 2003, 1.88 million Turks were living in Germany, equaling approximately a quarter of all foreigners.[6] Of these 73.6 percent have been living in Germany for at least ten years.[7] The emergence of the Turkish migrant community in Germany is rooted in the labor market needs of the 1950s and the West German government's decision to recruit "guest workers." At that time, the German government sought to procure agreements with several labor-rich countries.[8] These immigrants provided a willing source of labor that contributed much to Germany's "economic miracle."[9] The economic regulation of the movement of labor into Germany continued into the 1960s and early 1970s.

In a shift similar to that in the Netherlands, a major change occurred in the mid-1970s. By 1974, the number of foreign residents in Germany had reached a total of 4.1 million and the German government, increasingly aware of the "absorption" problem and confronted with an economic recession, responded with a recruitment ban. The ban was followed by restrictive measures introduced to encourage return to the country of origin. These included differential child benefit payments, restrictions on the employment of family members and progressively more severe restrictions on family reunion.[10] Although the ban and repatriation policies did not drastically reduce the inflow of foreigners, Germany was fairly successful in containing and stabilizing the flow of new immigrants.

In the late 1970s, both the Christian Democratic Union (CDU) and Christian Socialist Union (CSU) had framed the issue of foreigners as a "problem" (*Ausländerproblem*); thus, when returned to power in 1982, the new government cited "Aliens policy" (*Ausländerpolitik*) as one of its urgent policy items. Chancellor Kohl stated his policy principles as integration, restriction and promotion of repatriation. His three points, rejected by most of the relevant policy institutions (church, trade unions, and welfare organizations), were accepted by the Federal Cabinet on March 2, 1983. In November 1983, the Bundestag passed a law providing financial incentives to encourage foreign workers to leave Germany, which led to the return of roughly 150,000. The incentives were abandoned, however, in 1985. The basic tenets of the Aliens policy set forth in October 1982 were repeated by Chancellor Kohl in the Bundestag on March 18, 1987. A draft for a new Aliens Act was leaked in spring 1988 and caused heated discussions among the German public. Its hostility to foreigners caused widespread protests and its withdrawal led to the replacement of the Minister of the Interior in 1989. A somewhat revised version, the Aliens Act of July 9, 1990, came into force on January 1, 1991 while public attention was occupied with German unification. This law, in contrast to the first Aliens Act of 1965, is much more detailed and differentiates between foreigners according to length of residence. It is also more restrictive.[11] The ban on dual nationality continued. Furthermore, nothing was mentioned regarding integration. The new conditions, like "appropriate" housing and not benefiting from social allowances when applying for a residence permit or renewal, were openly criticized by the Greens and the Social Democrats on the grounds that they are discriminatory measures. Political activities and hence participation of migrants were still restricted. The new law had options on re-immigration of children and assistance for return and reintegration to the country of origin. Repatriation assistance in general was abandoned, but certain related measures remained in force.

Up until the early 1990s, the German government rejected the *de facto* development of immigration into permanence on the basis that Germany is not an immigration country. Consequently, integration remained rather a controversial and limited option. Recent policy changes show a shift in Germany's attitude. The Aliens Act 1999 and Amendment to the Law on Foreigners and Aliens 1999 hint at the change.[12] These two acts together introduced new rules about citizenship requirements. Conditions are outlined for the naturalization of foreigners who have lived in Germany for at least eight years, and their spouse and minor children. It introduced the requirement that newborns are considered German citizens if at least one parent has lived in Germany for at least eight years or at least one parent has unlimited right to residence or an unlimited permit to live in Germany. In July 1999, the Citizenship Law Reform Act was published in the German official gazette. This act entered into force on January 1, 2000. It established that children born to foreigners in Germany could automatically receive German citizenship.[13]

Another important and more recent development was the new German Immigration Law 2005. The discussions around this law also show how difficult this issue has been for Germany, especially since the debate on an immigration law for Germany dragged on for four and a half years. Finally, on July 1, 2004, the German Bundestag approved the law, which will regulate migration in the future. German politicians began to deal with this issue in 2000 by proposing to draft a modern immigration law. However, the Social Democrat–Green Party coalition that ran the federal government initially did not want to push this legislation through the Bundestag, where it holds a narrow majority. So attempts were made to build a wider consensus. In mid-2000, an independent commission was created, chaired by a prominent CDU opposition politician, Rita Süssmuth. The Süssmuth Commission's extensive report, published in 2001,[14] included three key recommendations: the active selection of qualified immigrants, following the example of the classic immigration countries; the active promotion of integration via language and cultural orientation courses for immigrants; and an overhaul of asylum rules. Of these, the proactive selection of immigrants via a skills-based point system was the critical element intended to give Germany an advantage in the international competition for economically attractive migrants. Nonetheless, a much watered down version was passed in late June 2004 and took effect in January 2005. The critical item of the original immigration law was lost. There will be no selection of economically attractive migrants according to a point system. Instead, the recruitment ban that was passed in 1973 will remain in effect. The new immigration law differentiates now only between two residence titles: the (unlimited) settlement permission and the (limited) residence permit. An important development with this law is that new immigrants will have the right to participate in state-funded German language classes and receive an introduction to the country's justice system, culture and history. The government has earmarked over 200 million for this purpose. The authorities may also force foreigners already living in Germany to participate in the courses or forfeit their residence permits or social benefits.

The Netherlands

As with other European countries, immigration in the Netherlands gained momentum in the aftermath of the Second Word War, with the main inflow beginning in the 1960s and early 1970s.[15] A change of policy occurred by the late 1970s, when it became clear that immigrant numbers had become very large and the issue of integration needed to be addressed. In 1990, foreign residents were about 4.6 percent of the total Dutch population of 15 million and migration inflow reached a peak level of almost 85,000 in 1991. Despite substantial immigration, the Netherlands has never defined itself as an immigration country, mainly because of its already dense population.

The 1980s were marked by multiculturalist policies. In 1979, the Netherlands Scientific Council for Government Policy (*Wetenschappelijke Raad voor het Regeringsbeleid*, WRR), the government's official policy advisory body, published a report that recommended the abandonment of the fiction of temporary immigrants and the development of an integration policy.[16] This report was a turning point in immigration policy. The aim was to bring about the integration of immigrants by lessening deprivation, strengthening their legal status, fighting against discrimination and motivating political participation. In this context, minority policy targeted discrepancies in education, housing, employment, well-being and health. In 1980, the government formally admitted the unlikelihood of the eventual return of foreign workers to their home countries. In 1983, an official minorities policy was adopted, which acknowledged the need for explicit social policies to integrate minorities and which stated that it was necessary to deal with the issues on the basis of ethnic groups and not just individuals (Minorities Act or *Minderhedennota*).[17] Two goals were underlined in this minority policy: the creation of a multicultural society and the compensation of disadvantages. Groups to which the government feels a special responsibility and which are disadvantaged in public life were regarded as minorities. The mission was integration while retaining the cultures from the home countries. This aim was to be achieved via equitable access to Dutch institutions, subsidized cultural activities and initiatives. Furthermore, the revised constitution of 1983 introduced municipal voting rights for immigrants.

However, multiculturalism came increasingly under attack in the mid-1980s. The changed economic climate and the high unemployment rates among minorities (and native Dutch) introduced a new dynamics to immigration. It was also becoming increasingly apparent that the migrants were there to stay. In 1989, the Scientific Council published a new report (ten years after the first one), entitled "Immigrant Policy" (*Allochtonenbeleid*) in which it noted that both immigrants and immigration are a permanent feature in Western Europe. The new focal point was the fight against the high unemployment of immigrants through measures in the labor market and education. The basic principles were a restrictive Aliens policy, a cultural policy, as determined by immigrants themselves through their organizations, and an integration policy aiming to improve the performance of immigrants in the labor market and in education. It was argued that until then integration policy had failed because the safeguarding of the culture of origin overly prioritized the components of culture and religion at the expense of structural integration in the society. It was recommended that the group approach should be discarded in favor of a more individually based approach for more integration and participation in the domains of work, education and adult training. Furthermore, the report asked for measures to promote employment equity, and more emphasis on integration and education. Laws prohibiting racial defamation, incitement to racial hatred, discrimination and violence were also passed.

The 1991 Government Action Program on Minorities Policy stressed the need for measures to reduce economic and social deprivation, to prevent discrimination and to improve the legal situation for minorities. The program was aimed at established immigrants and newcomers. It was in the same period that the words *inburgering* (adaptation, integration) and *nieuwkomers* (newcomers) appeared. In 1994, the government published the *Contourennota integratiebeleid etnische minderheden* (Framework memorandum, integration policy ethnic minorities), which was meant to replace the *Minderhedennota*. In this memorandum, integration was defined as a process leading to the full and equal participation of individuals and groups in society, for which mutual respect for identity is seen as a necessary condition.[18] In 1996, a bill regarding settlement programs for newcomers, namely *inburgeringsprogramma*, was presented to the Dutch parliament. This bill eventually became law and took effect in September 1998 (*Wet Inburgering Nieuwkomers* (WIN), or Newcomer Integration Act). The settlement programs had already been in operation for some time before 1998. According to this law, newcomers are required to sign a contract with the Dutch government. This contract requires newcomers to attend and participate in integration programs and obliges the government to provide these programs. If newcomers do not comply, their benefits can be reduced. Technically, these programs last on average 600 hours per person, and consist of courses in Dutch and courses on Dutch society as well as professional orientation. Social guidance is also part of the integration program. People with a temporary asylum residence permit are also included in the WIN.

At the end of 2001, the Advisory Council on Government Policy (WRR) issued a new report, entitled "the Netherlands as Immigration Society." This third report focuses on three basic guiding principles: "the principle of participation," "the principle of the responsibility of the involved players," and "the principle of encounter." These principles are treated in this report as being central to an immigration society:

- immigrants and their descendants participate in and contribute towards Dutch society; in particular this calls for participation in employment and education;
- the realization of such participation makes demands on individual responsibility;
- the participation does not remain confined to isolated segments of society.

This report reflects the change of discourse, which took off at the beginning of the 1990s when VVD (*Volkspartij voor Vrijheid en Democratie*; People's Party for Freedom and Democracy) politician Frits Bolkestein broke the silence and ended the politically correct period by saying that integration problems were primarily a concern about Moroccans and Turks.[19] The report argues that the normative multicultural notion of integration policy—based on the preservation of the migrant's own cultural identity and the equality of all cultures—led to the problematic situation in which ethnic minorities were not internalizing basic Western norms. The new report stresses that responsibility is now on the individual immigrants to become citizens and thus to abide by the laws and the basic norms of Dutch society. Most of the recommendations concern newcomers. Regarding established immigrants there is a call for the discontinuation of all group-specific policies including the labeling of target groups, support for immigrant associations, the central consultation platform, specific knowledge centers of particular immigrant groups, etc. The Integration of Newcomers Act 1998 tightens integration policy further. It obliges all Dutch municipalities to offer state-subsidized integration programs responding to individual needs of new immigrants. The Amended Netherlands Nationality Act 2003, which requires a demonstration of integration with Dutch society is now a prerequisite for being naturalized, and applicants must pass an examination showing proficiency in Dutch language, institutions and culture.

The tightening of policy has been accompanied by a politicization of the issue among politicians and the public. Until the 1980s, the Netherlands was able to claim a conspicuous absence of racist politicians. This changed with the emergence of the extreme right party, the *Centrum Partij* (CP), whose leader was elected to parliament in 1989.[20] The other parties responded with silence. In the early 1990s, the liberal-conservatives put the immigration issue on the agenda, suggesting German-style immigration restrictions. Again the other parties did not respond, to avoid politicization of the matter. In the May 15, 2002 elections the four-month-old LPF (*List Pim Fortuyn*) won a resounding victory (in the context of a brand-new party in a multiparty, proportional representation system) by coming in second with 26 seats, the result of winning 17.9 percent of the votes. The defining position taken by the party was to limit new immigration into the Netherlands. The platform called for halting new immigration while integrating existing immigrants more effectively. Despite the fact that the leader of the LPF, Pim Fortuyn, was condemned for his statement, and he was later assassinated, his message lifted the taboo on anti-immigration statements and policies, and the issues he and his party raised are still on the agenda.

Selected Indicators of Integration: Labor Market Participation and Education

Unemployment and Self-Employment

Integration policies are first and foremost focused on increasing labor market participation and educational attainments among the second generation of migrants.[21] The underlying idea is that integration without labor market participation is very difficult. In the 1960s immigrant workers were hired because the labor market in Europe was booming. The immigrant workers got jobs in industries with low paid labor. This changed in the early 1970s. For example, since the early 1970s the Dutch labor market has undergone radical change: the share of part-time jobs has more than doubled, the share of flexible employment contracts has doubled and the female participation ratio has increased from 26 percent in 1970 to 57 percent in 1998. At the same time, the share of immigrants in the Dutch labor force has risen from 7.8 percent to 9.3 percent.[22] During this period, the Dutch economy went through a process of radical post-industrial restructuring, resulting in high levels of unemployment that reached double-digit levels in the mid-1980s. Since the industries with low-paid labor were predominantly affected by the economic recession of the 1980s, many immigrant workers lost their jobs and became long-term unemployed.

The labor market position of many immigrant workers is weak because of their low educational level and lack of Dutch or German language skills. Comparing the Dutch and German case is difficult since there are different ways of looking at it. In the Netherlands, the unemployment rate among ethnic minorities has gone down substantially since 1995. Still, the unemployment rate for Turks in the Netherlands is almost three times as much as the Dutch average. At the same time, only 8 percent of the Dutch Turks are unemployed (compared to 18 percent in Germany).

In Germany, the Turks have twice the level of unemployment of the natives and about 18 percent of German Turks are unemployed. Of course, one important consideration for both cases is that integration policy cannot be decoupled from larger economic policies and should be evaluated in a grander scheme than just integration policy.

In Europe, similar to the North American experience, self-employment among immigrants has been growing steadily. This is often seen as a positive sign. Immigrants of Turkish descent have also increasingly turned to self-employment. Nonetheless, despite a declining failure rate and a small tendency toward diversification, immigrants are still overrepresented in the cleaning, retail, and restaurant trades, as they tend to reproduce the entrepreneurial strategies of fellow countrymen. As a consequence, immigrant entrepreneurs are primarily active in markets

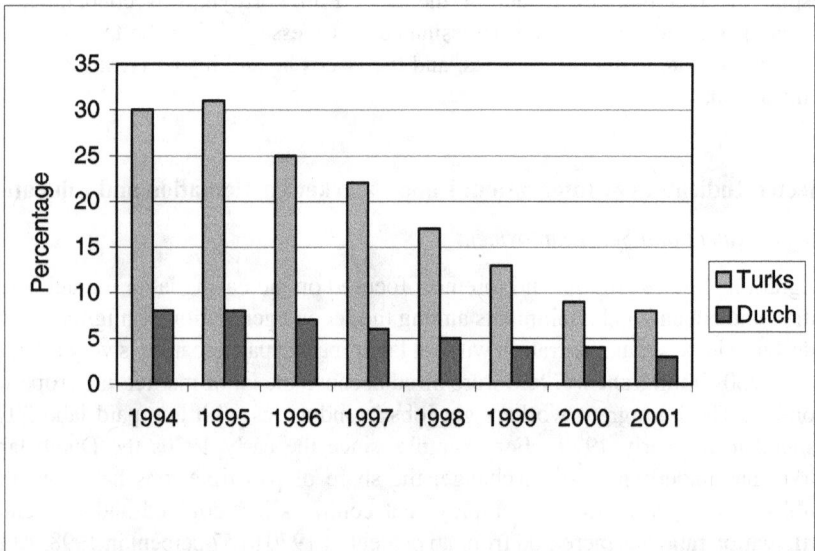

Figure 1.   Unemployment levels within Turkish and Dutch subgroups in the Netherlands. *Source:* Instituut voor Sociologisch-Economisch Onderzoek (http://www.iseo-eur.com/ downloads/IM_06_hoofdstuk4.pdf).

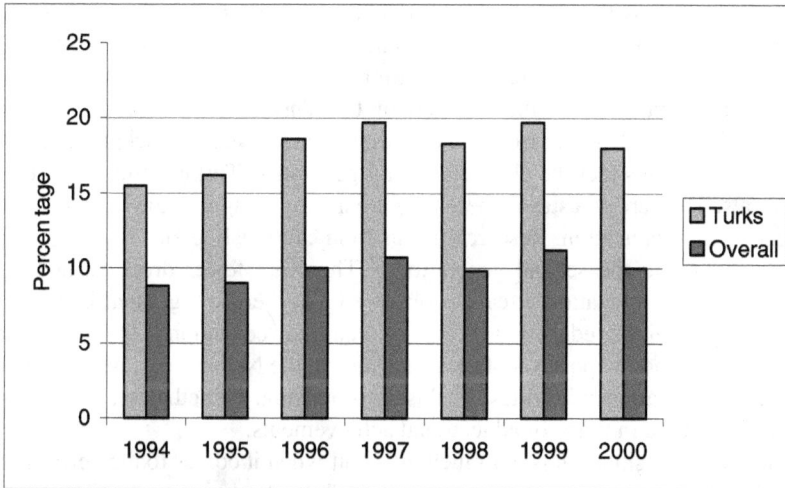

Figure 2. Unemployment levels among Turks and overall level of unemployment in Germany. *Source:* Beauftragte der Bundesregierung für Ausländerfragen, *Daten und Fakten zur Ausländersituation*, February 20, 2002.

that are easily accessible and have a low growth potential. This implies that due to crowding-out effects their existence as entrepreneurs is uncertain. This leads to a relatively high failure rate, low profitability, long working days and weeks, and a high level of informality.

Turkish immigrant entrepreneurs in the Netherlands have increased over time. Their absolute numbers were 1,895 in 1986–87, 5,385 in 1992, 6,561 in 1998 and 9,047 in 2000.[23] The respective numbers for the Dutch were 28,748 (1992), 35,796 (1998) and 43,926 (2000).[24]

In Germany, it is estimated that in 1998, there were 51,000 businessmen of Turkish origin, providing jobs to 265,000 persons. This represents 18.3 percent of the total number of economically independent non-Germans.[25]

Education

Since 1985, the Educational Priority Policy (EPP) has been in effect in the Netherlands. This policy is aimed at reducing the educational disadvantage of children due to their social, economic and cultural circumstances. In terms of education, two big problems stand out for the Turkish community. A high percentage of people (between 15 and 24 years) leave secondary school without any qualifications. There is a relatively low level of participation of Turks in higher education. "Black schools" are a problematic phenomenon. Furthermore, many Turkish children have problems with the Dutch language.[26] Analyses show that social class largely determines test results.[27] As most Turks (and Moroccans) belong to the lowest socio-economic category, the factor of ethnic origin is so closely intertwined with the factor of social class that it is not really possible to differentiate between the two. Gender barely plays a role, while the influence of ethnic origin is also limited. Crul claims that when the socio-economic position of the parents is taken into account, the educational position of the children of the Turkish (and Moroccan) second generation is not so different from Dutch children with a similar background.[28]

Crul further states that the children of first generation Turkish migrants are now adolescents. They are at a stage where they are now moving into the labor market or completing their education. Research in this field cautiously points to an encouraging change among the second generation.[29] There are fewer dropouts and more students in higher education. It can be observed that there is a gradual intergenerational change to higher education levels.[30] Given that "education is the prime factor for the socio-economic position of the minorities in the Netherlands, particularly for the second generation minorities,"[31] this is promising. Nonetheless, there is still much to be desired in terms of educational achievements.

In Germany the situation is not much different when it comes to the performance of Turkish students in the educational system. While almost a quarter of all Turkish students go to the *Hauptschule* (the lowest track of secondary education), which only 13 percent of all West German students do, the situation is the opposite with regard to the *Gymnasium*: almost a quarter of the latter attend this most advantageous school type whereas only 6 percent of Turkish students do so. There is also a higher probability that Turkish students end up in the *Sonderschule*, which are special schools for pupils with learning disabilities. The lack of language skills makes it more likely for Turkish students to attend these special schools.[32]

Contested Features of Integration

An entire literature has grown up in the social sciences around the concept of "transnationalism." What it in effect means is that people can move easily between different national, linguistic and cultural spaces, while keeping professional and family contacts in each. Integration is no longer spatially bounded in the way it was (or was believed to be) in the past. It is argued that transnational activities emerge because they become sources of information and offer opportunities for political mobilization despite existing barriers.[33] The consequences and impact of transnational activities on integration are disputed. Some argue that transnational political loyalty and political incorporation are not mutually exclusive.[34] Still others argue that it may inhibit integration.

Transnationalism is also disputed in the sense that some scholars like Ewa Morawska argue that it is nothing new and has always been part of migration. She argues that "life worlds and diaspora politics of turn-of-the-century immigrants share many of the supposedly novel features of present-day transnationalism."[35] Still it cannot be denied that given today's opportunities there is much more room for transnationalism.[36] In the American example, transnationalism is considered interwoven with integration and not necessarily seen as counter-effective to its logic. Mexican migrants in the United States and their continued political involvement in their home country's politics is a good example of this.[37] In our present case, the relevant realms of transnational tendencies can be seen in dual citizenship, the media, political activism of migrants and low rates of intermarriage/high rates of "imported" spouses from Turkey.

Naturalization and Dual Citizenship of Migrants

Migrants can formally become part of their new communities through naturalization. Many choose to maintain ties to their home country via dual citizenship. This technically can allow them to influence policy in both countries. Opponents of dual citizenship usually argue for a nation-state order, in which individuals ought to belong to one single nation-state, which is manifested in national citizenship. Just as a "single" nationality can be linked to integration, dual citizenship of migrants and transnationalism are often seen as interconnected.[38] Hence Jones-Correa claims that

> Where once state sovereignty might have been thought of as total and complete, each state occupying a unique and mutually exclusive political and territorial space, that is ... increasingly *not* the case. Instead we would be better served by seeing the relations between immigrants and states as a system of overlapping sovereignties.[39]

In this context, the policies of the host country are important. The Dutch naturalization process used to be one of the more open in Europe. The vesting period was five years, only basic language skills were required, and willingness to integrate was equated with basic language proficiency. Furthermore, since January 1992 dual citizenship was allowed. Children of immigrant descent but born in the Netherlands could acquire Dutch nationality by simple declaration when they reached the age of 18. Dutch nationality was granted automatically at birth if either the father or the mother was born in the Netherlands, the so-called double *jus soli* requirement.[40] Recently, because of the growing political saliency of issues of immigration and integration in the Netherlands, the Dutch naturalization regime has become much more restrictive. Since 1997, the possibility of dual citizenship has been annulled, resulting in an immediate and steep decline in the number of applications, while participation in a so-called settlement process, consisting of language lessons and courses in Dutch history and society, has been made mandatory. In 1983 the number of naturalizations was 7,000. In 1995, the number of naturalizations had risen to 68,000 and in 1996 to 79,000. In comparison, the number of naturalizations in 2001 was 43,000 and in 2003 it was 25,000. A declining trend can also be observed specifically with Turks and their naturalization (Table 1).

Since the reform of the citizenship law, effective as of January 1, 2000, all foreigners who have resided in Germany for at least eight years have a right to naturalization as long as they fulfill certain criteria. They will need to have a limited or unlimited residence permit or a right to residence, agree to the liberal democratic basic order of Germany, have sufficient German language skills and generally be able to sustain themselves financially. Dual or multiple citizenship is principally to

Table 1.   Acquisition of Dutch Citizenship by Turkish Nationals

Year	Turkish Nationals Acquiring Dutch Citizenship
1996	29,295
1997	19,851
1998	12,755
1999	4,324
2000	3,913
2001	4,728
2002	4,678
2003	2,818
2004	2,723

Source: Statistics Netherlands (CBS, Centraal Bureau voor de Statistiek).

be avoided and is only accepted in certain cases. Dual citizenship is only tolerated until the child reaches adulthood, and between the ages of 18 to 23 he or she must choose between his or her Turkish or German passport. In Germany, Turks were the largest group naturalized with 39 percent out of 140,731 in 2003.[41] Between 1984 and 2003 a total of 623,000 Turks were naturalized (Table 2).

Political Activism of Migrants

Political participation in the host country is a crucial measure of the extent of the integration of migrants. In the Netherlands, compared to other ethnic groups, Turks

Table 2.   Turkish Nationals Acquiring German Citizenship

Year	Naturalizations
1984	2,000
1985	2,000
1986	2,000
1987	2,000
1988	2,000
1989	2,000
1990	2,000
1999	104,000
2000	83,000
2001	77,000
2002	65,000
2003	56,000
Total	399,000

Source: Federal Statistics Office Germany

participate more in politics, have a greater trust in the local and governmental institutions and are more interested in local news and in local politics.[42] Turks vote more often than Moroccans, while Moroccans vote more often than Surinamese and Antilleans.[43]

Migrants not only have the right to vote in the Netherlands, they also have the right to stand for election. In the municipal elections in the Netherlands on March 6, 2002, 208 migrant politicians were elected into the municipal council of their municipality (out of a total of 9,080 councilors in the Netherlands). This was an increase of 38 percent compared to the elections of 1998, and an increase of more than 50 percent compared to the elections of 1994. Of these 208 city councilors more than half are of Turkish origin. In the national elections on January 22, 2003, 14 migrant politicians (out of 150 total seats) were elected as members of the Second Chamber of the Dutch parliament.[44]

In Germany, Turks (if they do not have citizenship) have neither active (possibility to vote) nor passive (possibility to be elected) voting rights and cannot cast ballots in local, state, federal or European elections. Therefore, they lack a stake in the exercise of state power. Hence, even though they are directly affected by political decisions, they cannot influence the shaping of these decisions, either directly or through elected representation. In the current Bundestag, among the 603 members, there are two people of Turkish descent: Ekin Deligöz, a Green Party member who received German citizenship in 1997, and Lale Akgün of the ruling Social Democrats.

Yet one of the important discussions in the Netherlands and Germany is around the ties of migrant organizations to their country of origin. The transnational nature of migrant organizations elicits the fear that these ties "exhibit" or imply nationalism. There is concern that migrants will focus on homeland politics rather than orient themselves towards what is happening in their new home country. Another *problématique* is that ideological disputes are "imported" and that the host country has continued to enjoy political influence over migrants. Examples of past "imported" controversial issues are the Kurdish question and the polarization between the extreme left and extreme right in Turkey. Examples of possible influence of the home country are officials of Diyanet that are sent by the Turkish government. The latter is a matter of concern for the Netherlands as well as Germany.

There is a very high number of Turkish migrant organizations in Europe. In the Turkish community in the Netherlands there is one organization per 291 inhabitants, in the Moroccan community there is one organization per 462 inhabitants and in the Surinamese Community (the biggest ethnic group) there is one organization per 770 inhabitants. Most of the Turkish organizations represent the divisions in the home country, while their agenda is mixed with issues concerning Turkey and the host country. Both of the host countries discourage any influence of Turkey on migrant organizations and the Turkish migrant community. The transnational links maintained via migrant organizations are considered a problematic signal whereby migrants continue to be deeply involved in the life of their countries of origin even though they no longer live there permanently.

Homeland-originated Media

In most cities of Europe where Turkish populations exist it is possible to buy many Turkish-language publications including numerous daily newspapers. New technologies such as satellite television, cellular telephones, and the Internet further broke down state borders and provided the diaspora with a stronger influence on developments "at home." In Europe for many years the availability of media from Turkey was limited to print. In the early 1990s, the Dutch cable began to carry Turkish radio and television's international public channel. Later on, private television carried by satellite became available at a reasonable cost. Turks now have instant access to news on current events in their homeland as well as to contemporary popular culture.[45]

In Germany, nearly a million televisions are tuned into Turkish television by satellite every night.[46] Sixty percent of Germany's Turks had satellite television connections in 1998 in order to receive half a dozen Turkish channels.

In 1995, a survey of Dutch migrants found that 43 percent of the Turkish respondents owned a satellite dish, 52 percent subscribed to cable and 34 percent had a master antenna.[47] In 1999, 76 percent had cable and 73 percent owned a satellite dish.[48] In the same 1999 study it was found that eight out of the eleven Turkish channels that could be received via cable or satellite in the Netherlands were watched by more than half of the Turkish respondents, which indicated a rise since 1995. At that time, the majority watched only four out of the available nine channels. Although some research suggests that satellite channels are far from discouraging the integration process, it is evident that the above statistics reflect high rates for watching Turkey-originated media. It is also suggested that there is a need for Turkish satellite channels as well as Dutch channels among Turkish viewers, and that the main reason for watching these channels is to stay informed about the social and political situation in Turkey.[49] For Dutch news, viewers watch the Dutch news channels. It is of course possible to view the migrants as "localized cosmopolites"[50] having attachments to several places in the world. It is also possible, however, to consider the influence of the media as reinforcing ties to the country of origin and undermining or complicating integration.[51]

Low Levels of Intermarriage and High Levels of "Spouse Migration"

The choice of partners from the home country reinforces transnational ties and is considered a challenge for integration. The extent to which ethnic intermarriage occurs is widely accepted as an important indicator of assimilation and identification. Turks increasingly are "strategizing marriage." In other words, the large majority of Turks, including the second generation, choose a partner of the same ethnic background.

In the Netherlands, nine out of ten married persons born in Turkey or Morocco have a partner born in the same country.[52] In Germany the situation is not much different. Since 1970, the numbers of German–Turkish marriages has increased although the overall numbers are very low. For example, in 2003 there were 7,414 marriages between Turks and Germans.[53] These numbers indicate a low level of intermarriage among Germans and Turks but many Turks have German nationality and do not appear in the statistics.

Conclusion

In the Netherlands, multiculturalism was the buzzword and the explicit principle of the government's approach from the mid-1980s onwards. The Dutch integration concept did not arise from policy designed specifically for the integration of immigrants. It was merely a continuation of the known national model. The Dutch "polder" model (model of consensual policymaking)[54] provided the basis for the integration of new groups. The migrants were organized as groups and social participants. This has radically changed. The new stipulation is that people must integrate as individuals into Dutch society, learning to understand its norms and values.

Although the German approach did not start out as an "open" one, over time German policy has made it easier to be naturalized. The legal integration requirements introduced with legislation in 2005 resemble the Dutch approach. Germany and the Netherlands face similar problems when it comes to labor market participation and educational performance of Turkish migrants despite differing approaches. No matter how the comparison is done, Turkish migrants are behind the natives in both countries. Nonetheless, there are positive trends for Turkish migrants in education and the labor market in both. Yet despite such progress there is still much room for improvement.[55] Furthermore, progress has come to a standstill in the labor market in the face of the current economic slowdown, and decline may even be setting in. The educational level of people of foreign nationality is rising faster than for "native" nationals in some categories. Nevertheless, despite having gained some ground in terms of educational levels, people of Turkish nationality still lag far behind. Yet politicization, continued immigration inflow, and transnational tendencies form powerful constraints for policymaking.

Legislation and policy of the host countries increasingly target transnational features of immigrant communities. Dual citizenship is limited. Mandatory language and cultural orientation courses oblige migrants to focus on the host country. Marriage with partners from the home country is discouraged through strict entry requirements, long bureaucratic waiting periods and language criteria. The host countries do not appreciate political activism tied to Turkey. These policy initiatives and attitudes inevitably lead to the question of whether it is possible to be an immigration country without being transnational, what the "dangers" of targeting transnational features are and whether focusing on transnational features would actually lead to greater integration.

Notes

1. See *NRC Handelsblad* (national daily), January 19, 2004.

2. The assimilation model refers to the elimination of ethnic differences/groups. Multiculturalism is a model for national identity used in societies with highly heterogeneous populations (e.g. Australia). It rejects cultural assimilation and emphasizes cultural pluralism and the role of ethnic organizations in the provision of welfare services.

3. See for example Immigration and Integration Minister Verdonk in *Trouw* (national daily), February 24, 2004 on exams after integration courses or the liberal proposal by VVD (*Volkspartij voor Vrijheid en Democratie*; People's Party for Freedom and Democracy) on residence permits for spouses in *NRC*, February 23, 2004.

4. R. Koopmans, "Good Intentions Sometimes Make Bad Policy: A Comparison of Dutch and German Integration Policies," 2004, available online http://www.wz-berlin.de/zkd/zcm/pdf/koopmans_good _intentions.pdf.

5. Due to the lack of a specific body in charge of economic migration in Germany, the information content and reliability of data on labor immigrants are limited. For a more detailed discussion see http://www.eumap.org/journal/features/2004/migration/germanylabour/.

6. http://www.integrationsbeauftragte.de/download/Strukturdaten.pdf.

7. Ibid.

8. Agreements were made with Italy (1955 and 1965), Spain (1960), Turkey (1961 and revised in 1964), Greece (1960 and renewed in 1962), Portugal (1964), and Yugoslavia (1968). Besides these, labor agreements were also made with Morocco (1963), Tunisia (1965) and Korea (1970, for miners only). However, in the Korean case the number of workers involved was rather small.

9. Ch.P. Kindleberger, *Europe's Postwar Growth: The Role of Labor Supply* (Cambridge, MA: Harvard University Press, 1967).

10. S. Castles, H. Booth and T. Wallace, *Here for Good. Western Europe's New Ethnic Minorities* (London: Pluto Press, 1984); OECD-SOPEMI, *Trends in International Migration* (Paris: OECD, 1981).

11. Different categories are distinguished: the residence permit, right of unlimited residence, residence title for specific purposes, and residence title for exceptional circumstances. The two most important provisions, the right of unlimited residence is given after an eight-year legal stay and the residence permit after five years. The first has the highest status and an increased protection against expulsion. It frees the migrant from the requirement to obtain a work permit provided that he or she has independent means of support, has made provisions for an old-age pension, has not been legally penalized and has adequate living quarters.

12. Aliens Act (*Auslaendergesetz*, AuslG); Long title: *Gesetz über die Einreise und den Aufenthalt von Ausländern im Bundesgebiet*; In the version published on July 9, 1990 (*Federal Law Gazette* I pp.1354, 1356), as last amended by Article 2 of the Act of July 23, 1999 (*Federal Law Gazette* I pp.1620 ff.).

13. Nationality Act (*Staatsangehoerigkeitsgesetz*, StAG); in the version published on July 22, 1913 (*Reich Law Gazette* I p.583—*Federal Law Gazette* III 102-1), as last amended by the Act of July 23, 1999 (*Federal Law Gazette* I pp.1618 ff.)

14. For the full report see http://www.bmi.bund.de/cln_012/nn_174266/Internet/Content/Broschueren/ 2001/Zuwanderung__gestalten__-__Integration__Id__48169__de.html.

15. For an extensive review of the development of migration to the Netherlands, see L. Lucassen and R. Penninx, *Newcomers. Immigrants and their Descendants in the Netherlands 1550–1995* (Amsterdam: Het Spinhuis, 1997).

16. Scientific Council for Government Policy (WRR) *Etnische minderheden* [Ethnic Minorities], Reports to the Government, 17 (The Hague: Sdu, 1979).

17. *Minderhedennota* [Minorities Act] Tweede Kamer 1982–83, 16102, No.21 (The Hague: Ministry of Interior, 1983).

18. *Integratiebeleid etnische minderheden. Contourennota* [Framework memorandum, integration policy ethnic minorities], Second Chamber of the Parliament, Meeting Year 1993/1994, 23684, Nos.1–2.

19. The discussion was triggered when Frits Bolkestein published a controversial editorial "Integration of Minorities Calls for a Get-Tough Policy" in the national daily *De Volkskrant* (September 12, 1991).

20. Their predecessor, the Centrum Democrats, had occupied one seat out of 150 in the Second Chamber of the Parliament for most of the past ten years.
21. J. Doomernik, "Data Availability for Secondary Analysis in The Netherlands," EFFNATIS Working paper 24, available online http://www.unibamberg.de/projekte/effnatis/Paper24_IMES.pdf.
22. Sociaal Cultureel Planbureau, *Sociaal en Cultureel Rapport 1998. 25 Jaar Sociale Verandering* [Social and Cultural Report 1998: 25 Years of Social Change] (The Hague: SCP, 1998).
23. H. van den Tillaart, *Monitor Etnisch Ondernemerschap: Zelfstandig Ondernemerschap van Etnische Minderheden in Nederland in de Periode 1990–2000* [Monitor Ethnic Entrepreneurship: Independent Entrepreneurship of Ethnic Minorities in the Netherlands from 1990–2000] (Nijmegen: ITS, 2001), 117. These figures refer to first-generation immigrants only.
24. There are no numbers available for the total Dutch economy in 1986–87.
25. Zentrum für Türkeistudien, *Die Regionalen Transferstellen für ausländische Existenzgründer und Unternehmer in Nordrhein Westphalen. Ökonomische Daten der türkischen und ausländischen Selbständigen in NRW und Deutschland* [Regional Transfer Offices for Foreign Startups and Entrepreneurs in North Rhine-Westphalia, Economic Data of Turkish and Foreign Entrepreneurs in NRW and Germany] (Essen: Zentrum für Türkeistudien, 1999).
26. F. Lindo, "Does Culture Explain? Understanding Differences in School Attainment between Iberian and Turkish Youth in the Netherlands," in H. Vermeulen and J. Perlmann (eds.), *Immigrants, Schooling and Social Mobility. Does Culture make a Difference?* (London: MacMillan, 2000).
27. G. Driessen and H. Dekkers, "Educational Opportunities in the Netherlands: Policy, Students' Performance and Issues," *Review of Education*, Vol.43, No.4 (1997), pp.299–315.
28. M. Crul, "The Educational Position of the Second Generation in the Netherlands: Results, Career Routes and Explanations," EFFNATIS Working Paper No.35 (2000), available online http://www.uni-bamberg.de/projekte/effnatis/Paper35_IMES.pdf.
29. M. Crul, "Onderlinge hulp en schoolsucces van Marokkaanse en Turkse jongeren. Een optimistische visie" [Mutual Help and Success in School of Moroccan and Turkish Youth. An Optimistic Vision], in I. Van Eerd and B. Hermes (eds.), *Pluriform Amsterdam* (Amsterdam: Vossiuspers AUP, 1998), pp.51–69.
30. A. Ode, *Ethnic-cultural and Socio-economic Integration in the Netherlands: A Comparative Study of Mediterranean and Caribbean Minority Groups* (Assen: Van Gorcum, 2002), p.50.
31. Ibid., p.109.
32. For a detailed discussion see the contribution by V. Özcan and J. Söhn to this volume.
33. L. Yalçın-Heckmann, "The Perils of Associational Life in Europe: Turkish Migrants in Germany and France," in Tariq Madood and Pnina Werbner (eds.), *The Politics of Multiculturalism in New Europe* (London: Zed Books, 1998), pp.95–110.
34. E.K. Østergaard-Nielsen, "Trans-State Loyalties and Politics of Turks and Kurds in Western Europe," *SAIS Review*, Vol.20, No.1 (2000), pp.23–38; M. Fennema and J. Tillie, "Participation and Political Trust in Amsterdam: Civic Communities and Ethnic Networks," *Journal of Ethnic and Migrant Studies*, Vol.25, No.4 (1999), pp.703–26.
35. E. Morawska., "Immigrants, Transnationalism, and Ethnicization: A Comparison of this Great Wave and the Last," in G. Gerstle and J.H. Mollenkopf (eds.), *E Pluribus Unum? Contemporary and Historical Perspectives on Immigrant Political Incorporation* (New York: Russell Sage, 2001) p.178.
36. For a distinction between old versus new transnationalism see P. Levitt, *The Transnational Villagers* (Berkeley: University of California Press, 2001); L.E. Guarnizo, "On the Political Participation of Transnational Migrants: Old Practices and New Trends," in Gerstle and Mollenkopf (2001), pp.213–63; N. Glick Schiller, "Transmigrants and Nation-States: Something Old and Something New in the U.S. Immigrant Experience," in Ch. Hirschman, Ph. Kasinitz and J. DeWind (eds.), *The Handbook of International Migration: The American Experience* (New York: Russell Sage, 1999), pp.94–119.
37. See for example, M. Jones-Correa, "The 'Return' of the State: Immigration, Transnationalism, and Dual Nationality," available online http://drclas.fas.harvard.edu/publications/revista/latinos/jonescorrea.htm.

38. I. Bloemraad, "Who Claims Dual Citizenship? The Limits of Postnationalism, the Possibilities of Transnationalism, and the Persistence of Traditionalism," *International Migration Review*, Vol.38, No.2 (2004), pp. 389–426.
39. M. Jones-Correa, see note 37.
40. *Jus soli* is a rule of law that stipulates that a child's citizenship is determined by his or her place of birth.
41. See note 6.
42. Fennema and Tillie (1999).
43. A similar pattern can be observed in Belgium too, even though Turks achieve elected office less than Moroccans do. See the contribution by D. Jacobs, K. Phalet and M. Swyngedouw to this volume.
44. For more extensive reviews on city councilors and advisory board members see M. Berger and R. Wolff, *Een gekleurd advies? Een onderzoek naar de participatie van etnische minderheden in landelijke adviescolleges en gemeentelijke overlegstructuren* [A Biased Advice? Research into the Participation of Ethnic Minorities in National Advisory Council and Municipal Communication Platforms] (Amsterdam: Imes, 2001); M. Berger *et al.*, *Politieke participatie van etnische minderheden in vier steden* [Political Participation of Ethnic Minorities in Four Cities] (Amsterdam: IMES, 2001); and L. Michon and J. Tillie, *Amsterdamse polyfonie: opkomst en stemmgedrag bij de gemeenteraads- en deelraadsverkiezingen van 6 maart 2002* [Amsterdam Polyphonics: Electoral Turnout and Voting Behavior at Municipal Elections of March 6, 2002] (Amsterdam: Imes, 2003).
45. For a detailed discussion, see Project Hermes at http://www.quest-et.org/ec/issues.asp?mode =turkish_comm.
46. A. Aksoy, "The Possibilities of Transnational Turkish Television", available online http://www.photoinsight.org.uk/text/aksoy/aksoy.pdf.
47. Veldkamp Marktonderzoek, *Media-onderzoek etnische groepen 1995* [Media Research Ethnic Groups 1995] (Amsterdam: Veldkamp, 1995).
48. Veldkamp Marktonderzoek, *Mediagebruik etnische publieksgroepen—1998* [Media Consumption among Ethnic Groups—1998] (Amsterdam: Veldkamp, 1999).
49. R. Staring and S. Zorlu, "Thuis voor de buis: Turkse migranten en satelliet-teevee" [At Home in Front of the TV: Turkish Migrants and Satellite TV], *Migrantenstudies*, Vol.12, No.4 (1996), pp.211–21; and M. Millikowski, "Stoorzender of katalysator? Turkse satelliet tv in Nederland" [Interfering or Catalyst], *Migrantenstudies*, Vol.15, No.3 (1999), pp.170–90.
50. A. Çağlar, "Mediascapes, Advertisement Industries and Cosmopolitan Transformations: Turkish Immigrants in Europe," Robert Schuman Center Working Papers No. 2002/53 (2002).
51. Ch. Ogan, *Communication and Identity in the Diaspora: Turkish Migrants in Amsterdam and their Use of Media* (Lanham, MD: Lexington Books, 2001).
52. C.D. Harmsen, "Cross-Cultural Marriages," *Monthly Bulletin of Population Statistics* (Voorburg/ Heerlen: Statistics Netherlands, 1999).
53. The number of German women marrying Turkish men was 71 (1960), 404 (1970), 3,339 (1980), 2,767 (1990), 3,399 (1995), 3,720 (1996), 3,934 (1997), 4,106 (1998), 3,971 (1999), 4,320 (2000), 5,005 (2001), 5,642 (2002), and 5,564 (2003). The number of German men marrying Turkish women was 12 (1960), 182 (1970), 426 (1980), 691(1990), 948(1995), 937(1996), 1,073(1997), 1,247 (1998), 1,188(1999), 1,464 (2000), 1,738(2001), 1,983 (2002) and 1,850 (2003).
54. The coexistence of several population groups (protestant, catholic, socialist and liberal) was institutionalized in the 20th century in the "verzuiling" (system of pillarization). Each group had its own pillar and because there was no majority, the groups always needed to consult with each other and eventually reach a compromise. The Netherlands have rapidly secularized since the Second World War, but the institutional structures still reflect the marks of pillarization.
55. See the October 2003 annual minorities report of the Social and Cultural Planning Office (*Sociaal Cultureel Planbureau*, SCP) and the November 2003 report of the Central Statistical Office (*Centraal Bureau voor de Statistiek*, CBS).

The Turkish Community in Austria and Belgium: The Challenge of Integration

JOHAN WETS

Katholieke Universiteit Leuven (University of Leuven), Belgium and Katholieke Universiteit Brussel (Catholic University of Brussels), Belgium

Introduction

Turkish migrant workers make up a significant proportion of the immigrant population of Austria and Belgium. The first arrivals of Turkish migrant workers in these countries was part of the wave of Turkish immigration that began in the early 1960s in response to a labor shortage in the Federal Republic of Germany, which signed a bilateral agreement with Turkey in October 1961, regulating the short-term immigration of Turkish workers. The economic situation in many other European countries was similar to the German one and shortly after Austria (1964), Belgium (1964), and other European countries (Netherlands, France, Sweden and Switzerland) signed bilateral agreements with Turkey. The immigration that had been meant to be temporary had become long term. The 40th anniversary of the bilateral agreement has been celebrated recently. Turkish immigrants have been part of the scene in various European countries for many years, but does this mean that they fully participate in society? Are they well integrated? This study will try to answer these questions.

Austria and Belgium have a different history and a different geopolitical position. The context in both countries is, however, fairly similar. Austria and Belgium are both highly developed "corporatist welfare states." Together with the other countries of the so-called "continental regime type," France, Germany and Luxemburg, they have well-developed social security schemes, but not as universalistic as

Correspondence Address: Johan Wets, K. U. Leuven, HIVA, Parkstraat 47, B-3000 Leuven, Belgium. Email: johan.wets@hiva.kuleuven.ac.be in the Nordic countries. In general, there is a strong relationship between previous occupations and entitlement to provisions, and generous income protection for families with children. Employees are well protected against dismissal. The number of special schemes for occupational groups is high, and there is extensive collective coverage for civil servants. Pension benefits in the continental regime are slightly above the European average.[1] The continental welfare system is an expensive system, with a broad coverage that might attract immigrants, and consequently bring about anti-immigrant sentiments. On the other hand, the system might need immigrant labor power to keep it turning in the future.

Austria and Belgium continue to deny that they are officially immigration countries, but in fact the migrant community has gained access to the welfare system and has become very much settled. This has led in both countries, as in many other European countries, to political reaction. Right-wing, anti-immigrant parties are a major force in both countries. The Austrian *FPÖ (Freiheitliche Partei Österreichs)* and the Flemish *Vlaams Belang*[2] are both right-wing parties. While the FPÖ is more of a populist party, and the Vlaams Belang is more a one-issue anti-immigrant party,[3] and the profile of the electorate voting for both parties might differ, nevertheless, both parties campaign against immigration. They oppose the entry of new immigrants and demand that settled immigrants must assimilate or leave. These ideas and the political context are far from unique. Similar anti-immigrant parties are on the rise in countries such as Denmark, France, Italy and Switzerland. Similar developments are observed even in countries that traditionally held a more tolerant attitude, such as the Netherlands.

The position of the Turkish population in West European countries is important in the discussion of problems associated with the integration of immigrants since it represents a large share of the (non-EU) foreigners living in these countries, including in Austria and Belgium. The largest groups of non-EU foreigners in Austria are the nationals of the former Yugoslavia and Turkey. The two main non-EU nationalities in Belgium are Moroccans and Turks. In both countries, Turks are often presented as the least integrated group of immigrants.

One of the first questions that arise when addressing the issue of how well Turkish migrants are integrated within their guest societies is what is meant by integration. Integration can be defined as a continuous long-term two-way process. The two-way process implies the involvement of the immigrant (the individuals, institutions and organizations) and individuals, institutions and organizations of the receiving society. Successful integration can be determined by how well migrants participate in the social, economic and political life of the host community. Nonetheless, there is no generally accepted theory of integration. Research approaches differ both between and within disciplines. An often used distinction is the one between social integration, cultural integration and structural integration.[4] *Social integration* refers to the degree of interaction between immigrant and native population groups. The policy concern here is about segregation versus mixing. *Cultural integration* relates to the degree to which various population groups share the same norms, values and preferences. Examples given here are, for instance, ideas and attitudes towards gender equality or on the role of religion in the organization of society. *Structural integration* implies here that immigrants and their descendants have equal access to the major institutions of society, such as education, the labor and housing markets, the political system, health care services, and so on. The obvious policy goal here is the elimination of differences between immigrant and native population groups.[5]

The purpose of this contribution is to examine some of the challenges associated with the structural integration of Turkish immigrants in both countries. The primary focus will be on integration into the labor market and in the area of education. Other important issues like access to health care and housing will not be covered. The issue of political participation of Turkish immigrants in Belgium is scrutinized by Dirk Jacobs, Marc Swyngedouw and Karen Phalet, while Christiane Timmerman examines the issue of gender in the context of the integration of Turkish immigrants in Belgium elsewhere in this volume.

Turkish Immigrants and the Challenges of Integration in Austria

Austria, a country with a population of eight million, has experienced over the last two centuries various forms of international migration: immigration, emigration and transit migration, the latter due to the geopolitical position of the country. In the postwar period there were four waves of immigration in the form of refugees to Austria. These flows occurred as a result of events stemming from Soviet dominance and repression in Eastern European countries. These flows consisted of Hungarians (1956), Czechs (1968), Poles (1981) and Jews from the Soviet Union. Subsequent to the instability and violence after the collapse of the Soviet Union and former Yugoslavia, Austria also experienced a significant flow of refugees into the country in the first half of the 1990s. Additionally, there were Turkish nationals who sought asylum in Austria in the 1980s and 1990s.

However, there was also significant economically motivated immigration into Austria. The economic situation of Austria in the early 1960s was of almost full employment and there was need for extra manpower. From the beginning of the 1960s until the mid-1970s this led to the recruitment of guest workers, mainly from Turkey and the former Yugoslavia, to meet the employment demands of a growing economy. Originally, the goal of most of these "guest workers" was to be employed abroad and to save enough money to take back home. By the early 1970s, it became clear that the presence of the Turkish community changed from temporary to permanent. The reaction to the oil crisis of 1973 was similar in most western countries: to stop further immigration, to encourage those who had arrived previously to return home and to require from those who stay to assimilate into the host society. The Yugoslavs on the whole opted to return home. The Turks chose to stay, which subsequently led to an increase in family reunification. The proportion of Turkish residents in Austria grew from 7.7 percent of all foreigners in 1971 to 22.2 percent in 2001 or 160,000 Turkish citizens.[6] An economic boom in the late 1980s created renewed labor shortages in some sectors, following which employers looked to the traditional sources of labor from South-Eastern Europe to fill these slots. The number of Yugoslavs residing in Austria rose due to the crisis and the war in Yugoslavia. In 1990, Austria's policymakers also regularized the employment status of 29,100 foreigners hitherto illegally employed. The number of non-nationals in Austria doubled from 344,000 in 1988 to 690,000 in 1993. The share of foreign workers of all employed people rose from 5.4 percent to 9.1 percent.[7]

Austria's diverse immigrant population has become even more so in recent years. According to the 2001 census, of Austria's eight million inhabitants more than 730,000 (or 9.1 percent) were foreign residents, with 62.8 percent of them coming from the successor states of the former Yugoslavia and from Turkey. Between 1985 and 2001, over 254,000 foreigners were naturalized. Austria's proportion of foreign-born residents in 2001 was even higher than that of the United States, reaching a level of 12.5 percent.[8]

Yet Austria does not consider itself a traditional country of immigration. This is clearly reflected by recent immigration policies. Widespread public discontent over levels of immigration in the early 1990s led to a curtailment of the traditional labor migration and family reunification programs, supporting the official line that Austria is not a traditional country of immigration. On the other hand, this does not mean that Austria wishes to close all possibilities for entering the country legally. The country's accession to the European Union (EU) and the joining of the Schengen Agreement has brought more open borders in a sense that there is free circulation between Schengen countries.[9] Furthermore, there are quotas for foreign seasonal workers, which enabled the admittance of thousands of temporary workers. Austria has a long tradition of seasonal labor to meet companies' exceptional short-term demand for labor, especially in typically seasonal branches such as tourism and agriculture. The legal status of foreign seasonal workers differs considerably from that of all other resident or foreign workers in Austria. Their employment and residence permits are limited in time, they are prohibited from bringing their family to Austria and their residence permit is linked to their contract with a single employer, to whom they are bound: they are prohibited from moving freely on the labor market and finding another employer. When the employment term is up, the foreign worker must subsequently leave the country, since termination of employment also means the loss of residence permit. These foreign seasonal workers are not looked upon as immigrants but as part of an "international labor supply system" that can be utilized without having to maintain welfare and integration standards in regard to these foreign workers. The foreign workers have to pay unemployment insurance contributions, but are not entitled to unemployment allowances. In recent years, seasonal labor has been playing an increasingly important part in Austria's labor market, since the government has pursued a generous quota policy for foreign seasonal workers and has opened access to this kind of employment to all sectors.[10]

Critics have argued that this regulation may initiate a new "guest-worker regime," with thousands of foreign workers coming into Austria—even if interrupted by short periods of absence—for whom all legal paths to consolidate residency are closed. The history of the guest-worker regime in Austria has been similar to that of many other non-immigration countries of Europe: It is a system where temporary migration has a tendency to become permanent. This has had, of course, long-run repercussions in terms of the size and composition of the immigrant population in Austria. This naturally will continue to keep the issue of integration of especially non-EU immigrants high up on the agenda of Austrian policymaking and politics.

How these conflicting policies are to be reconciled remains an unanswered question.[11] The immigrant himself/herself has become involved directly through the so-called 2002 "Integration Contract" (*Integrationsvertrag*), which is a recent political measure of Austrian integration policy. It is, according to Böse and others, a one-sided obligation on the part of the immigrants, who have to deliver specified evidence of being "integrated" as defined in the regulations, such as passing a German-language proficiency exam. In case of failure the immigrants can lose their residency permits.[12]

Due to Austria's conservative political culture and the special form of its postwar nation-state building, the integration and naturalization of these immigrants and their descendants is, according to Fabian Georgi, even more problematic than in most of the other European countries.[13] The Austrian nation-building process stems from that of the Austro-Hungarian period, contending on the one hand with a heterogeneous population and on the other hand with the formation of German nationalism. Austria's assimilation or "nationalization" policy towards cultural minorities was a clear and conscious strategy implemented by the ruling elite of the time. This policy has led to an almost complete assimilation of most of the non-German groups in the Republic of Austria by the mid-twentieth century. The Austrian conception of the integration of migrant communities is a continuation of the strategy adopted towards the national minorities: integration is understood as a form of assimilation. According to Georgi, there is wide-ranging social and political exclusion in comparison with other Western European countries towards migrants. Moreover, the legal situation concerning political rights, security of residence and naturalization is one of the most restrictive in Europe.[14]

This situation is reflected in the new Naturalization Act that was passed in 1998, which retained the principle of *jus sanguinis*[15] and a regular waiting period of ten years for naturalization. According to the new law, the individual immigrant who wishes to acquire Austrian nationality has to show that he or she is integrated into Austrian society and has to give proof that he or she is economically self-sufficient—that is, not in need of social assistance—and sufficiently proficient in German. Minor criminal offences now constitute reasons for denial of citizenship.[16] A migrant may now acquire citizenship based on a legal claim after a period of 15 years on grounds of good integration. Still, in the majority of cases, Austrian citizenship is awarded to people without a legal claim on a discretionary basis after 10 years of continuous residence.[17] Since 1998, the number of naturalizations has continued to increase from 17,786 in 1998 (of whom 5,683 were Turks) to 31,731 in 2001 (of whom almost one-third were Turks). According to the Essen-based Center for Studies on Turkey, 53 percent of Turks living in Austria are naturalized.[18] This is largely due to demographic reasons: most migrants who entered Austria in the period of renewed immigration between 1988 and 1993 are now eligible for citizenship on a discretionary basis.[19] The Austrian Labor Force survey,[20] which provides information on both place of birth and citizenship of individuals surveyed, shows that around 40,000 Austrians have their place of birth in Turkey. Adding these people to the number of Turkish citizens residing in Austria gives a total of 200,000 Turks living in the country.[21]

Immigration policy until 1987 was seen purely as a function of labor-market policy and was mainly under the responsibility of the Ministry for Social Affairs. The Ministry of the Interior, after having played only a minor role in the past, joined the former as an actor from 1991 onwards, when immigration policy was influenced by factors other than solely the labor market policy.[22] The political landscape had changed in Austria and immigration issues began to emerge on the political agenda. At the beginning of the 1990s, the considerable influx of immigrants and the rising unemployment rates caused heated discussions in the media and in the political arena about immigration into Austria.

At first, the legal framework that regulated residence and labor-market access for non-Austrians was not altered (apart from some minor changes to the existing regulations). The approach to "guest-worker" schemes was maintained. A national quota system (*Bundeshöchstzahl*) was introduced for work permits. The yearly-fixed quotas varied from 8 percent to 10 percent of the total workforce. However, the political atmosphere eventually led to more restrictive regulations concerning labor market access and immigration which were modified several times in recent years.[23] In 2002, for instance, the immigration quota for less skilled labor was abolished completely, with the result that poorly qualified "third-country nationals" seeking to enter the Austrian labor market have had little chance of success since then. The government is expected to maintain its restrictive policy line regarding immigration.

The Foreigners' Employment Act (*Ausländerbeschäftigungsgesetz*) from 1975 states that after eight years of permanent employment a foreigner can obtain the so-called "Befreiungsschein" (exemption document)—limited to two years, but renewable—which allows the employee to change employer.[24] The Foreigners' Employment Act remains one of the primary control mechanisms of foreign employment. This type of regulation has been an important factor in causing ethnic segmentation of the labor market, curtailing the integration of immigrants in general. Also, as migrant workers cannot change jobs as a rule, they become heavily dependent on their employers and are open to abuse or exploitation.[25] These developments have put the migrant population in Austria in an uncertain position. The regulations were adapted in 1997. In that year, the new Aliens Act merged two previous Acts, the 1992 Aliens Act and the 1993 Residence Act, into a single law aiming at the promotion of integration of aliens already present in Austria. The 1992 Aliens Act tightened up regulations on the entry and residence of foreigners and the 1993 Residence Act, established *contingents* for different categories of migrants. In contrast to the quota used for the issuing of work permits, the contingents for residence permits defined the absolute number of permits that would be issued in any single year.[26] A major feature of this 1997 reform included an improvement of the legal position of immigrants residing in Austria for at least eight years and children born in Austria, by removing the possibility of expulsion in their case. The Act weakened, however, the position of immigrants residing in Austria for less than eight years, for whom expulsions have become a more realistic threat. To be in employment and obtain sufficient income is still a vital requirement for non-Austrian citizens. Extended periods of unemployment can cost immigrants the legal base of their stay.[27] These factors constitute additional challenges to ensuring a better integration of immigrants.

In January 2000, the Austrian Freedom Party (FPÖ), which ran an anti-immigrant campaign, formed a coalition government with the People's Party (ÖVP). In July 2002, parliament adopted major amendments to the Aliens Act and the Asylum Law. The reforms introduced new regulations in three important areas. Jandl and Kraler summarize them as follows.[28] First, labor immigration has been restricted mainly to key personnel, with a minimum wage requirement of around 2,000 per month for prospective migrants. Second, and in stark contrast to the first category of migrants, the employment of seasonal workers will be greatly facilitated by allowing such laborers in areas outside agriculture and tourism and extending the employment period to up to one year. Third, all new immigrants from non-EU third countries (plus those who have been living in Austria since 1998) are required to attend "integration courses" consisting mainly of language instruction and a basic introduction to the law, history and politics of Austria. Non-participation will lead to sanctions, both financial and legal, for instance the denial of more secure residence titles. The ultimate fate of non-compliant foreigners could be expulsion from Austria.

Another major challenge that Turkish immigrants face in respect of structural integration is in the area of education. Schooling is compulsory in Austria for all children between the ages of 6 and 15, regardless of their nationality and whether they have a residence permit or not. The situation of children with an immigrant background is marked in the Austrian education system by inequality. The segregation of migrant children in the education system is to a large extent due to the social position of the parents. The first Turkish "guest workers" had a rural background and a fairly low level of education. These unfavorable conditions were to a large extent inherited by the following generations. Three-quarters of the Turkish migrant population have attained only primary education. Another 15 percent has completed an apprenticeship. In terms of education, no other migrant group has fared as poorly as the Turks.[29]

A direct effect of the low educational qualifications is a poor position in the labor market. The Turkish laborers work mainly as blue-collar workers, earning less than their Austrian counterparts. They are employed as unskilled or semi-skilled workers. Only a minority is employed as white-collar workers. Turkish laborers are overrepresented in a number of sectors of the Austrian labor market. Their niches are mainly industry and the service sectors. Employment in the manufacturing industries has decreased during the last few decades while the service sector showed a rising share of employment.[30] The sectors with the largest shares of immigrant workers are construction, catering, and cleaning, which are also the sectors with the highest concentration of unskilled labor and very limited chances for upward mobility.[31] The first-generation migrants worked in these "ethnic niches," but so did a large part of the second generation. The next generations are not significantly better educated than the generation of their parents, and thus take up similar positions in the labor market. A glance at the statistics presented in the Austrian Labor Force Survey shows that Turks with an Austrian nationality do only slightly better than Turkish nationals working in Austria. According to the same Labor Force survey, Turks are significantly less often self-employed than the Austrian population or other migrants. Compared to the 12.5 percent of self-employed among the Austrian population and 7.6 percent among the (non-Turkish) migrant population, only 1.4 percent of the Turkish residents are self-employed. According to the survey, Turks with an Austrian nationality fare almost as well as the group called "other foreigners." This is due to the legislation: A basic requirement for obtaining a trade license is to be an Austrian or to have an Austrian partner.[32] Ethnic entrepreneurs can be found in the areas of Vienna with a high concentration of foreigners.

Male Turks have a higher employment rate than the average Austrian (male) population. The Turkish women, however, are less present on the labor market. As extended periods of unemployment can cost immigrants the legal base of their stay, there is more pressure on foreign workers to find a new job as soon as possible than there is for unemployed Austrians. Therefore they are much more likely to accept even low-paid or low-quality jobs. This tends to enforce the segmentation of the labor market. The economic and political pressure on immigrants leads to a situation in which, contrary to many other countries, activity rates for foreign women and men are considerably higher than those of Austrians.[33] Also the average unemployment rate of immigrants in Austria exceeds the overall unemployment rate only by 1–2 percent.[34]

Georgi observes that since the beginning of the twentieth century, assimilation has been the major strategy for integrating cultural and linguistic minorities in Austria. He describes Austria as an apparently homogeneous society that still experiences conflict with and discrimination against its "old minority groups"[35] while "new" immigrant minorities (mainly Turks and people from the former Yugoslavia), pose new problems and challenges. Georgi concludes that on the one hand new minorities still experience pressure to assimilate and that on the other hand, as a result of Austrian society's hostility towards them, they nevertheless experience structural social segregation and political exclusion.[36] As a result, these groups, including the Turks, remain marginalized and segregated, and even the third-generation descendants of the former guest workers in Austria tend to have higher unemployment rates, lower wages, less educational success and poorer housing conditions than that of the Austrian host society.[37]

Turkish Immigrants and the Challenges of Integration in Belgium

Belgium, a country with a population of 10 million, is home to many immigrants and asylum seekers. Immigration into Belgium was and is mainly European due to its strong attraction for many EU citizens, especially the French and the Dutch. Approximately 63 percent of foreigners in Belgium are EU nationals. Non-EU immigration to Belgium began first with Southern European migrants and later with Moroccans and Turks who were recruited in the 1960s to work in the coal mines. The Belgian government signed up several bilateral agreements to bring in foreign labor to compensate for the declining domestic workforce. These agreements were first signed with Italy in 1946, followed by Spain in 1956, Greece in 1957, Morocco and Turkey in 1964, Tunisia in 1969, Algeria in 1970, and Yugoslavia in 1970. The Moroccan and Turkish communities are the most numerous migrant communities among non-EU citizens. More than 8.8 percent of Belgium's population is of foreign origin. However, if one considers the total number of persons who at birth did not have Belgian nationality, it is found that the population of foreign origin is much higher, reaching almost 13 percent of the Belgian population. Thirty-six percent of the 202,786 persons who received Belgian nationality between 1995 and 2000 were Moroccans; 24 percent of them had a Turkish background and 6 percent were Italian.[38]

Turkish migrants mainly originate from a cluster of central Anatolian provinces. Nearly 60 percent of first-generation Turkish migrants living in Belgium were born in the countryside or in a small village.[39] According to data on migrants from the State Institute of Statistics in Ankara, the three provinces that provided the most Turkish immigrants are Afyon, Eskisehir and Kayseri. Almost one-third of the Turkish immigrants in Belgium originate from Afyon, in particular Emirdağ.[40] Contrary to some other immigrant groups, Turks settled just about everywhere and are distributed equally over the urban areas of the country, in Brussels and in Antwerp, but especially in Ghent and Limburg. The Turkish community in Belgium is composed of persons of diverse ethnic, religious and cultural backgrounds, including Turks of Kurdish origin, Christians, Sunnis, and Alevis.

Economic recession and the crisis that struck the coal industry (leading to increased unemployment), in the early 1970s, led to a restrictive migration policy and left many of the guest workers who were already in the country unemployed. It was difficult for the Turkish miners to adapt to the labor market after the mines closed down for they were unable to speak Flemish or French. However, despite the fact that work opportunities ceased to exist and there seemed to be no future prospects due to the new restrictive policy, immigration was not brought to a halt. The Moroccans and Turks stayed in the country and, although there was a "migration stop" for labor migration, new immigrants from Morocco and Turkey kept on entering the country through the process of family reunification and family formation.

In the mid-1980s, the Belgian government accepted the fact that the planned temporary migration seemed to have a more permanent character and began to develop policies to encourage immigrants to settle in the country and to integrate into society. The law on the entrance, residence, settlement, and return of foreigners, which is still in force, was passed in December 1980. This law provided more legal security regarding residence and it introduced a legal process for foreigners to contest measures questioning the legality of their stay. In 1981 an anti-racism law was passed. At that time, the political class still refused to grant voting rights at the local level to foreigners.[41]

In the mid-1980s the country suffered from a high and persistent level of unemployment. The immigrant population became easy scapegoats. The government implemented, with not too much success, a policy to encourage immigrants to return home. Simultaneously, an integration policy was established. In 1984, the Nationality Code, which was almost 50 years old, was replaced by a new one. The new Nationality Code introduced the principle of *jus soli*[42] and simplified the procedure for naturalization. Children born on Belgian soil to foreign parents who themselves were born in Belgium became Belgian citizens. Although simplified, the naturalization process still required individuals to demonstrate a "desire to integrate" measured arbitrarily by the administration. The right to political participation of the migrant communities was heavily debated. The government decided not to grant political rights, but to relax the conditions for acquiring Belgian nationality. This had a significant impact during this period. The number of applications more than doubled the year after the adoption of the new law. The Nationality Code was revised again and passed in its new form on March 1, 2000. Since then, any foreigner legally residing for at least seven years in Belgium who has a permanent residence permit can become Belgian with a simple declaration without a check on his or her "desire to integrate." Between 1990 and 2002, over 400,000 foreigners have become Belgians under this provision.[43]

The so-called "new Belgians"—foreigners who acquired Belgian citizenship—participated in all social activities and could join political parties. Since 1994, many cities and regions have elected "new Belgians" to political office, at the local, regional, as well as national level. Some even hold posts in executive functions, thus giving evidence of their integration into Belgian society. While successful by many accounts, the Belgian government's policies for integrating immigrants, like those of neighboring countries, have been accompanied by restrictive policies on newcomers.[44]

The impressive electoral success of the *Vlaams Blok* in the city of Antwerp in the 1989 elections (the first in a series of electoral victories) led to the creation of a government service that would monitor the position of the immigrant population called the Royal Commissioner for the Policy on Immigrants. This task has been taken up since 1990 by the successor organization, the Center for Equal Opportunities and the Fight against Racism.

Of the first wave of Turkish immigrants, 30 percent were illiterate. The profile is slowly changing. The number of Turkish students has doubled since the 1970s. Technical and vocational schools are not popular among Belgian students: approximately 10 percent attend these schools. In comparison, 70 percent of Turkish students prefer to attend technical and vocational schools. Second-generation students show a stronger preference for these schools and they often leave after completing higher secondary education.[45] Data on the qualifications of newcomers are hard to find and are often incomplete, but ongoing research shows that the Turkish newcomers in Flanders are still lower skilled than the people arriving from other countries.[46]

Education among the second generation, especially compared to other groups, is still quite limited and many of them have turned to trade.[47] The third generation deviates from the previous ones with a higher rate of university graduates. The numbers of Turkish students who attend university have increased over the decades even if in real terms their numbers still remain low in comparison to natives and other immigrant youth. Approximately 40 percent of them are female. Even though they are concentrated in Flemish regions, success rates are higher in French-speaking universities. Nearly half of the Turkish females who study at this level prefer to study medicine while the male population who reach this level prefer economics, international trade, political science, and the like. Seventy percent of those who begin university are able to graduate.[48]

One reason for the poor level of education among Turkish migrants is the fact that the children do not master the language of education sufficiently. Preschool attendance is still quite low amongst Turkish children, and this directly affects school performance later on. Children are not able to grasp the language or socialize with the Belgian children, thus causing frustration and learning problems once they start primary school. However, the situation seems to be changing in the third generation. The role education plays in the integration process is further elaborated in the piece by Veysel Özcan and Janina Söhn, elsewhere in this volume.

The direct consequence of poor schooling is the lack of vocational qualifications. Europe's Turks suffer greatly from this. As a result, the majority of Europe's working Turks have insecure low-paid unskilled jobs. In most cases the children follow in their parents' footsteps. The number of young Turks who have university degrees is rather small even if it is growing. These socio-professional characteristics marginalize the Turkish community on the labor market.[49] Low educational qualifications result in a poor position in the labor market. Turkish immigrants in Belgium are more likely than any other group to be blue-collar workers, earning less than the Belgians or other migrant groups.[50] They are mainly situated in industry and the service sector, and are heavily represented in agriculture and horticulture, metallurgy and the waste processing industry. Contrary to the Austrian situation, male Turks have a much lower employment rate than the male Belgian population. Also Turkish women are less active in the labor market.[51] And yet research by Martens and others found that Turks with a Belgian nationality do slightly better than Turkish nationals working in Belgium.[52]

The first-generation unskilled labor force was relatively less affected by unemployment or the problems it incurred. Nevertheless, the second generation was affected by the Belgian market's multiple crises since the 1970s. Hence, they experience higher unemployment rates.[53] In the year 2000, nearly half of the active Turks living in the Walloon region were unemployed. In the Flemish region, Turks' unemployment was only 25 percent. It reached 35 percent in Brussels. Turkish women account for 40 percent of the unemployed Turkish population.[54]

The average unemployment rate of Turks in Belgium is much higher than the overall unemployment rate. An analysis of some labor market data for 2003 in Flanders illustrates the poor position of the Turkish population in the labor market.

The Turkish population represents only 0.5 percent of the working population in Flanders, but represents 1.9 percent of the unemployed. The overall unemployment rate was 8 percent. For people with a Belgian nationality it was 7 percent, for non-Belgians 15 percent, for the Moroccan population it was 27 percent and for the Turkish population it was 29 percent.[55] The pressure of unemployment and the increasing difficulty of getting work have played a critical role in the initiative taken by some immigrants to set up their own businesses. The number of these businesses has doubled in the last 25 years. The preferred businesses are grocery stores, fruit and vegetable stores, bakeries, "doner" takeaway shops, restaurants and cafes. These account for 75 percent of preferred businesses,[56] in which sector Turkish immigrants are heavily represented.

Conclusion

Austria and Belgium are relatively small countries. A significant proportion of the population residing in both countries consists of immigrants from non-EU countries. Both countries have similar histories of (recent) immigration. In the 1960s and 1970s, guest workers were encouraged to come and settle temporarily. However, the economic downturn that followed the oil crisis in 1973 accompanied by major structural changes in each economy led to the decision to stop the recruitment of labor from abroad. However, guest workers not only stayed on and became immigrants, but immigration has continued through family reunification. Immigrants of both countries have difficulties integrating into the labor market and lag significantly behind the host society in respect of educational performance, which in turn aggravates their employment situation. The difficulties that immigrants face regarding integration have played a critical role in fueling anti-immigrant feelings. The rise of the Right in the domestic politics of both countries impacted on the evolution of immigration policies in each country in respect of employment and especially citizenship rights. Often these policies have caused the challenges of integration that immigrants face to become even greater.

On the labor market, Turkish migrants fare worse than the other migrant communities, both in Austria and Belgium. There are, however, some remarkable differences between the countries regarding unemployment figures. The unemployment rate is much higher in Belgium than in Austria. In Belgium, foreigners in general and Turks in particular are much more frequently unemployed than the Belgians. In comparison, the unemployment rate of foreigners in Austria is only slightly higher than the unemployment rate of the Austrians. The employment rate of the foreigners in Austria is higher than that of the Austrians. The situation in Belgium is the opposite: here, the Turkish population participates less in the labor market than the Belgium population.

Austria sanctions unemployment. An extended period of unemployment can cost immigrants the legal base of their stay. This is not the case in Belgium, where there is no limit to the duration of unemployment benefits for breadwinners and single persons. There is no link between any benefit entitlement and the right to stay in the country. Belgian unemployment insurance leads to what is called the unemployment trap, since it discourages the labor force from re-entering the labor market. This is one of the factors accounting for the high unemployment rate of the Turkish population in Belgium.

The Turkish population in Austria and Belgium emigrated from Turkey around the same period in history. Forty years later, the socio-economic position of the Turkish migrants in both countries is very similar. The Turkish men, as well as Turkish women, have a low level of education, even when compared with other migrant groups. This is a central factor that leads to a poor labor market position. They are often unemployed or occupy positions in the least favorable sectors and earning less than other laborers. The second generation generally has not done much better than their parents. Turks who naturalized and acquired the nationality of the host country occupy apparently slightly better positions, but it is hard to prove any causality.

Another difference between the countries is their approach to the acquisition of citizenship. Naturalization is difficult to achieve in Austria, even for children of the third generation. The Austrian legislation is based on the principle of *jus sanguinis*; in comparison, the new Belgian Nationality Code introduced the principle of *jus soli* and simplified the procedure for naturalization. The naturalization process is a relatively simple administrative process, open to a large group of foreigners. Acquiring the nationality of the country of residence improves the legal situation of the immigrants. For instance, foreigners enjoy social and civil rights, although no political rights. This is, in the Belgian case, the reason why foreigners remain excluded from national and regional elections. The logic behind it is that if one wishes to integrate and to participate actively in political life, one can easily apply for Belgian citizenship.

If *structural integration* implies that immigrants and their descendants have equal access to the major institutions of society, among which are education and the labor market, it can be concluded that the integration of the Turkish population was not a complete success story, either in Austria or in Belgium. Do these findings imply the unmitigated failure of the Austrian and Belgian integration policy? To answer this question, it is useful to go back to the question raised in the introduction: *how can we define integration*. Should we rely on the definition given today or on the definition society used one, two, three or four decades ago? What sort of indicators can measure successful integration? And which sorts of policy measures introduced in different countries have been successful? Why, for which groups and in what domain?

There is a need for further research to answer these questions and question *why*? Why do many *Turkish* immigrants fail to integrate? To answer this, it will be necessary to go beyond the structural elements of integration and also look at social and cultural integration. Structural elements like the integration of immigrants into the labor market are relatively easy to measure and compare. But the other aspects of integration and especially their interplay with structural integration should not be overlooked. Social integration, the level of social interaction between immigrants or ethnic minorities and the wider society is crucial, as well as cultural integration, the degree of identification with various norms and values of the host country. These dimensions of integration are clearly more difficult to measure than labor market participation and school enrollment.

Regardless of the differences and similarities between the countries studied and the particularities within each country, it can be stated as a general conclusion that both countries—like many other European countries—still have to learn how to handle immigration and how to deal with the question of citizenship. A better integration of the migrant population, however it is defined, can only be achieved within a society that tolerates and respects all groups it is composed of, whatever their ethnic origin, cultural background or religious affiliation. The receiving countries have to offer the structural setting that allows newcomers to find their place in the host society. But integration is a *two-way process* that also implies the involvement of the migrant population and their descendants. Integration is not a matter of adaptation or assimilation, but a matter of respect, mutual acceptance and participation. This also means the willingness of immigrants to accept responsibility for this process, participate actively and take up their roles and responsibilities in a permanent dialogue.

It remains to be seen how it would be possible to break out from the vicious circle of weak immigrant integration, the rise of anti-immigrant feelings and adoption of legislation that is discriminatory against immigrants and immigration, and actually succeed in initiating an integration process that is actually and genuinely two-way.

Acknowledgment

With thanks to Rana Çakırerk.

Notes

1. Arjan Soede, Cok Vrooman, Pier Marco Ferraresi and Giovanna Segre, *Unequal Welfare States: Distributive Consequences of Population Ageing in Six European Countries* (The Hague: Social and Cultural Planning Office, June 2004).
2. *Vlaams Belang* was previously called *Vlaams Blok*, but the party changed its name after a conviction for racism of three associations linked to the Vlaams Blok.
3. Yves De Weerdt, Hans De Witte, Patrizia Catellani and Patrizia Milesi, *Turning Right? Socio-Economic Changes and the Receptiveness of European Workers to Extreme Right. Report on the Survey Analysis and Results* (Leuven: HIVA, 2004).
4. See for instance Jeannette Schoorl, "Information Needs on Stocks of Migrants for Research on Integration," Paper submitted at the UNECE/Eurostat Seminar on "Migration Statistics," Geneva, March 21–23, 2005.
5. Ibid.
6. Heinz Fassmann, "Social Position and Social Mobility of Turkish Immigrants in Austria," Paper presented at the workshop on "Integration of Turkish Immigrants in Austria, France, Holland and Germany," Boğaziçi University, Istanbul, February 27–28, 2004.
7. Michael Jandl and Albert Kraler, "Austria: A Country of Immigration?" *Migration Information*, available at http://www.migrationinformation.org/Profiles/display.cfm?ID=105, 2003.

8. Ibid.
9. The Schengen countries are the EU-15 countries minus the UK and Ireland. On March 25, 2001, Norway joined the treaty of Schengen.
10. Georg Adam, "Controversy Over Quota for Foreign Seasonal Workers," *European Industrial Relations Observatory On-Line*, 2004, available at http://www.eiro.eurofound.eu.int/about/2004/03/feature/at0403202f.html.
11. Ibid.
12. Martina Böse, Regina Haberfellner and Ayhan Koldaş, *Mapping Minorities and their Media: The National Context—Austria*, Centre for Social Innovation, available online at http://www.lse.ac.uk/collections/EMTEL/Minorities/papers/austriareport.pdf, 2001.
13. Fabian Georgi, "Nation-State Building and Cultural Diversity in Austria," in Jochen Blaschke (ed.), *Nation-State Building Process and Cultural Diversity*, European Migration Centre, http://www.emz-berlin.de/projekte_e/pj50_pdf/Austria.pdf, 2004. Fabian Georgi discusses in this article the history and the specific elements of the Austrian nation-state building process and gives an overview of the tradition and practice of Austrian minority politics, with a focus on the strategy of assimilation for the integration of cultural and linguistic minorities and the continuity of this paradigm when dealing with new immigrants.
14. Ibid., p.22.
15. *Jus sanguinis* ("right of blood") is the Latin concept determining that a child's citizenship is determined by that of his or her parents. This is in contrast to *Jus soli* ("right of the territory" or "right of soil"), which refers to rights which are acquired as a result of one's place of birth.
16. Jandl and Kraler (2003).
17. More information about obtaining citizenship based on a legal claim or on discretionary grounds can be found at http://www.wien.gv.at/english/citizenship.
18. *The European Turks: Gross Domestic Product, Working Population, Entrepreneurs and Household Data* (Essen: Centre for Studies on Turkey, 2003), available at http://www.tusiad.org/haberler/basin/ab/9.pdf.
19. Ibid.
20. *Austrian Labour Force Survey*, quoted in Fassmann (2004).
21. Fassmann (2004).
22. August Gächter, *Migrants and Ethnic Minorities on the Margins: Report for Austria 2001*, cited in Böse, Haberfellner and Koldas (2001); Karin König and Bernhard Perchinig, "Austrian Country Report on Immigration Management," in Jan Niessen, Yongmi Schibel and Raphaële Magoni (eds.), *EU and US Approaches to the Management of Immigration* (Brussels: MPG, 2003).
23. Böse, Haberfellner and Koldas (2001).
24. Rainer Bauböck, "Migrationspolitik" [Migration Policy], in Herbert Dachs *et al.* (eds.), *Handbuch des politischen Systems Österreichs. Die zweite Republik* [Manual on the Austrian Political System. The Second Republic] (Wien: Manz, 1997).
25. August Gächter, "Integration und Migration" [Integration and Migration], *SWS-Rundschau*, Vol.35, No.4 (1995), pp. 435–8.
26. Jandl and Kraler (2003).
27. König and Perchinig (2003).
28. Jandl and Kraler (2003).
29. Fassman (2004).
30. Böse, Haberfellner and Koldas (2001).
31. Heinz Fassmann, *Arbeitsmarktsegmentation und Berufslaufbahnen. Ein Beitrag zur Arbeitsmarktgeographie Österreichs* [Labor Market Segmentation and Job Careers. A Contribution to the Austrian Labor Market Geography] (Vienna: Verlag der österreichischen Akademie der Wissenschaften, 1993).
32. Fassmann (2004).
33. The activity rate (%) is the number of residents who are economically active (this means employed and unemployed) multiplied by 100, divided by the number of residents of working age.

34. Böse, Haberfellner and Koldas (2001).
35. "Ethnic minorities" still living in Austria are mainly groups related to the population in neighboring countries like Hungarians (in Burgenland), Slovenes (in Carinthia and Styria), Croats (in Burgenland), Slovaks, Czechs and Serbs.
36. Georgi (2004).
37. Ibid.
38. Nouria Ouali, *Immigratie in België, aantallen, stromen en arbeidsmarkt: rapport 2001* [Immigration in Belgium, Numbers, Flows and the Labor Market: Report 2001] (Brussels: Federal Public Service Employment, Labour and Social Dialogue, 2003).
39. George Reniers, "On the Selectivity and Internal Dynamic of Labor Migration Processes: A Cross-cultural Analysis of Turkish and Moroccan Migration to Belgium," *IPD-Working Paper* 1997-7, p.8.
40. Ibid., p.9.
41. Marco Martiniello and Andrea Rea, "Belgium's Immigration Policy Brings Renewal and Challenges, Country profile Belgium," *Migration Information Source*, 2003, available at http://www.migration-information.org/Profiles/display.cfm?ID=164; Sonia Gsir, Marco Martiniello and Johan Wets, "Belgian Country Report on Immigration Management," in Niessen, Schibel and Magoni (eds.) (2003).
42. See note 15.
43. Data National institute of Statistics. Available at http://www.statbel.fgov.be/figures/d22_nl.asp.
44. Martiniello and Rea (2003).
45. Karel Neels and Reinhard Stoop, "Social Mobility and Equal Opportunities: The Case of Turkish and Moroccan Minorities in Belgium," *IPD Working Paper* 1998-3, p.6.
46. These findings stem from an ongoing and not yet published research on Flemish Integration Policy carried out by the higher Institute of Labour Studies (HIVA) of the University of Leuven and OASeS, of the University of Antwerp.
47. Altay Manco, *Sociographie de la population turque et d'origine turque. Quarante ans de présence en Belgique (1960–2000) Dynamiques, problèmes, perspectives* [Sociological Description of the Turkish Population and the Population of Turkish Origin in Belgium (1960–2000). Dynamics, Problems and Perspectives] (Brussels: Centre de Relations Européennes, Ed. Européennes, 2000).
48. Ibid.
49. Ural Manço, "Turcs d'Europe: de l'image tronquée à la complexité d'une réalité sociale immigrée" [The Turks of Europe: From a Truncated Image to the Complexity of an Immigrated Social Reality], *Hommes et Migrations*, No.1226 (July–August 2000), Paris, pp.76–87.
50. Hans Verhoeven, *De vreemde eend in de bijt, arbeidsmarkt en diversiteit* [The Stranger in our Midst: Labor Market and Diversity] (Leuven: Steunpunt WAV, 2000).
51. Ibid.
52. Albert Martens, Nouria Ouali, Marjan Van de Maele, Sara Vertommen, Philippe Dryon and Hans Verhoeven, *Etnische discriminatie op de arbeidsmarkt in het Brussels Hoofdstedelijk Gewest. Onderzoek in het kader van het Sociaal Pact voor de Werkgelegenheid van de Brusselaars* [Ethnic Discrimination on the Labor Market in the Brussels Capital Region. Research in the Framework of the Social Pact for Employment of the Brussels Population] (Brussels/Leuven: ULB/K.U.Leuven, 2005); Verhoeven (2000).
53. Manco (2000).
54. Ibid.
55. Data: Statistics Belgium (Nationaal Instituut voor de statistiek), The National Employment Office (RVA) and the Flemish Public Employment Service (VDAB). Calculations by Steunpunt WAV (http://www.steunpuntwav.be).
56. Manco (2000).

The Educational Attainment of Turkish Migrants in Germany

JANINA SÖHN[*] & VEYSEL ÖZCAN
*Social Science Research Centre Berlin (WZB), Germany

Introduction

Education is the main prerequisite for the successful socio-economic integration of immigrants and for their social mobility. For immigrant children and children of immigrants in particular, their participation and attainments in the education system of the country of immigration are key components of their integration into those societies. While in previous decades labor migrants easily found employment as un- and semi-skilled workers, such jobs are now rapidly diminishing and employment increasingly depends on at least medium-range educational qualifications. Thus, the educational attainment of immigrant children at present is an important indicator of how the integration of immigrants will develop in future.

The OECD Programme on International Student Assessment (PISA) has drawn renewed attention to the fact that so far, in many immigration countries, immigrant children do not have equal educational opportunities. In most OECD countries, an achievement gap exists between native students and children of parents born abroad. In countries with a substantial proportion of migrants of Turkish origin, such as Germany, Belgium, the Netherlands, Switzerland and Austria, these discrepancies are particularly large.[1] The large majority of (adult) immigrants from Turkey who live in these states are of working class and rural background that were recruited in

Correspondence Address: Janina Söhn, Reichpietschufer 50, 10785 Berlin, Germany. Email: soehn@wz-berlin.de; Veysel Özcan. Email: mail@veysel-oezcan.de

the 1960s and 1970s as un- or semi-skilled workers or immigrated as family members. Their children face similar problems in school education. Yet the discrepancies in academic performance and educational degrees between those of Turkish origin and native students vary across European countries—despite a similar socio-economic background and migration history. Germany performs especially poorly when it comes to offering Turkish youths equal opportunities in the education system.[2]

This study focuses on the educational attainment of Turkish immigrants in Germany, the country with the largest number of migrants of Turkish origin in Europe. In 2004, Turkish citizens were the largest national group among the 6.7 million foreigners in Germany. While the official figure is 1.8 million, the number of people with a Turkish background is even higher when taking into account those immigrants who have been naturalized and become German citizens. Then, the number of Turkish citizens *and* other persons with a Turkish background in Germany is about 2.5 to 3 million.

Given the socio-economic position of first-generation immigrants—almost exclusively either in low-skilled jobs or unemployed—how do Turkish youths fare in the education system? Even if their educational attainment is better than their parents'—are they on a par with native students?

In this contribution, we describe and discuss the position and performance of Turkish students in pre-school and the general education system in Germany. As a preliminary remark we first illustrate the problems arising from a lack of specific data on integration and education in Germany. In the succeeding section we will first describe generic features of the German education system as the determining institutional setting of integration in this area. This is particularly important as international comparative research indicates that different outcomes of academic achievement of immigrant youths seem to depend more on the general institutional arrangements and regulations than on educational policies explicitly geared at immigrants.[3] We then present a chronological picture of the educational situation of Turkish migrants in pre-school, primary and secondary education. Whenever possible, we will refer to research which focuses on Turkish students, but sometimes important findings pertain to all students with non-German citizenship. In the following section we discuss relevant explanations of the discrepancies between German and Turkish (and other immigrant) students. These explanations refer to a number of factors such as students' socio-economic background, aspects of migration biography or the lack of support in the acquisition of German language skills. In the final part we summarize research findings and propose measures suitable for enhancing the educational achievement of Turkish students.

Lack of Significant Data

An important precondition for implementing political measures aimed at changing and improving educational opportunities is an accurate assessment of the educational situation. It is all the more remarkable that detailed and continuous census data on education in Germany is hardly available. Furthermore, the value of existing data is limited, as stressed in the first *Educational Report for Germany*: "The available statistical material includes solely citizenship, but disregards native tongue or other important criteria for migration background,"[4] such as parents' country of origin.

Citizenship is the central indicator in official statistics for migration background, but this has lost significance since the 1990s. Based on citizenship, Turkish children are the largest group of migrant children: Almost every second foreign student in Germany is a holder of a Turkish passport. However, the data provided by PISA for the first time allow us to look beyond citizenship. According to PISA, the largest group of immigrant students consists of *Aussiedler* from the former Soviet Union and Poland.[5] If we define migration background as having at least one parent born abroad, about 16 percent of all 15-year-old immigrant students (in the western part of Germany[6]) are of Turkish background compared to 34.2 percent of Polish and former SU background.[7]

Those who are registered as foreign citizens in Germany did not always immigrate themselves. A considerable share were born in Germany: for 35 percent of the 1.8 million Turkish citizens, their country of birth is Germany. Additionally, there are also German citizens with a migration background. The quantitative dimension becomes clear when we consider that 620,000 persons of Turkish origin have become German citizens since 1980. It is not possible, however, to identify the naturalized population in official statistics. The same is true for children of non-German parents who have become German citizens by birth since 2000, when a new citizenship law came into effect. The number of migrant children benefiting from the rule of *jus soli* is about 35,000 to 40,000 each year. Given these multiple blind spots, the analysis of the educational situation of migrants on the basis of official statistics is imprecise. Moreover, it is impossible to disclose separately those successful Turkish migrants who have been naturalized and therefore no longer appear in the statistics among the Turkish students.[8]

Turkish Students in the German Education System

The German Education System—General Implications for Educational Opportunities

The education system in Germany is characterized by two major conditions: First, education is under the legislature of the regional states (the *Länder*), not the federal state. Thus there are differences in the structure of the school systems among the 16 German Länder. Second, as will be explained in more detail below, the German school system promotes student selection according to school performance rather early in their school careers.

In Germany, kindergartens are the most important pre-school institutions. Crèches for toddlers under the age of three are still exceptional. Pre-school education in kindergartens usually starts at the age of three. Since 1996, children of this age have the legal right to a place in kindergarten until they start school at the age of six. Attendance, however, is not mandatory. In the western part of Germany, where most migrants live, there is still a shortage of places in kindergartens for children in this age group.[9]

At the level of primary education, elementary schools are comprehensive schools for all children aged six to ten, or, in two Länder, from age six to 12. Only a small minority of primary schools are privately run. Usually all children have to attend the school closest to their home. Thus, the mix of the children at a primary school mirrors the socio-economic and ethnic composition of the immediate neighborhood. Sending a child to a different school requires parents to apply for an exemption from the rules.

Apart from these mainstream schools, there are schools for special education (in both primary and secondary education) to serve children with physical and mental impairments, as well as schools for children with learning disabilities, speech defects and behavioral problems.[10] Attending special education schools for students with learning disabilities increases one's risk of completing compulsory education without any school certificate.[11]

Secondary education in Germany is characterized by its three different tracks, i.e. school types, which lead to different certificates with a clear hierarchical order. Only the *Abitur* certificate, acquired at a grammar school (*Gymnasium*), provides entrance to university. The certificate of the lowest track (*Hauptschule*), acquired after the ninth or tenth grade, has been greatly devalued over the last decades, putting young adults in an unfavorable position when applying either for vocational training or a qualified job.[12] The intermediate type of secondary education, *Realschule*, takes up the position in between. The certificate gained at this type of school ensures better prospects for vocational training. Comprehensive schools (*Gesamtschule*), which exist in some Länder as a fourth type of school, integrate these three different tracks, facilitating movement between them.[13]

At the end of primary education each child—aged ten to 12—gets a recommendation to continue in one of these three types of school tracks. It varies according to Länder legislation whether the child's performance is the decisive factor and whether parents have to follow the recommendation of the schools regarding their children's placement.[14] Compared to the school systems in other countries, the German school system channels students into different tracks of secondary education at a very young age.[15] This decision in a child's life strongly influences his or her future life chances and is hardly reversible at a later stage in a child's school career or in adulthood.

Turkish Students in Pre-School Education

Pre-school care is of great importance for the integration of migrant children. This holds true especially for children whose mother tongue is not German or whose parents have no or only little knowledge of German. Kindergarten is often the only place where these children can learn German before they enter school. Despite the undisputed importance of pre-school education and child care for migrant offspring, hardly any systematic research has been done in this area so far.

Figures for Turkish children show that in 2000 there were only negligible differences in attendance rates compared to German children. However, nothing can be said about regional differences and about the age at which Turkish children start going to the kindergarten, i.e. at the age of three or only in the last year before entering primary school. Participation rates for different age groups are only available for the total group of non-German children.

In 2000, 47.1 percent of the foreign three-year-olds attended kindergarten compared to 56.3 percent of all children. The differences between the groups decrease with age, but there is still a gap between children aged five to six. Thus, foreign children still attend kindergarten less often, although the rate has increased and regional differences have to be taken into account. Furthermore, as Table 1 shows, day care for children below the age of three is still an exception in Germany. In 2000, the share of foreign children aged 0 to three who attended a crèche was 6.4 percent. Hence, there is hardly any systematic promotion of migrant children's knowledge of the German language in this age group.

The relevance of kindergarten attendance for migrant children is made strikingly clear by a study conducted with survey data.[16] Whereas for German children there is no clear correlation between kindergarten attendance and later school success, this observation does not hold in the case of non-German children. Of those foreign children who had attended kindergarten 51.4 percent succeeded in entering intermediate or higher secondary school tracks. In contrast, only 21.3 percent of the children who had not attended kindergarten reached the same school level. In a multivariate analysis the positive effect on the school career of kindergarten attendance is confirmed for foreign but not for German children. It seems that German children acquire certain abilities and knowledge through family socialization which non-German children can only attain in kindergarten, above all the acquisition of the German language.

The reasons why only a minority of Turkish families take advantage of kindergarten education for their children are not known in detail. It seems plausible that employment of the mother has an effect on children's attendance. Unemployed

Table 1. Kindergarten Attendance Rates, 2000

	Total[1]	Below Age 3	Age 3–4	Age 4–5	Age 5–6
All Children in Kindergarten, as % of all Children	47.5	9.5	56.3	82.9	89.8
Foreign Children in Kindergarten, as % of all Foreign Children	42.3	6.4	47.1	75.7	85.5

[1] Basic population: children aged 0 to eight (excluding children already attending school).
Source: Federal government's commissioner for migrants, refugees and integration 2002

migrant mothers often decide to take care of their children themselves. This might be true especially when parents are not aware of the positive impact of pre-school education on language acquisition. Additionally, financial reasons might play a role since kindergarten and care facilities are not available free of charge.

Turkish Students in Primary Education

Primary education is the first institutional context of learning every child experiences. The competences a child acquires within the four (or six) years in primary school are the foundation upon which the decision about the secondary education track is based. The international study PIRLS (Progress in International Reading Literacy Study at the fourth grade) is the equivalent to PISA for the primary education level. Findings were first published in 2003. Before this, little research had been done on immigrant children in German primary education. While there are no specific data according to national origin of children, the results nevertheless are useful indicators for the educational situation of children with a Turkish background.

PIRLS measures the competencies in reading, mathematics and the sciences.[17] Children from families without a migration background (defined by country of birth) scored best, while children with both parents born abroad did worst. The share of so-called "weak pupils"[18] with and without migration background is remarkable. As to reading comprehension, 5 percent of pupils without migration background and 13 percent of children with one parent born abroad were classified as weak, while this classification applied to a quarter of the children whose parents were both born abroad. However, the influence of migration background on children's competences should not be examined without considering other influential factors. A large share of migrant families has a rather low socio-economic status, a factor which has a clear negative effect on the competencies of children (see section five).

Although primary school is meant to be a comprehensive school for all children, attending a specific school in a specific context can have an impact on educational attainment. Kristen[19] focuses on the beginning of primary education as an early turning-point in a child's school career: She compares parents of German and Turkish origin in the German town of Essen and their decision on what kind of primary school they send their children to. Why do they enroll them in the public school which is located nearest to their home and what kind of parents explicitly opt for Catholic or Protestant primary schools (not necessarily due to religious beliefs but because those schools reputedly offer a better learning environment)? Only few Turkish parents, the more educated and those with better knowledge of German, have enough information to even consider these alternatives. Turkish children are left behind in the common primary schools, while middle-class German parents, making use of exemptions from the rule, choose schools with a larger share of native middle-class children.

Radtke,[20] too, strongly emphasizes that it is not migrant parents who choose segregated schools, but rather German parents of middle-class background who take decisions which lead to higher segregation. Additionally, Radtke studied how schools themselves initiate and reinforce ethnic segregation. In his case study, he found that (primary) schools tend to specialize as schools with a certain profile favored by German middle-class parents (e.g. focus on music, early learning of English, alternative pedagogical approaches) or as schools allegedly suitable for immigrant children (extra language tuition, social workers). These kinds of specializations tend to lead to ethnically and linguistically as well as socio-economically more homogeneous classes which form a more or less favorable learning environment for the children enrolled.[21] Decisions by organizations (school administrations and local authorities) as well as individuals, i.e. parents, thus have the unintended consequences of enforcing ethnic segregation in schools, which is officially deplored by some and silently approved of by others.

Already during primary education, selection of students into different school types takes place to a certain extent. Children who cannot meet the requirements of a regular school are thought of as having "special needs" and can be transferred to special schools for pupils with learning disabilities. Diefenbach makes the point that it is controversial and unclear how the decisions about this referral come about and, more importantly, whether these decisions are justified. When migrant children are sent to these school types, it might often be the case that language problems become mixed up with cognitive deficiencies as perceived by the teachers.[22] The special schools for learning disabilities are supposed to meet the students' particular needs. In contrast to the migrant children's special situation as second language learners, however, the teaching staff of these schools is rarely trained for teaching German as a second language.[23] An unjustified referral to these schools for special education can be considered an indicator of indirect discrimination since the chances of achieving a higher school certificate are very low.[24]

In 2000 4.4 percent of all foreign pupils, compared to 2.1 percent of all German children, attended special schools for learning disabilities.[25] Putting these values in

Table 2. Relative Risk (compared with Germans) of Attending a Special School, 1998–2000

	1998	1999	2000
Turkish	1.73	1.76	1.90
Greece	1.27	1.42	1.52
Spain	1.14	1.03	1.19
Italy	2.27	2.32	2.05
Serbia and Montenegro	4.50	4.33	4.90
Croatia	0.82	0.9	1.05
Bosnia	1.18	1.33	1.71
All Foreigners	1.93	1.93	2.10

Source: Reimer Kornmann and Aline Kornmann, "Erneuter Anstieg der Überrepräsentation ausländischer Kinder in Schulen für Lernbehinderte," *Zeitschrift für Heilpädagogik*, Vol.54, No.7 (2003), pp.286–9.

relation to each other results in the Relative Risk Index (RRI), which is a common measure to illustrate the overrepresentation of pupils.

Turkish children's risk of attending a special school is almost twice as high (1.9) as German children. Though there was an increase compared to 1999 (1.8), it was still lower than in 1991 when the RRI was 2.3.[26] There are children of other nationalities who show a much higher probability of attending a special school. The RRI was highest for children from Serbia and Montenegro (4.9). The value for Italian children was 2.05, the Greek RRI was 1.52. Thus, Turkish children's risk of ending up in this dead-end road of education is high but not the highest when compared to other immigrant students.

Transition to Secondary Education

For the large majority of pupils in Germany, the most crucial stage in their school careers is at the end of primary school when it is to be decided in what school track the children are to continue their secondary education. Depending first of all on their grades (especially in German and in mathematics), but also on the schools' recommendation and the parents' choice, children continue either at a *Gymnasium* (higher secondary track), a *Realschule* (medium secondary track) or a *Hauptschule* (lower secondary track).

In the German PIRLS study, researchers have, for each fourth grader tested, gathered information on the schools' recommendation for secondary school track. Thus, it is possible to analyze how far these recommendations were in line with the proficiency levels measured and whether they varied with respect to aspects unrelated to actual performance, such as migration background and social stratum. In multivariate statistical models which control for reading proficiency (according to PIRLS, not according to the grades given by teachers) and social class, the likelihood of children with German-born parents being recommended for the highest or medium secondary school track is significantly higher compared to pupils whose parents were born abroad.[27] When the influence of additional factors on the teachers' recommendation, such as grades and the motivation of the pupils, are taken into account, the influence of socio-economic background overrides that of having parents born abroad—a migration background in itself surprisingly has a marginally positive effect.[28]

Kristen[29] analyzes the transition from primary to secondary education on the basis of school records in the state of Baden-Württemberg, which allows the singling out of Turkish children for analysis. According to her results, grades are the main reason why children of non-German background tend to end up in the least favorable type of school. However, compared to Germans with the same grades, Turkish and Italian children (but not ex-Yugoslavs and ethnic Germans) are still more likely to be recommended for the lowest *Hauptschul* track.[30]

Thus, as will be discussed in section four in more detail, ambiguities remain as to whether migrant children face (institutional) discrimination because of their ethnic background or whether their working class background is the main stumbling block.

Furthermore, teachers' recommendations might indeed be fair, yet it could be the case that the instruction given during primary education does not meet these students' needs and does not enable them to fully develop their potential.

Attainment of Turkish Migrants in Secondary Education

Studies which analyze immigrant children's integration in the field of education usually use or choose among three indicators of academic achievement: the kind of school track students attend during secondary education, test scores of standardized achievement tests and the school certificates they end their school career with (the latter is most common regarding surveys of adults). In the following we will first present descriptive results on these perspectives on educational achievement and later on we will discuss research which tries to explain the differences between groups of students.

Table 3 shows the distribution of students with Turkish citizenship across the three school tracks. The type of school children attend as young teenagers predicts rather precisely the kind of certificate they will ultimately achieve.[31] In order to illustrate the unequal chances of achieving higher education degrees, the distribution of Turkish students among school types is compared to the distribution of all (West German[32]) students. One must bear in mind that official school statistics can only be differentiated with regard to citizenship.

While almost a quarter of all Turkish students attend *Hauptschule*, the lowest track of secondary education (and only 13 percent of all West German students do), the situation is the reverse with regard to grammar school: almost a quarter of the latter attend this most advantageous school type whereas only 6 percent of Turkish students do so. About the same share of Turkish students (7 percent) attends a

Table 3. Distribution of Turkish Students across Different School Types in (West-) Germany, 2003/04 (%)

Selected School Types	Turkish Students	All Students	Difference
Primary School	40	34	+6
Lower Secondary School (*Hauptschule*)	23	13	+10
Medium Secondary School (*Realschule*)	10	15	−5
Higher Secondary School (*Gymnasium*)	6	23	−19
Comprehensive School	8	5	+3
Special Education (including learning disabilities)	7	4	+3
Other Types of Schools	5	6	−1
Total	100	100	

Source: Statistisches Bundesamt, *Bildung und Kultur. Allgemeinbildene Schulen. Schuljahr 2003/04* [Education and Culture. General Schools, School Year 2003/04], Fachserie 11, Reihe 1 (Wiesbaden: Statistisches Bundesamt, 2004), Table 4.4.1 and 3.1, author's calculation.

school for special education. There is no data about how the educational participation of Turkish students in particular has developed over the last few decades. However, for all students of non-German nationality from the 1970s until the early 1990s a slow but steady improvement in favor of higher over lower school track has been recorded. Since then stagnation has occurred, showing a distribution of about the same as reported in Table 3.[33]

PISA is an important information resource as it provides representative data on how children of immigrant families (not only those with a foreign passport) fare in the German education system. The data allow the possibility to identify the group of 15-year-olds with at least one parent born in Turkey. As to the distribution across school tracks in the year 2000, 56.6 percent of them attended *Hauptschule* (versus 23.6 percent of those with a father born in Germany), 19.3 percent *Realschule* (versus 34.5 percent), 13.9 percent comprehensive school (versus 9.3 percent) and only 10.2 percent grammar school (versus 32.5 percent).[34] Students of Turkish origin showed the least favorable distribution compared to all immigrant groups, only students with ex-Yugoslavian fathers tended to score as badly.[35]

Results are similar when we consider the PISA tests, which measured actual literacy, numeracy and proficiency in science (irrespective of the school track attended and the grades given by the teachers). Regarding the three tests, Germany scored below average in the international comparison and far below countries like Finland, Canada or New Zealand, the top scorers of PISA 2000.[36] The results of students with a migration background were even more devastating: One in five students with parents born abroad (versus one in ten students of German-born parents) did not reach the lowest of five levels of literacy.[37] Students whose father was born in Turkey scored at 389 on average, the lowest mean score compared to those of other countries of origin.[38]

Results are similar in the mathematic test of PISA 2003,[39] where half of the Turkish students do not exceed the lowest of five competence levels. These analyses of Ramm and others[40] offer a unique comparison between students of Turkish (and ex-Yugoslav) origin in different receiving countries, namely Germany, Austria and Switzerland, on the common basis of the same achievement test (in mathematics). Despite a similar socio-economic status, both second (382) and first (382) generation Turkish students score lowest in Germany (with differences of 22 to 30 points compared to their peers in the two other countries).

The poor performance of Turkish immigrant children is also reflected in final school results. Statistics on the level of certificate which students achieved by the time they left school shed light on the most disadvantaged groups of youths: those who leave school with no certificate at all, not even with that of the lowest school track, the *Hauptschule*-certificate. This includes students of special education schools. For the federal level, there is no specific information about Turkish students. Therefore, we present the example of the regional state of North Rhine-Westphalia.[41] Figure 1 demonstrates that Turkish students clearly lag behind

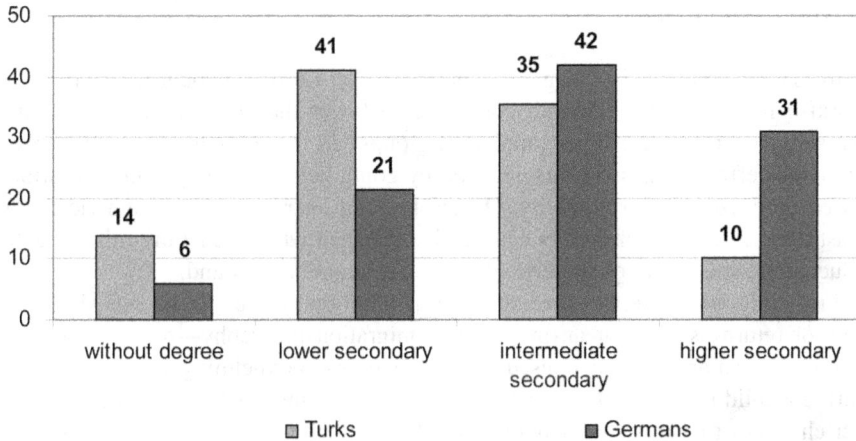

Figure 1. Completion of compulsory education, Turkish and German students, North Rhine-Westphalia, 2003 (%). *Source:* Statistical Office North Rhine-Westphalia, 2003.

German students in terms of certificates. In 2003, 14 percent of all Turkish students left school without any certificate, while the share among Germans was much lower, 6 percent. At the same time we see a clear gap between Turkish and Germans students who finished with a higher secondary certificate. The share among Turks was 10 percent while the share among Germans was about three times as high.[42]

How does the educational achievement of these young adults of Turkish background compare to the level of schooling of the total Turkish population in Germany? In 2000, one in four Turkish citizens did not have a school certificate at all.[43] The comparable share among persons who had German as well as Turkish citizenship was 16 percent whereas only 1 percent of Germans did not finish school with a certificate; 57 percent of Turkish citizens had a lower certificate (*Hauptschule* or comparable qualification). The share with higher certificates (*Abitur*) which allows entrance to university was 7 percent. It was higher for Turkish-Germans where 15 percent had the highest school certificate but still lower than compared to Germans (23 percent). As can be seen, the average level of formal education of Turkish citizens is clearly lower than that of Germans, whereas dual citizens occupy a position in between.

When we distinguish generations, the educational levels of the first and second generation differ clearly:[44] 39 percent of the first generation has no school certificate at all whereas the share among Turks of the second generation is much lower, at 7 percent. The proportions of those with a lower intermediate certificate are more or less similar. Concerning higher school certificates, however, differences are evident. 33 percent of the second generation has an intermediate or higher school certificate while the corresponding share in the first generation is only 5 percent.

Discussion of Findings

Why is it the case that, in Germany as in many other European countries, students of Turkish immigrant background tend to score lower than the average native and worse than most of the other immigrant groups? In the literature there have been numerous efforts to answer this question by going beyond essentialist explanations based on citizenship or ethnicity. On the level of characteristics of individuals at least three categories of factors can be distinguished which generally influence the educational attainment of students with an immigrant background.

First, migration itself—especially age at immigration, length of stay, intent to stay or return as parts of an individual's migration biography—has a number of possible direct and indirect consequences. There is overwhelming evidence that the earlier a child immigrated (or when born in the receiving country), the higher his or her chances of a successful school career.[45] Apart from the negative consequences of a school career interrupted by migration, the students' immigrant parents are less familiar than natives with the structure of the school system in the receiving country, as well as its formal and informal norms. They are less able to make the right choice for their children at the right time. Furthermore, the expectation or hope of one day returning to one's country of origin might keep some parents from supporting their children's school careers as much as they would if they knew they would settle for good.[46]

Second, language itself forms an important part of a migration background: a migrant's first language often differs from the official language of the receiving society. Additionally, some languages are linguistically more similar to each other than others and therefore easier to learn. This factor of language is influential not only for children who immigrated with their parents, but also for second generation children who were born in the receiving country, yet nonetheless learned their parents' native language as their own first language.

Lastly, it is the parents' own education and socio-economic status which is most commonly referred to when explaining the educational performance of immigrant children in Germany. Students of lower social strata in general are less likely to attend the highest track of secondary education (and university).[47]

Traditionally, sociological studies have focused on these factors of the individual students and their parents' choices made during a child's school career. Research has primarily investigated to what extent these factors explain why children of immigrant parents in general and students of Turkish origin in particular have more trouble in school than the average native student. Over the last decade, studies have used a limited number of data sets[48] with which they tested hypotheses about these different sets of factors by means of multivariate statistical analyses.

As regards the differences between natives and immigrants in general, migration biography, language and social class are indeed powerful predictors of variations in educational performance. Analyses of PISA data, for instance, show that the large discrepancies between children with or without foreign-born parents is partly due to the lower socio-economic status of immigrant parents, the length of stay in

Germany (i.e. the fact of immigration during the student's childhood) and family language (a different language than German spoken at home). Once statistically adjusted for these key variables, the difference between the mean scores of students with parents born in Germany and abroad was no longer statistically significant.[49]

The opportunity of the immigrant child to acquire knowledge in the societal language is a major reason why duration of stay has such a strong influence on educational achievement.[50] In the case of 15-year-old students in PISA, 30 percent of those of Turkish origin were born abroad, a higher percentage than among those of Greek and Italian origin. This might be an explanation for the lower performance among Turkish immigrant children compared to their Greek and Italian counterparts. However, many more ethnic German students emigrated from Russia and Poland during their childhood, but on average fare better than Turks.[51] The explanatory power of duration of stay thus seems limited. The language spoken in migrant families might be more relevant.

Both duration of stay and educational background influence migrant parents' familiarity with the local school system, their knowledge about "good" and "bad" schools and about the long-term consequences of certain decisions. There are no representative studies on Turkish parents' knowledge about the German school system (of secondary education). The importance of informally gained information about the educational system is confirmed by Lindo's[52] qualitative study about Turkish, Spanish and Portuguese youths in the Netherlands. The interviewees' mothers who had informal contact with Dutch parents learned to choose better, i.e. less ethnically segregated, schools for their children.[53] Turkish mothers had these kinds of contacts to a lesser extent than Iberian mothers, who also had a higher level of education.

Although it is rather obvious that proficiency in the societal language is essential for a child's academic advancement, there are no studies on migrants in Germany which measure both the exact level of language proficiency and performance at school. Only in one standardized large-scale study on the mathematic proficiency of eighth graders in the Land Rhineland-Palatine did researchers collect data on the students' first and dominant languages. This is the appropriate information in linguistic terms, as in the case of bilingual children a dominant language other than German means by definition that proficiency in this other language is higher than in German.[54] Students with Turkish as their first and dominant language scored very low in the mathematics test (60 percent of one standard deviation below the average), only students with an Italian and Albanian mother tongue scored worse.[55] These descriptive results, however, were not controlled for factors such as social background or duration of stay in Germany.

The central result of all research is the primary significance of parents' education and/or socio-economic status—irrespective of the exact operationalization of school success (e.g. as attendance of different school tracks or school certificates already achieved) and of the data base.[56] Class bias in the German school system, one has to stress again and again, is one or even *the* major reason why a majority of students of Turkish background fare so poorly at school. As most migrants of Turkish origin are of low socio-economic status, children of these parents have to bear the brunt of the German education systems' tendency to reproduce social inequality more strongly than any other OECD country: it is characterized by the highest correlation of parents' socio-economic status and their child's reading competence.[57]

Researchers disagree on the issue of whether, all in all, being of Turkish origin has an additional negative effect on academic achievement once characteristics like migration biography, parental education and socio-economic status are taken into account. Von Below, Alba *et al.* and Wagner *et al.*[58] find an independent negative effect of being Turkish *ceteris paribus*: Turkish as well as Italian children are still more likely to attend or have attended the lowest track, *Hauptschule*, compared to "comparable" Germans and other nationalities like the Greeks, who have the reputation of being the most successful group among the "guest worker nationalities." In studies by Kristen, Esser as well as Kristen and Granato,[59] however, the significant influence of a Turkish background vanishes in the full models of multivariate analyses. It remains a point of debate whether a remaining negative effect for Turkish students is due to discrimination on the schools' part or whether one has to consider further characteristics of the Turkish population in Germany.

Despite vague speculations about the role of culture and religion (Islam in particular) brought forth in public debate, there is no evidence of an impact of the aspect of culture. The main objection is that Italian students—predominantly Roman Catholics—do not perform any better than Turks. Looking beyond the aspect of religion, there have been only very few studies of (Turkish) immigrants and the importance of culture, traditions and values with respect to the importance of educational success and other goals in life.[60] In a survey among young adults of German, Italian and Turkish origin, some indications were found that traditional views on gender relations correlate with lack of higher school degrees (*Abitur*), controlling for parents' education. These views were more common among Turkish than Italian or German respondents.[61] In his comparison of Turkish and Iberian young adults in the Netherlands, Lindo[62] tries to answer the similar question why more Turkish respondents discontinued their education after secondary school. He observed that more migrant youths of Turkish origin married early, which in turn implied an end to education both for males and females. Their parents' pressure to do so was increased by their ties to their ethnic community both in the Netherlands and in Turkey. Ties within Turkish communities are constantly reinforced by continuous chain migration and can result in moral pressure. The immigration process of the Iberians has come to an end and was more individualized from the beginning—these families can be less influenced by what their co-ethnics might say about the behavior of their offspring. Although the scope of this study does not allow a generalization of its results, it underlines that norms and values regarding education among Turkish migrants must be analyzed in the social context of migration and ethnic communities (or the absence thereof).

Irrespective of the background of the individual child, his or her family and further ethnic ties, however, the school context, the teachers' behavior and characteristics of the classes may have an impact on the amount and quality of knowledge and final certificate students acquire in school. Potentially influential features include financial resources of the school, the quality and methods of teaching as well as the social, ethnic and linguistic composition of the pupils. Mainly the last aspect, ethnic and social segregation at school, has lately gained the attention of a number of researchers.

Schools with a large share of German-language learners (or, depending on the specific operationalization, students of non-German nationality), seem to offer less favorable learning opportunities for the individual child—the child of German or foreign origin. This has been shown for various regional contexts and with different sets of data.[63] More Turkish children tend to go to schools with a large share of migrant children. In the multivariate analyses of Esser and Kristen,[64] for instance, the decisive factor which overrides the negative influence of the variable "Turkish citizenship" on educational performance is ethnic segregation in school. As on the micro level of the individual, migration background and low socio-economic status at the level of school class composition is closely connected empirically: Classes with a high percentage of ethnic minority students tend to have a high percentage of low socio-economic status students as well, and in secondary education these are usually found at the school type of the lowest track, *Hauptschule*. Both factors have a negative effect on educational achievement of the individual, though it is hardly possible to disentangle the exact causal relationships.[65]

There are contrasting views on whether low performance by Turkish children and other migrant groups can be interpreted as resulting from discrimination against immigrant children. Kristen[66] believes that it is not teachers who actively discriminate against Turkish and other migrant pupils. Rather, their lower achievement is, in her view, due to structural factors like ethnically segregated schools, which offer a poor learning environment, or family resources, e.g. parents' limited knowledge of the German school system as well as their low level of education. Although grades given by teachers are not totally arbitrary, PIRLS provides evidence that grades reflect actual competences only to a limited extent. Fourth graders who had achieved the same PIRLS test scores had not been given the same grade by their teachers, rather grades varied considerably across the sample.[67] Consequently, a narrow focus on the characteristics of the individual and familial background of students might neglect what goes on in schools and to what degree schools are responsible for the below-average performance of students with migration background.

Gomolla and Radtke,[68] for instance, highlight "institutional discrimination," decisions and institutional arrangements of the school which result in unequal educational attainment of native and immigrant students. They stress the importance of decisions which lead to selection among students, like channeling migrant students more often to special education for children with learning disabilities and to lower secondary school tracks, thus fostering ethnic segregation (more or less) unintentionally. According to Gomolla and Radtke's observations, these decisions do not only depend on the pupil's performance or even the teacher's possible prejudices, but they also arise from complex organizational interests. For example, schools tend to prefer more homogeneous school classes (with regard to academic performance and "normal" student social behavior and language proficiency) as they are considered easier to instruct in a manner considered adequate. As a consequence, if a class at a primary school is regarded as too crowded, migrant pupils with insufficient knowledge of German are seen as "problematic" students deviating from the ideal norm and thus stand a higher risk of being referred to a special school.[69] While legal regulations do not allow language deficiencies to form the main reason for these decisions, low levels of German-language proficiency are sometimes reinterpreted as indicators of poor overall performance.[70] Likewise, "perfect" German is seen as a precondition for a recommendation to the highest secondary education, while only in the lowest track, *Hauptschule*, do schools provide for extra language training. Hence, otherwise gifted children who by the fourth grade have not reached the proficiency of native speakers stand little chance of receiving the instruction their cognitive capacities would actually allow for.[71]

Indeed, schools in Germany are ill-prepared for dealing with second language learners as "normal" students and a mainstream phenomenon. Training in teaching German as a second language is clearly insufficient.[72] Yet without appropriate instruction in this field it is not surprising that migrant children have a hard time learning subjects at an equal pace with their native peers.

Conclusion

Turkish migrants (in Germany and other European countries) on average have a considerably lower level of schooling compared to the native population. Though the educational level attained by the younger generation has increased compared to the early labor migrants, they still do worse than Germans of the same age group.

The processes which explain the educational disadvantages of migrants in general and Turkish migrants in particular have not yet been studied in detail and in a satisfactory manner. This problem is also exacerbated by the absence of appropriate data. Until now research has suggested several major causes of the unequal educational attainment, ranging from the immigrant parents' socio-economic status to the ethnic composition of school classes and the impact of institutional discrimination. Diefenbach[73] even speaks of an ethnically segmented school system, because school types leading to higher school certificates are (more or less) reserved for Germans while schools of the lowest track have become the last resort for immigrant youths. In general, more qualitative as well as quantitative research is necessary in order to enable a better understanding of the interaction of different factors.

As a common denominator, most studies hitherto stress the significant influence of the socio-economic background of parents. A central finding of PISA is that the correlation of parental socio-economic status and educational success in Germany is stronger than in any other OECD country. This reproduction of social inequality by the German education system pertains to natives and immigrants alike. In education policy, this crucial issue of social inequality has in general rarely been at the center stage. So far the German school system has clearly not succeeded in compensating for the disadvantageous social background of Turkish children.

However, the impact of social status and educational distance is aggravated in the case of migrant students as they often speak a language other than German among their families. And the international comparison of PISA data shows that Germany (along with countries like Belgium, the Netherlands or Switzerland) is particularly bad at dealing with pupils who do not speak the official language at home.[74] Realizing that language proficiency is a prerequisite of school success, some German Länder have recently introduced tests for language assessment of five-year-old children in order to detect whether they need language training during the last year at kindergarten before attending school.[75] Whether these new language assessments will indeed lead to better promotion of language acquisition, or—as a worst case scenario—to further negative selection of children with specific needs into dead-end "special treatment" remains to be seen.

Up to now empirical school research in Germany has not examined what might further enhance the achievement of migrant children. No study has systematically evaluated factors like class size, team teaching, teaching methods or language instruction on the academic achievement of this group of students.[76] Given this absence of evaluation of pedagogical practices, what kind of political measures seem likely to enhance the educational attainment of immigrant children? As the socio-economic background of parents can hardly be changed overnight, these measures should concentrate on changing public institutions as well as school–parent relationship.

Firstly, language support at an early stage in a child's life is of fundamental importance. If Turkish families do not have the material and immaterial resources to support their children in learning German, the only institution which can fulfill this task is the kindergarten. Therefore political efforts should, above all, concentrate on care facilities like kindergartens, but also on expanding the supply of crèches for the youngest children. The latter's potential for language acquisition has not yet been fully exploited due to low attendance rates and the small number of care facilities for toddlers. Furthermore, the quality of care and education should be improved. An OECD study on early childhood education in Germany demonstrated that there is a clear need for better training of pedagogues in order to adequately cater to the diverse social and cultural backgrounds of the children.[77] Furthermore, full-time schools—both in elementary and secondary education—are still unusual in Germany. Full-time care and support could foster especially language acquisition as well as the overall performance of migrant children provided the quality of care and teaching is constantly monitored and improved.

Additionally, Turkish parents should be offered more information about the German school system, and counseling might help them take the right decisions on what kind of secondary education their children should strive for and how to continue thereafter. Turkish organizations such as parents' associations and Germany-based Turkish media could play an intermediate role between schools and parents and take a more active part in supporting the educational integration of children of Turkish background. Training more teachers with a migration background seems promising as a more representative work force could not only encourage immigrant families to send their children to early child care but also contribute to better relations with parents.

Furthermore, an increasing number of foundations in Germany now successfully offer special educational programs and scholarships for talented migrant children of a non-privileged social background,[78] the promotion of positive role models for other migrant children being one aim besides the support of the individual. These talented migrant children would otherwise possibly fall through the cracks of the school system. The example of such innovative programs of foundations, which involve parents and mentors as well as cooperation with the state, show that successful educational integration is indeed possible by the joint efforts of all actors involved.

Finally, it is of utmost importance that an unfavorable composition of schools and classes is not allowed to impede the development of the children. The three-tiered system of secondary education itself seems to be a major cause of ethnic and social segregation in schools. Reforming this hierarchical system would imply teaching all children together at comprehensive schools for a longer period than the usual four years of primary education. In addition, teachers should be better trained to adequately handle classes which are and will be culturally, linguistically and socially more heterogeneous than in the past. From these kinds of reforms, not only migrant children but all students with a disadvantaged background might benefit and German society would be able to profit from at present undisclosed talents and potential of these children.

Acknowledgments

We wish to thank Roric McCorristin, Karen Schönwälder and the participants of the workshop on "Immigration Issues in EU–Turkey Relations" in June 2005 for helpful comments on the draft paper.

Notes

1. OECD, *Lernen für das Leben. Erste Ergebnisse von PISA 2000* [Learning for Tomorrow's World: First Results from PISA 2003] (Paris: OECD, 2001), p.182; Viola Sylke Schnepf, "How Different Are Immigrants? A Cross-Country and Cross-Survey Analysis of Educational Achievement," Discussion Paper No. 1398 (Bonn: IZA, 2004), p.12; Arbeitsgruppe Internationale Vergleichsstudie, *Vertiefender Vergleich der Schulsysteme ausgewählter PISA-Teilnehmerstaaten* [School Systems of Selected PISA Countries: A Detailed Comparison] (Bonn: Bundesministerium für Bildung und Forschung, 2003), p.198.
2. Maurice Crul and Hans Vermeulen, "The Future of the Second Generation: The Integration of Migrant Youth in Six European Countries," *International Migration Review*, Vol.37. No.4 (2003), pp.979; Gesa Ramm *et al.*, *Sozio-kulturelle Herkunft: Migration* [Socio-Cultural Descent: Migration], in Deutsches PISA-Konsortium (ed.), *PISA 2003. Der Bildungsstand der Jugendlichen in Deutschland—Ergebnisse des zweiten internationalen Vergleichs* [PISA 2003—The Education of Young People in Germany—Results from the Second International Comparison] (Münster *et al.*: Waxmann, 2004), pp.254–72.
3. Crul and Vermeulen (2003), pp.983–4.

4. Author's translation of Hermann Avenarius *et al.*, *Bildungsbericht für Deutschland. Erste Befunde* [The Education Report for Germany. First Results] (Opladen: Leske und Budrich, 2003), p.213.

5. The *Aussiedler* immigrants are officially considered as of ethnic German origin and receive German citizenship upon arrival. Their first language, however, is often Russian or Polish, rather than German.

6. As hardly any foreigners live in the eastern part of Germany, the new Länder are typically left out of most analyses on integration issues.

7. Jürgen Baumert and Gundel Schümer, "Familiäre Lebensverhältnisse, Bildungsbeteiligung und Kompetenzerwerb im internationalen Vergleich" [Family Background, Educational Participation and the Acquisition of Competences: An International Comparison], in Deutsches PISA-Konsortium (ed.), *PISA 2000—Die Länder der Bundesrepublik Deutschland im Vergleich* (Opladen: Leske und Budrich, 2002), p.190.

8. Recent research indicates that Germans with a Turkish background do better in terms of integration than Turkish citizens: Kurt Salentin and Frank Wilkening, "Ausländer, Eingebürgerte und das Problem einer realistischen Zuwanderungs-Integrationsbilanz" [Foreign and Naturalized Citizens— The Problem of How to Realistically Evaluate the Integration of Immigrants], *Kölner Zeitschrift für Soziologie und Sozialpsychologie,* Vol.55, No.2 (2003), pp.278–98.

9. Eurydice—The information database of education systems in Europe, *The Education System in Germany (2002/2003)*, available online at http://www.eurydice.org/Eurybase/Application/frameset. asp?country=DE&language=EN.

10. Ibid.

11. Heike Solga, "Jugendliche ohne Schulabschluss und ihre Wege in den Arbeitsmarkt" [Young People without School Certificates and their Routes into Employment], in Kai S. Cortina *et al.* (eds.), *Das Bildungswesen in der Bundesrepublik Deutschland* [Germany's Education System] (Reinbek: Rowohlt, 2003), p.715; Sandra J. Wagner and Justin J.W. Powell, "Ethnisch-kulturelle Ungleichheit im deutschen Bildungssystem. Zur Überrepräsentanz von Migrantenjugendlichen an Sonderschulen" [Ethno-cultural Inequalities in the German School System: The Overrepresentation of Migrant Youths in Schools for Special Eeducation], in Günther Cloerkes (ed.), *Wie man behindert wird. Texte zur Konstruktion einer sozialen Rolle und zur Lebenssituation betroffener Menschen. Materialien zur Soziologie der Behinderten* [On Becoming Disabled] (Heidelberg: Universitätsverlag Winter GmbH, 2003), p.199.

12. Solga (2003), pp.725–6.

13. Heike Diefenbach, "Ethnische Segmentation im deutschen Schulsystem. Eine Zustandsbeschreibung und einige Erklärungen für den Zustand" [Ethnic Segmentation in the German School System. The Current Situation and Some Explanations], in Forschungsinstitut Arbeit, Bildung, Partizipation e.V. (FIAB) (ed.), *Bildung als Bürgerrecht oder Bildung als Ware* [Education as a Civil Right or as an Economic Good], Band 21/22 des Jahrbuchs Arbeit, Bildung, Kultur (Recklinghausen: Forschungsinstitut Arbeit, Bildung, Partizipation e.V., 2004), p.246.

14. Wilfried Bos *et al.* (eds.), *IGLU. Einige Länder der Bundesrepublik Deutschland im nationalen und internationalen Vergleich* [IGLU. Selected Länder of the Federal Republic of Germany—A National and International Comparison] (Münster *et al.*: Waxmann Verlag, 2004), pp.191–2.

15. Wolfgang Einsiedler, "Unterricht in der Grundschule" [Teaching in Elementary Schools], in Kai S. Cortina *et al.* (eds.), *Das Bildungswesen in der Bundesrepublik Deutschland* [Germany's Education System] (Hamburg: Rowohlt, 2003), pp.285–341.

16. Katharina Spiess *et al.*, "Children's School Placement in Germany: Does Kindergarten Attendance Matter?" Discussion Paper No. 722 (Bonn: IZA, 2003).

17. Kurt Schwippert *et al.*, "Heterogenität und Chancengleichheit am Ende der vierten Jahrgangsstufe im internationalen Vergleich" [Heterogeneity and Equal Chances at the End of Grade Four—An International Comparison], in Wilfried Bos (eds.), *Erste Ergebnisse aus IGLU. Schülerleistungen am Ende der vierten Jahrgangsstufe im internationalen Vergleich* [First Results from IGLU: Student Performance at the End of Grade Four: An International Ccomparison] (Münster: Waxmann, 2003), pp.265–302.

18. In the competence area of reading comprehension, so-called weak pupils did not understand the sense of short sentences. In the area of mathematics they were only able to calculate basic additions, but not subtraction and multiplication.

19. Cornelia Kristen, *School Choice and Ethnic School Segregation. Primary School Selection in Germany* (Münster et al.: Waxmann, 2005).

20. Frank-Olaf Radtke, "Die Illusion der meritokratischen Schule. Lokale Konstellationen der Produktion von Ungleichheit im Erziehungssystem" [The Illusion of Meritocratic Schools. Local Constellations Producing Inequality within the Education System], in Klaus J. Bade and Michael Bommes (eds.), *Migration—Integration—Bildung. Grundfragen und Problembereiche* [Migration—Integration—Education. Fundamental Questions and Problem Aareas], IMIS-Beiträge 23 (Universität Osnabrück: Institut für Migrationsforschung und Interkulturelle Studien, 2004), pp.143–78.

21. Ibid., p.171.

22. Diefenbach (2004).

23. Wagner and Powell (2003), p.197.

24. In the regional state of North Rhine-Westphalia 10,283 pupils of all nationalities finished special school in 2004, 68% of them without a degree; see also Reimer Kornmann, "Migrantenkinder in der Sonderschule—Sonderfälle?" [Migrant Children in Schools for Special Education—Special Cases?] paper presented at conference on "Migrantenkinder in NRW—Sozialer Aufstieg oder Verelendung?" [Migrant children in North Rhine-Westphalia—upward mobility or impoverishment] in Wuppertal-Barme on December 2, 2003.

25. Reimer Kornmann and Aline Kornmann, "Erneuter Anstieg der Überrepräsentation ausländischer Kinder in Schulen für Lernbehinderte" [The Overrepresentation of Foreign Children in Schools for Pupils with Learning Disabilities further Increases], *Zeitschrift für Heilpädagogik*, Vol.54, No.7 (2003), pp.286–9.

26. Ibid.

27. Bos *et al.* (2003), p.211.

28. Ibid., p.217; Rainer H. Lehmann, *Aspekte der Lernausgangslage und der Lernentwicklung von Schülerinnen und Schülern, die im Schuljahr 1996/97 eine fünfte Klasse an Hamburger Schulen besuchten. Bericht über die Erhebung im September 1996 (LAU 5)* [Aspects of Learning Preconditions and Learning Development of Students who in 1996/97 attended Fifth Grade in Hamburg. Report on the Survey in September 1996 (LAU 5)] (Hamburg: http://www.hamburger-bildungsserver.de/lau/welcome.htm, 1997), Ch. 5.1.

29. Cornelia Kristen, "Hauptschule, Realschule oder Gymnasium? Ethnische Unterschiede am ersten Bildungsübergang" [*Hauptschule, Realschule* or *Gymnasium*? Ethnic Differences in Educational Decisions at the End of Primary Education], *Kölner Zeitschrift für Soziologie und Sozialpsychologie*, Vol.54, No.3 (2002), pp.534–53.

30. Kristen (2002), p.544.

31. Changing between different school tracks is possible from the beginning until the end of secondary education and about one in five students does change. Upward mobility happens more often than downward mobility and is slightly more common for immigrant children, see Heike Diefenbach, "Bildungsbenachteiligung und Berufseinmündung von Kindern und Jugendlichen aus Migranten-familien. Eine Fortschreibung der Daten des Sozio-Ökonomischen Panels (SOEP)" [Disadvantages of Children from Immigrant Families in Education and in the Transition to Employment. Further Results from the Socio-Economic Panel (SOEP)], in Sachverständigenkommission 11. Kinder- und Jugendbericht (ed.), *Migration und die europäische Integration. Herausforderungen für die Kinder- und Jugendhilfe* [Migration and European Integration] (München: Verlag Deutsches Jugendinstitut, 2002), pp.32–3.

32. See note 6.

33. Leonie Herwartz-Emden, "Einwandererkinder im deutschen Bildungswesen" [Immigrant Children in the German Education System], in Kai S. Cortina *et al.* (eds.), *Das Bildungswesen in der Bundesrepublik Deutschland* [Germany's Education System] (Reinbek: Rowohlt, 2003), p.681.

34. Baumert and Schümer (2002), p.196.

35. Students at schools for special education were not tested, thus PISA data present a picture still too positive with respect to the Turkish students' position.

36. OECD, *Literary Skill for the World of Tomorrow. Further Results from PISA 2000. Executive Summary* (http://www.pisa.oecd.org/dataoecd/59/31/2960581.pdf), p.6.

37. Jürgen Baumert and Gundel Schümer, "Familiäre Lebensverhältnisse, Bildungsbeteiligung und Kompetenzerwerb" [Family Background, Educational Participation and the Acquisition of Competences], in Deutsches PISA-Konsortium (ed.), *PISA 2000. Basiskompetenz von Schülerinnen und Schülern im internationalen Vergleich* [PISA 2000. Basic Competences of Students: An International Comparison] (Opladen: Leske und Budrich, 2001), p.375.

38. Baumert and Schümer (2001), p.378.

39. Ramm *et al.* (2004), p.264.

40. Ibid., p.268.

41. With 18 million inhabitants (2003), North Rhine-Westphalia has the largest population of all 16 German Länder. The number of Turkish citizens is 627,000, a third of the total Turkish population in Germany.

42. As regards gender, research finds either no differences between Turkish boys' and girls' academic achievement or an advantageous position for females (regarding *Abitur*), which is the general trend among students in Germany as a whole. There is a dramatic change, however, when it comes to vocational training. Young women of Turkish origin are significantly more likely to have no vocational training than their male co-ethnics and youths of other nationality, see Susanne von Below, *Schulische Bildung, berufliche Ausbildung und Erwerbstätigkeit junger Migranten. Ergebnisse des Integrationssurveys des BiB* [Education, Training and Employment of Young Migrants. Results of the Integration Survey of the BiB] (Wiesbaden: Bundesinstitut für Bevölkerungsforschung (BiB), 2003); Cornelia Kristen and Nadia Granato, "Bildungsinvestitionen in Migrantenfamilien" [Migrant Families and their Investment in Education], in Klaus J. Bade and Michael Bommes (eds.), *Migration—Integration—Bildung. Grundfragen und Problembereiche* [Migration—Integration—Education. Fundamental Questions and Problem Areas], IMIS-Beiträge 23 (Universität Osnabrück: Institut für Migrationsforschung und Interkulturelle Studien, 2004), pp.123–42; Diefenbach (2004), p.235.

43. Veysel Özcan, "Aspekte der sozio-ökonomischen und sozio-kulturellen Integration der türkischstämmigen Bevölkerung in Deutschland" [Aspects of the Socio-Economic and Socio-Cultural Integration of People of Turkish Origin in Germany], in Cem Özdemir *et al.* (eds.), *Die Situation der türkischstämmigen Bevölkerung in Deutschland. Gutachten im Auftrag des Sachverständigenrates für Zuwanderung und Integration* [The Situation of People of Turkish Origin in Germany. Report on Behalf of the Council on Immigration and Integration] (Berlin, 2004).

44. Ibid. First generation refers to Turks who immigrated before 1973 and were at least 20 years old at that time. Second generation are Turks who were either born in Germany or immigrated before the age of 4 and therefore still had time to learn German in kindergarten before school enrollment.

45. e.g. see Baumert and Schümer (2001), p.378; Hartmut Esser, "Integration und ethnische Schichtung," [Integration and Ethnic Stratification] Working paper No. 40 (Mannheim: Mannheimer Zentrum für Europäische Sozialforschung, 2001), pp.59f.

46. Kristen and Granato (2004), p.127.

47. For theoretical discussions on reasons for this see e.g. Robert Erikson and Jan O. Jonsson, "Explaining Class Inequality in Education: The Swedish Test Case," in Robert Erikson and Jan O. Jonsson (eds.), *Can Education Be Equalized? The Swedish Case in Comparative Perspective* (Oxford: Westview Press, 1996), pp.1–63.

48. Besides PISA for instance the Socio-Economic Panel (SOEP), a data base which is often used in immigrant-related studies as it includes an oversampled group of immigrants of typical "guest worker" nationalities: see Richard D. Alba *et al.*, "Ethnische Ungleichheit im deutschen Bildungssystem" [Ethnic Inequality in the German Education System], *Kölner Zeitschrift für Soziologie und Sozialpsychologie*, Vol.46, No.2 (1994), pp.209–37; Gert G. Wagner *et al.*, "Education as a Keystone of Integration of Immigrants: Determinants of School Attainment of Immigrant Children in West Germany," in Hermann Kurthen *et al.* (eds.), *Immigration, Citizenship, and the Welfare State*

in Germany and the United States: Immigrant Incorporation (Stanford/London: Jai Press, 1998) pp.35–46; Diefenbach (2004). For the Mikrozensus, a 1% sample of the resident population, see Kristen and Granato (2004), and for the "Integration Survey" of the Federal Institute for Population Research, see von Below (2003), as further important data sources.

49. Baumert and Schümer (2001), p.378.
50. As regards transnational migration during a student's school career, detrimental effects from this disruptive event are likely. In a study of young adults of Turkish and Italian origin, Diehl found that visiting the home country for at least six month during the entire school career (applying to 19% of the Turkish respondents) has an indirect negative effect on educational achievement: These long-term visits lead to a loss of language proficiency in German which in turn decreases the chances of reaching the goal of higher level certificates. Claudia Diehl, "Die Auswirkungen längerer Herkunftsland-aufenthalte auf den Bildungserfolg türkisch- und italienischstämmiger Schülerinnen und Schüler" [The Effects of Extended Stays in the Country of Origin on the Educational Success of Students of Turkish and Italian Origin], *Zeitschrift für Bevölkerungswissenschaft*, Vol.27, No.2 (2002), pp.165–84.
51. Baumert and Schümer (2001), p.343; Diefenbach (2002), p.53.
52. Flip Lindo, "Does Culture Explain? Understanding Differences in School Attainment between Iberian and Turkish Youth in the Netherlands," in Hans Vermeulen and Joel Perlman (eds.), *Immigrants, Schooling and Social Mobility* (London: Macmillan Publishers, 2000).
53. Ibid., pp.213–14.
54. In a survey on language usage, children at primary schools in the city of Hamburg were asked about the languages spoken in their families. Of those children whose family spoke Turkish to some extent, about every second is dominant in German, about one-third is dominant in Turkish and about one child in ten states that his or her German is as proficient as Turkish, see Sara Fürstenau *et al.* (eds.), *Mehrsprachigkeit in Hamburg. Ergebnisse einer Sprachenerhebung an den Grundschulen in Hamburg* [Multilingualism in Hamburg, Results of a Language Survey at Primary Schools in Hamburg] (Münster *et al.*: Waxmann Verlag, 2003), p.56.
55. Andreas Helmke and Hans H. Reich: "Die Bedeutung der sprachlichen Herkunft für die Schulleistung" [The Relevance of Linguistic Origin for School Performance], *Empirische Pädagogik*, Vol.15, No.4 (2001), pp.567–600.
56. Kristen and Granato (2004), p.139; von Below (2003), p.84; Esser (2001), p.62; Wagner *et al.* (1998), pp.41–2.; Alba *et al.* (1994), pp.222–3; Bernhard Nauck *et al.*, "Familiäre Netzwerke, inter-generative Transmission und Assimilationsprozesse bei türkischen Migrantenfamilien" [Family Networks, Intergenerative Transmission and Processes of Assimilation of Turkish Migrant Families], *Kölner Zeitschrift für Soziologie und Sozialpsychologie*, Vol.43, No.3 (1997), pp.477–99.
57. Baumert and Schümer (2001), pp.381–5.
58. Von Below (2003), p.84; Alba *et al.* (1994), pp.222–3; Wagner *et al.* (1998), pp.41–2.
59. Kristen and Granato (2004), p.139; Esser (2001), p.62; Cornelia Kristen: "Ethnische Unterschiede im deutschen Schulsystem" [Ethnic Differences in the German School System], *Aus Politik und Zeitgeschichte*, Vol.53, No.21–22 (2003), p. 347.
60. Hans Vermeulen and Joel Perlmann (eds.), *Immigrants, Schooling and Social Mobility. Does Culture make a Difference?* (London: MacMillan Press Ltd., 2000).
61. Von Below (2003), pp.71–2, 88–9.
62. Lindo (2000).
63. Petra Stanat, "Schulleistungen von Jugendlichen mit Migrationshintergrund: Differenzierung deskriptiver Befunde aus PISA und PISA-E" [School Achievement of Youths with Migrant Background: Differentiation of Descriptive Results from PISA and PISA-E], in Deutsches PISA-Konsortium (ed.), *PISA 2000. Ein differenzierter Blick auf die Länder der Bundesrepublik Deutschland* (Opladen: Leske + Budrich, 2003), p.256; Kristen (2002); Lehmann (1997).
64. Esser (2001); Kristen (2002).
65. Petra Stanat, "Migration and Educational Opportunities: Evidence from the PISA Study," Presentation at the AKI Conference on "The Integration of Immigrants: Language and Educational Achievement" at the WZB in Berlin on July 1, 2005.

66. Kristen (2002), p.549.
67. Bos *et al.* (2004), p.205.
68. Gomolla and Radtke (2002), p.264.
69. Ibid., p.272.
70. Ibid., p.271.
71. Ibid., pp.251–2.
72. As to the promotion of immigrant students' native tongue, educational policies vary across the regional states. Yet in general mother tongue teaching is being phased out in many Länder, see Ingrid Gogolin, "Bilingual Education—The German Experience and Debate," in: Arbeitsstelle Interkulturelle Konflikte und gesellschaftliche Integration (AKI) (ed.), *The Effectiveness of Bilingual School Programs for Immigrant Children,* Discussion Paper SP IV 2005-601 (Berlin: Wissenschaftszentrum Berlin für Sozialforschung, 2005), pp.133–45.
   Typically mother tongue instruction ranges from 2 to 5 hours per week, usually given in the afternoon. With the exception of the regional state of Hessen, attendance is voluntary (and not always possible, if there are too few students of the respective language group). In some Länder, mother tongue instruction is organized and financed by the consulates of countries like Turkey; in others, German state authorities are responsible, see: Cristina Allemann-Ghionda, *Schule, Bildung und Pluralität. Sechs Fallstudien im europäischen Vergleich* [School, Education and Plurality. Six European Case Studies in Comparison] (Bern *et al.*: Peter Lang, 1999); Ingrid Gogolin *et al.* (eds.), *Schulbildung für Kinder aus Minderheiten in Deutschland 1989–1999* [School Education for Children of Minorities in Germany 1989–1999] (Münster *et al.*: Waxmann Verlag, 2001).
   There are no federal statistics about how many Turkish pupils attend lessons in Turkish in Germany. In North Rhine-Westfalia in 1996, 65% of all students of Turkish origin attended mother tongue instruction classes, see Peter Broeder and Guus Extra, *Language, Ethnicity and Education. Case Studies on Immigrant Minority Groups and Immigrant Minority Languages* (Clevedon *et al.*: Multilingual Matters Ltd., 1999).
   In a survey of young immigrant women, 80% of the Turkish respondents had attended mother tongue instruction, 50% for more than 3 years, though due to the specific sample this share could be overestimated, see Bundesministerium für Familie, Senioren, Frauen und Jugend (ed.), *Viele Welten leben. Lebenslagen von Mädchen und jungen Frauen mit griechischem, italienischem, jugoslawischem, türkischem und Aussiedlerhintergrund* [Living Many worlds. Living Situation of Girls and Young Women with Greek, Italian, Yugoslavian, Turkish and *Aussiedler* Background] (Berlin: Bundesministerium für Familie, Senioren, Frauen und Jugend, 2005), pp.246–9.
   Mother tongue instruction for immigrant children has never been evaluated either regarding the language proficiency in these languages themselves or with respect to its effect on the acquisition of the German language, see Janina Söhn, *Zweisprachiger Schulunterricht für Migrantenkinder. Ergebnisse der Evaluationsforschung zu seinen Auswirkungen auf Zweitspracherwerb und Schulerfolg* [Bilingual Education for Immigrant Children: Results of Evaluation Studies on the Effects of Bilingual Education on Second-Language Acquisition and School Performance] (Berlin: Arbeitsstelle Interkulturelle Konflikte und gesellschaftliche Integration, 2005).
73. Diefenbach (2004), p.226.
74. OECD (2001), p.182; Ramm *et al.* (2004), p.259.
75. Lilian Fried, *Expertise zu Sprachstandserhebungen für Kindergartenkinder und Schulanfänger. Eine kritische Betrachtung* [Expert Report on Language Tests for Kindergarten Children and School Beginners] (München: Deutsches Jugendinstitut, 2004). One surprising result was that beside migrant children, a share of German children also did not have sufficient command of German.
76. For results of evaluations of bilingual education see Söhn (2005).
77. OECD, *Early Childhood Education and Care Policy in the Federal Republic of Germany*, available online at http://www.oecd.org/dataoecd/42/2/33979281.pdf (OECD: Paris, 2004).
78. Şükrü Uslucan, "Der Status Quo: Stiftungen in Deutschland und ihre Aktivitäten im Bereich der Bildungsintegration von Migranten" [Status Quo: Foundations in Germany and their Activities in

the Area of Educational Integration of Migrants], in Cem Özdemir and Körber-Stiftung (eds.), Integration stiften. Was leisten Stiftungen in Deutschland, um Kinder und Jugendliche mit Migrationshintergrund in das Bildungssystem zu integrieren? [Promoting Integration: How do Foundations Promote the Integration of Children and Youths with a Migrant Background in the Educational System] (Hamburg: Körber-Stiftung, 2004), pp.7–59.

Gender Dynamics in the Context of Turkish Marriage Migration: The Case of Belgium

CHRISTIANE TIMMERMAN
University of Antwerp, Belgium

Introduction

This study focuses on gender aspects of Turkish migration to Western Europe, more specifically to Belgium. The gender perspective is an essential element in evaluating correctly the dimensions and consequences of Turkish migration, as well as the integration of Turkish immigrants into Western European society.

During the last few decades, marriage has become one of the few means for foreigners to settle legally in Western Europe, especially for those, like the Turks, who had already established communities there. Looking to the Turkish communities in Western Europe, the connection between marriage and migration proves to be a crucial element in evaluating gender dimensions and the consequences for participation and integration in society and the socialization of future generations.

A great proportion of migration marriages fail and produce much social misery. In fact, migration marriages are associated with and even perpetuate the "integration

Correspondence Address: Christiane Timmerman, University of Antwerp, Prinstraat 14, B-2000 Antwerp, Belgium. Email: christiane.timmerman@ua.ac.be

problematique" that Turkish communities in Western Europe face. Notwithstanding this reality, migration marriages remain very popular both within the established Turkish communities in Western Europe and in emigration areas in Turkey. In order to understand the dynamics of this phenomenon, several elements have to be taken into account. First of all there is the appeal of Western Europe for people who in their regions of origin are confronted with difficult socio-economic conditions and who believe that emigration to the West will considerably improve their way of life and that of their children. These ambitions are accommodated into the existing socio-cultural tradition regarding marriage, which allows a very high degree of involvement of the families in the choice of partner and marriage arrangements. In Turkey, especially in the rural emigration areas but also in the Turkish immigrant communities in Western Europe, marriage remains first and foremost a family matter, the responsibility of the parents. Traditionally, the family of the boy proposes to the family of the girl and she is given to him in marriage when both families agree on the marriage terms. Especially among youngsters with a low level of education, it is not rare that the intended partners barely know each other, except when they are relatives. Among educated young people it is usual to choose one's own marriage partner. However, even then the approval of both families is crucial for the marriage to take place.

This concept of arranged marriages fits well with the migration ambitions of both the established Turkish communities in Western Europe and the emigration areas in Turkey. However, migration has an impact on these marriages, which in turn influences gender roles. In this context, traditional gender roles are often accentuated, although they prove to be rather inadequate for adjusting to Western society. The strong Turkish nationalistic identification within the Turkish communities in Western Europe and the often hostile climate in which they live, give fuel to the continuation of these dynamics. This applies to Turkish communities all over Western Europe but especially to the fairly small and closed communities found in Austria, Belgium, Denmark, the Netherlands and Switzerland. This study looks more closely at the Belgian case.

Turkish Migration to Belgium

In Belgium, the largest communities of residents from outside the EU are the Moroccan and Turkish ones. In 1998, there were 70,701 Turks (7.9 percent of the total foreign population) living in Belgium.[1] In 2000, the number of Turkish nationals dropped to 56,172 when in the same year 16,185 Turks acquired Belgian nationality. In 2003, there were 41,336 Turkish nationals; however, by 2005 the majority of people from Turkish origin had acquired Belgian nationality.[2]

Labor migration from Turkey to Belgium started with a bilateral agreement between Turkey and Belgium in 1962. At that time, the flow of Turkish and Moroccan immigrants was directed towards Flemish cities and the capital Brussels rather than the mining areas in Wallonia, as they had been at first. The current distributive pattern of foreigners in Flanders and Brussels confirms this: today, most foreigners live in the large towns within the triangle Brussels–Antwerp–Ghent, in

Limburg Province, in towns along the Flemish–Dutch border, and along the axis between Ghent and Kortrijk.

Although a moratorium on immigration was called in 1974, the Turkish population in Belgium continued to grow steadily. Since 2000, the impact of constant labor market shortages fed in Belgium the debate on the issue of the partial reopening of the borders which has since then emerged with new strength in the media and on the political agenda. However, the government is reluctant to adopt a more open approach towards immigration and Belgian immigration policy continues to be dominated by a discourse on control and closure.[3] Belgian migration policy cannot be seen independently from the restrictive European policy in this matter. Some have argued that the referenda in France and the Netherlands concerning the approval of the EU constitution (May 2005) can also be interpreted as "no" to enlargement of the EU (especially with Turkey) and "no" towards more non-EU immigration. This important political sign makes it very likely that the restrictive migration policy will be maintained.

The majority of the newcomers after 1974 came to Belgium on the basis of "family reunification" or "family formation." "Family reunification" allows children, parents or spouses of Belgian residents to settle in Belgium; we speak about "family formation" when a person enters Belgium with the purpose of marrying a Belgian resident. These two different ways of entering Belgium are called "chain migration."[4]

The initial chain migration applied exclusively to women who joined their husbands who were already in Belgium as *gastarbeiter* (guest workers). Before 1974, economic migration was male, marriage migration was female. In general, men chose to immigrate, while women and children merely followed their husbands or fathers. Gradually this pattern changed as the second generation grew up in Western Europe and started to marry. Contrary to expectations, the tendency to marry someone who grew up in the country of origin remained. However, the pattern of Turkish chain migration towards Flanders gradually changed, and is nowadays equally male–female. Population data show that from 2001 until April 15, 2005, 46 percent of the Turkish newcomers who entered Belgium on the basis of marriage were women.[5]

In 2003, 68,800 legal newcomers arrived in Belgium, the majority to Flanders (41.9 percent), followed by the Walloon (34.9 percent) and Brussels regions (23.2 percent). These people entered as chain migrants, refugees, asylum seekers and students. There were 3,828 Turks (5.6 percent) among them, the majority of whom were between 15 and 29 years of age. This is an indication that the majority came on the basis of marriage; they married in their region of origin a Belgium-resident partner and emigrated the moment their papers allowed them to enter Belgium.[6] Between 1994 and 1998, 75.3 percent of the Turkish newcomers in Flanders were between 15 and 34 years of age: the age distribution of men was 25–35 and of women was 18–24.[7]

In Belgium, the majority of marriages within the Turkish community are still contracted with a partner from the country of origin. In 1991, over 60 percent of

Turkish and Moroccan youngsters married a partner from their own country of origin.[8] On the basis of the population data of Flanders we see that in 2003 in 64.5 percent of the 17,386 married Turkish couples at least one partner was "imported." Of the newcomers, Turkish females in particular belonged to a precarious socio-economic category due to their young age and low educational background.[9]

In the Netherlands, for example, in 2000 about 75 percent of married Turks and Moroccans were married to a person raised in their country of origin. Nevertheless, the data also showed a tendency, mostly among Moroccans, by those who were married more recently, to marry a person who was raised in the Netherlands.[10]

The institution of marriage was affected dramatically since becoming such an important instrument for migration. This in turn affected gender relations and has had an impact on Turkish immigrants' integration into society, which will probably affect the socialization of future generations. For marriages in migrant communities much more is at stake than just love or the ambition to establish a harmonious household; it is often about the possibility of entering the "promised land," about economic and social benefits for the family of the one who is marrying and moving to Western Europe, about reviving the bonds with the region of origin, about loyalties and debts between families who wish to improve their socio-economic position, about young people who are dissatisfied with their current situation in society.

Nationalism and Socio-Cultural Frames of Reference

Atatürk's slogan *Ne Mutlu Türküm Diyene* ("Happy is the person who can call oneself a Turk") is still a significant reality for most Turkish residents in Belgium, irrespective of their ideological orientation. For example, in a study of ethnic Turkish girls who were born in Belgium and are likely to spend the rest of their lives there, it was found that they all defined themselves firmly as "Turks."[11]

Nationalism, both secular and religious, which is well-established in Turkey, also influences the way in which Turks living abroad experience their situation.[12] With Turkey coming closer to the EU, Turkish sentiments remain more salient than ever within the Turkish diaspora. The commitment to Turkey that is evident in Turks living abroad is great, and considerable effort is made by Turkey itself to maintain ties with its expatriates.[13] Nowadays, Turkish migration can no longer be seen as a fixed move from one point to the other. Instead, it is more a process of ongoing movement and interactions between several locations across different countries.[14] This phenomenon of transnational communities enables the maintenance of vibrant relations between the migrant society and the country of origin. It is evident that these dense relations between communities in the regions of origin and in Western Europe facilitate marriage migration and the transmission and influence of existing socio-cultural traditions, for example concerning gender relations. Strong transnational relations, as for example between Turkish communities in Flanders and in the region around Emirdag, even enable "transnational social control."[15]

People who are trying to find their way in a new society must inevitably deal with many uncertainties. They are confronted with different lifestyles, different mores and values and a different social, economic and material environment. Quite predictably in such circumstances, they will tend to question their own identity. In such confusing situations, people will often seek what they perceive as their "authentic" identity, defined by so-called tradition and culture, and legitimated by descent.[16] They will, in other words, seek an ethnic identity that, according to Frederik Barth,[17] classifies a person in terms of his basic, most general identity, presumptively determined by his origin and background. We have to be aware that the objective socio-cultural praxis that is used to legitimate one's ethnic identity can vary extensively within one ethnic group. For example, Turkish girls who identified with a secular Western way of life as well as girls who completely identified with an Islamic way of life both claimed that their socio-cultural praxis was truly Turkish.[18] This demonstrates that more than anything else it is the reference to perceived descent that defines ethnic identity.[19] So, it is clear that for the Turkish communities in Western Europe, Turkish nationalism, be it in its secular or religious form, remains an important element for modeling ones' "new" ethnic identity. Besides the strong transnational relations that exist between Turkish communities, this phenomenon also enhances the attraction of marriage migration: partners coming from the Turkish motherland are believed to be more authentically Turkish.[20]

In order to grasp the socio-cultural praxis in Turkish communities, several explanatory frames of reference and historical developments have to be taken into account.[21] Turkish Republican Nationalism, or Kemalism, changed the religious-dynastic state of the Ottoman Empire into a modern capitalistic state by making secularism one of the key principles of the new society.[22]

The Kemalist perception of secularism meant not so much separation of state and religion as control of the state over religion.[23] Within this modern nation, education was to play a crucial role.[24] Thus the frame was provided for a dramatic improvement of the legal, economic and educational conditions of the female population. Education became compulsory also for girls. Educated women were assumed to contribute in the private sphere of the home as more sophisticated mothers or in public life as teachers, nurses, medical doctors, lawyers, scholars or politicians. Men and women were in public life considered to be equal.[25]

Though Islam was to be excluded from public life, it was nonetheless allowed to keep its significance within the private sphere. Family life—and also marriage—remained within a traditional Islamic frame of reference in which patrilineality and the segregation between men and women are the guiding principles.[26]

While a traditional Islamic value system[27] dominated private life, a Kemalist-inspired world view determined public life. The *modus vivendi* between these two socio-cultural frameworks was disturbed by the emergence of a new frame of reference: Islamism.[28]

From a social perspective, Islamism strives for the establishment for a more just society based on traditional family values. But, contrary to a traditional Islamic frame of reference, Islamism aims to control all aspects of society, both private and public.[29] Also, compared to secular nationalism, Islamism claims to provide a better answer to the existential questions of life. As other religious ideologies, it gives meaning to profound human suffering, sickness, loss and death. For people who live in precarious economic and/or socio-cultural conditions—as migrants and ethnic minorities often do—Islamism gives a clear and all-embracing frame of reference.[30]

Gender in Turkish Communities in Belgium

Gender roles within Turkish communities in Western Europe are more or less in line with gender roles within the region of origin. However, migrants' life in Western society, which is experienced as alien at least by the newcomers, do influence the way gender roles are perceived.

There is a lot of evidence that the socio-economic situation of Turkish migrants in Western Europe is problematic compared with that of mainstream society. Unemployment is high, especially among young people. Research from 2005 demonstrates that ethnic minorities—mostly Moroccans and Turks—encounter considerable discrimination[31] in addition to their under-representation in the labor market due to their poor educational background.[32]

From the perspective of traditional gender roles, poor achievement at school and in the labor market have a negative impact especially on the status of men. Traditionally, they are responsible for the socio-economic well-being of their family, a task that for many is difficult to fulfill. As a consequence, many young Turkish men feel ignored or even threatened by Western society because they failed in their education and in finding a decent job. In addition, they are victims of overt racism to a much greater degree than women. Not only in the public domain do they have a hard time, but their patriarchal status in the private sphere is also under attack: Western public opinion has clearly chosen the side of the "poor oppressed women" in patriarchal clans and has shown an aversion to Muslim machismo.

Research has found that especially young men, mostly second generation, feel comfortable with an Islamist world view. The emphasis of the Islamist discourse on social justice is very appealing to youngsters who often feel ignored by society and threatened by socio-economic developments. Feeling insecure and searching for stability and a more positive identity elsewhere, they find refuge in an Islamist ideology. Militant Islamic movements often accentuate the hierarchical relations within the family, and fervently promote patriarchal ideas.[33] Felice Dassetto speaks in this context of a familial re-socialization to affirm the traditional roles. The mosque can have new significance for Muslim men who want to "re-legitimate" their male authority. Not only older men but younger ones, too, are urged to take their responsibilities towards their women more seriously and in particular to guard their moral behavior. Young migrant Turkish men who are seeking higher status in society are gratified by the new social concern offered by an Islamist frame of reference.[34]

Besides the Islamic world views, which mainly emphasize the family role for women, there exists another Turkish frame of reference, namely Kemalism, which stresses the role of women in public life. According to Kemalism, both men and women have to play their part in public life. For women, the key to this emancipation is education: Those who acquire knowledge deserve high status. Therefore, Turkish girls who pursue education have legitimate reasons to stand out within a Western-inspired (or Kemalist) frame of reference and, in consequence, to develop outside the family context. It is not the contact with Western culture as such that makes the transition possible to a "Western" model of society, but successful participation in the school system. However, in Belgium, as elsewhere in Western Europe, relatively few Turkish girls—but even fewer Turkish boys—are successful with their studies. Therefore, the majority of young Turkish girls have little choice but to stay within the confines of traditional family life. Nonetheless, the existence of this Kemalist-inspired frame of reference makes for those women who do study successfully, the participation in the Western public life more legitimate.

At the same time, active involvement in Islamist organizations may indirectly have an emancipating effect on migrant girls. This is because in addition to the ideological message these movements aim to transmit, they also offer the possibility of developing social networks. Islamist organizations pay a great deal of attention to young girls and women by organizing many activities for them, arguing that later, as mothers, they will play a key role in the transmission of Islamist ideas and embody Islamic authenticity, through their respect for Islamic family values, which forms the basis of a just society.[35]

Many Turkish girls in Belgium are trying to accommodate Islam within their lives. Recent research[36] showed that Islam is often used—especially by better-educated young girls—to claim equal rights for men and women. They interpret Islam—using more feminist interpretations of Islam—in a way that can distance them from the patriarchal traditions of their parents who are—according to them— not "authentic Islamic." In other words, they wish to get rid of the local Islamic traditions of their parents, which are in their eyes too restrictive and unjust for women. Often they have difficulties with restrictions on relations with members of the other sex, in other words, that refer to the sexual honor of the family ("namus"). At the same time, young educated women want to remain loyal to a more "women friendly" Islamic affiliation, in which they look for opportunities for women's emancipation.[37] On the basis of qualitative research methodology, we tend to conclude that girls see in Islam opportunities to challenge the male dominance in their communities where men invoke Islam rather to preserve the traditional male supremacy.[38]

Emigration Areas: The Case of Emirdağ

Some of the research used here concentrated on Emirdağ as a region of emigration.[39] However, to introduce a comparative perspective we also conducted some research in another Turkish region affected by emigration, in Sivas, the capital of the central-eastern Anatolian province of the same name.[40] In all these studies we used mainly qualitative research methodology which consists of participant observation and in-depth interviews.

The majority of Turks living in Belgium originate from one region, the district of Emirdağ, in the province of Afyon. This district consists of about 70 villages, of which the town Emirdağ (approximately 20,000 inhabitants) is the administrative center. This town is situated in a poor, arid area that is greatly affected by emigration. Contrary to the majority of other regions in Turkey, this region has stagnant economic growth and only a slight population growth. Daily life in Emirdağ is closely interwoven with that of the Turkish community in Belgium. The majority of houses in Emirdağ belong to people living in Western Europe. Local business is strongly interconnected with the Turkish communities in Western Europe and much oriented to the needs of European Turks who spend their holidays in their region of origin. Most important: the majority of families have relatives living in Western Europe with whom they maintain close relations. Emigration to Western Europe or the large urban centers in Turkey remains the major ambition of the region's inhabitants.[41]

As stated before, Turks continue to emigrate to Belgium and other Western European countries in the hope of building a better future. The lure remains great as a result of the rosy picture painted by the migrants. Yet a large group of "Emirdağlı" (i.e. inhabitants of Emirdağ) regrets this mass emigration from an economic as well as a social perspective. The exodus is detrimental to local investment and discourages youngsters from committing themselves to developing the region. Furthermore, as a result of the many instances of unsuccessful emigration the social cost is even higher: Many youngsters return home divorced and discouraged after a short "European adventure" that often lasted no more than a year, while the proportion of broken families among those who manage to hold out slightly longer is high.

On the basis of our field research it is clear that while many are eager to emigrate to Western Europe, few have any concrete notion of the life awaiting them there. The prospective newcomers have no specific conception of Belgium, and Flanders in particular. They only have an image of "Europe," which is shaped by migrants who return home for their summer holidays. Also, we found that in typical emigration areas the negative information coming from migrants who already live in Europe is often ignored or even denied.

The aspirant emigrants appeared to be heading for a "mythical" destination where all their worries would be resolved. Obstacles such as learning a foreign language, non-recognition of academic degrees, irrelevant work experience and a hostile society are, on the whole, taken lightly. In fact, few gave these obstacles any serious consideration at all.[42] Furthermore, they had heard stories about the prevailing Western mentality from their prospective spouses. They had been told about positive values such as tolerance, and negative aspects such as individualism. Almost all respondents spoke positively about the considerable degree of (political) freedom in Belgium/Western Europe. However, they also indicated that they had been warned that the Turkish community in Flanders was quite individualistic and showed little solidarity.

Community life in rural and semi-rural areas in Turkey, taking into account the different gender roles and the impact of education, nationalism, religion and modernization, is extensively described in several ethnographies.[43] On the basis of the knowledge we have on traditional socio-cultural frameworks of Turkish society it might be expected that especially boys would be interested in emigrating, due to their responsibility within the traditional frame of reference for the socio-economic well-being of their family. However, on the basis of our research[44] we could not find evidence for this: we found that women also have a clear interest in emigration to the West. Over the last few years, an equal number of Turkish women and men entered Belgium. In Flanders we spoke with female newcomers who had already achieved a degree of independence in Turkey and who hoped to be able to consolidate this freedom in Europe. In Turkey, we interviewed girls who liked the prospect of moving to a place with more opportunities for a higher standard of life. Turkish women living in Western Europe returning on holiday to their region of origin were especially positive about the Western European/Belgian healthcare system. The social security system was also evaluated very positively. These stories are attractive to many local girls who know how difficult it is to pay for good healthcare and who experienced the dramatic consequences that befell men—for example their fathers, brothers—on losing their jobs.[45] Both girls and boys saw the possibility to emigrate as an opportunity to improve their socio-economic status and to move to a more "modern" way of life. These findings are in line with earlier research conducted in Turkey.[46]

It emerged from our interviews with prospective emigrants that they considered mastering the language of the country of destination (Dutch or French) to be important. Men in particular indicated this, but women too found it indispensable, not only for finding work, but also for establishing contacts within Belgian society. Most respondents hoped to be able to take a language course, but their interest was also expressed in vocational training and more general courses. The interviewees were all very confident that they would receive assistance in Belgium from family and/or acquaintances already living there.[47]

We noticed during the interviews at which both prospective partners were present—the one living in Turkey, the other in Belgium—that they often had different expectations from marriage and their future life in Belgium.[48] The following section will discuss the reasons for these marriages.

Why a Partner from Turkey

It is a known phenomenon that marriages between partners who have been raised in Belgium and Turkey often tend to run into trouble during the first years due to the differences in background and expectations.[49] Notwithstanding this reality, a large proportion of Turkish youngsters in Western Europe marry someone who is raised in the country of origin.

They resort to this option since the alternative, marriage with a partner from their own Turkish community in Belgium, is often rejected due to the generally bad reputation of youngsters from the second and following generations. There is a feeling within the Turkish community in Belgium that many Turkish boys have gone astray and that many Turkish girls are too liberated.[50] Hooghiemstra[51] came to the same conclusion in her study conducted in the Netherlands. Also in the Netherlands the so-called too-Western and decadent attitude of the local Turkish youth was said to be a reason for preferring partners from the region of origin instead.

Youngsters who have grown up in the homeland therefore tend to be preferred as marriage partners: they are assumed to be "better behaved" and "more traditional." As mentioned earlier, migrant communities go to great lengths to consolidate in the country of destination what they regard to be their "authentic culture."[52] Research conducted in the Netherlands also found that one of the reasons why youngsters prefer to marry someone from the country of origin is their alleged "traditional" character.[53] Meanwhile, though, Turkey itself experienced societal developments that affected traditional socio-cultural praxis in a way that brought it more in line with the Western European way of life. On the basis of our year-long participant observation we see that these changes within the society of origin seem often to go unnoticed within Turkish communities in Western Europe.[54] Thus the Turks in Belgium are not sufficiently aware that the persons they import for marriage no longer come from the background they imagine.

Marriage migration often involves changes in traditional patterns. Traditionally, the bride leaves her family to join the family of her husband. She will be incorporated into the family of her husband that is now responsible for her and her conduct. It is the husband who must maintain his family and represent them in the public space. For male newcomers this pattern is reversed. Instead, he has to leave his family to join the family of his bride in Western Europe and often he will be dependent on her family.

Although it contradicts the traditional patterns regarding marriage, Turkish girls in Belgium see several advantages in marrying a man from their region of origin that are all linked to possibilities for acquiring greater independence within their marriage. In this case it is most probable that the parents of the bridegroom will remain in Turkey, which considerably diminishes their ability to interfere in the young household and to control their daughter-in-law.

The male newcomer is often unable to fulfill his traditional role appropriately, especially in the early stages of marriage, as his partner, who is already familiar with Belgian society, is the breadwinner and maintains all contacts with the outside world. In the Turkish community, these tasks are traditionally reserved for the male. In this phase, however, the female partner is the only one possessing the necessary linguistic and social skills. Moreover, the male often has to live with his in-laws. However, women's greater access to the public sphere and their heightened responsibilities are not perceived as an unambiguously positive development. Often the newly-arrived husband will not assume the typically female role, as taking care of the household and looking after the children, since these tasks are not prestigious and would cause him to lose his "masculinity." This frequently results in a double workload for the woman and lack of purpose for the man, with all the tensions this may cause within the household.[55]

On the other hand, over half of Belgian-Turkish men choose to marry a girl from their country of origin.[56] Again, the fact that these girls are regarded as being "better behaved" and "more traditional" plays a role. Especially rural girls with a low educational background are assumed not to hinder the husband's patriarchal position. They are considered to be more obedient and respectful towards their husband and their parents-in-law. Being ignorant about the new environment and not knowing the language of the new society, they are extremely dependent on their husband and his family. On the basis of our data we found that for some women it was self-evident that their husband was the household head and that he bore full financial responsibility. They felt protected in an alien society by their traditional role as a "housewife." Nevertheless, a number of female newcomers were prepared to make an effort to integrate formally and informally into Belgian society, and it was not uncommon for their partners to be supportive of this decision.[57]

What the male considers "protective," the female often regards as "domineering." In other words, much depends here on the perception of the newly-wed girl. Female newcomers who arrive in Belgium through marriage with a Belgian-Turkish man often have no support outside the husband's family and therefore they often experience problems with the social control exerted by the conservative Turkish community[58] or with their position as daughter-in-law in a patriarchal context. In some cases women are abused and confined to their homes, they receive death threats and suffer physical, sexual or psychological violence. There is no doubt that this group of maltreated, confined women exists, but there are no data available to determine its size.[59]

Although partners from Turkey are very much in demand, in recent years questions have been raised about their sincerity. Too many stories are circulating through the community about men who married Belgian-Turkish girls in order to obtain a residence permit and who ignored their marital obligations from the moment their residence status in Belgium was legally assured. In reaction, Belgian-Turkish parents try to protect their daughters from such opportunistic marriages by demanding a substantial dowry. The parents deposit this money until they feel certain about their son-in-law's motives for marriage. However, such a heavy financial burden can prove difficult to bear for the new family, and it happens that it is often the daughter herself who becomes responsible for repayment either during or after marriage.[60]

Often it is difficult to say what is most important for the one who is marrying and moving to Western Europe: the attraction of Europe or of the partner. We speak of "marriages of convenience" when the marriage—at least by one of the partners—is contracted with the sole aim of getting a residence permit. On the basis of figures of local administrations we see that this is an increasing problem: in the city of Antwerp the local administration noted an increase in the number of marriages that are refused compared to the total number of contracted marriages, 5.8 percent in 2003 to 8.3 percent in 2004. On the other hand it is a known phenomenon that people sometimes prefer to annul their marriage in order to avoid an expensive divorce or financial obligations towards the partner. The procedures of declaring a marriage "fake" are far less costly than a divorce and exempt the partners from paying eventual alimony.

So-called "forced marriages" are another phenomenon that is related to migration. Although it is obvious that this implies that at least one of the partners was forced to accept the marriage, in reality it is very difficult to distinguish between an arranged and a forced marriage. A marriage can be seen as "forced" by only one of the partners; or first be considered as "arranged" and later on, once the marriage failed, be evaluated as "forced." It is evident that it is impossible to quantify this phenomenon.[61] In ongoing research we see that some Turkish youngsters—especially young girls—tend to accept proposed marriage candidates because of factors unrelated to marriage, such as psychological pressure of the environment, problems at school, psychological problems, the longing for independence and an adult identity.[62]

Consequences for Participation in Society

Newcomers and their partners face several challenges in establishing a harmonious household. Besides the challenge of succeeding as a married couple, the newcomer is confronted with a new society while the settled partner has to learn about accommodating a foreigner in her/his household and into society. The challenges are rather different from a male and female perspective.

In the perception of newcomers—particularly men—finding employment is the main priority upon arrival in Belgium. This is the only possibility for the male to assume the traditional role of breadwinner and to repay the costs of the marriage/dowry and his journey to Belgium. In the case of most men, there is the additional burden of relatives who have stayed behind in the region of origin, and who regard the migration of their son as an "investment" that should pay off quickly. Consequently, these men easily fall prey to unlisted and therefore illegal employment, either in the migrant community (hotel, catering, and retailing) or in the Belgian community (fruit picking). The problem of unlisted employment is not restricted only to people without a residence permit.[63]

This eagerness to find a job hinders many of the male newcomers from participating in the "integration courses" organized by the Flemish community. These courses, which take some eight weeks, provide the possibility of learning Dutch, getting some basic information about Belgian society and receiving an orientation to the labor market. However, newcomers experience the language barrier as a serious handicap in their search for suitable work. Furthermore, their qualifications are often not recognized in Flanders, which makes them worthless on the labor market. This is doubly frustrating, especially for the highly skilled. Likewise, work experience in Turkey is usually deemed irrelevant. Most individuals, especially the low skilled, are very motivated to enroll for vocational training in combination with a language course, insofar as they can find paid labor during this training period in order to meet the most urgent financial needs. This is, however, often an impossible combination.[64]

We ascertained that female newcomers also want to work, but in their case finding employment is less imperative. They are motivated to find a job, and quite a number of women expressed the wish to enroll for vocational training or more general courses. In other words, they were hoping to realize their desire for emancipation through migration to Belgium and the opportunities that this entails in terms of work and training. On the other hand, there are also female newcomers who intend devoting themselves entirely to their role as housewife and who do not consider work outside the home an option.[65]

It emerged from the interviews that the expectations of women with regard to work sometimes clashed with the expectations of their husbands.[66] While the male often hopes to marry a "traditional housewife" by choosing a partner from his country of origin, the female newcomer expects to achieve emancipation by marrying a Belgian-Turkish partner. In other words, the myths that circulate about the two communities can be a source of conflict between many newly-weds.[67]

Few newcomers were aware before they left their homeland that Flanders has a reception policy. They had counted mostly on support from their partners and in-laws. Most female newcomers said explicitly that it was up to their partner, who had after all been raised in Flanders, to assist them. This expectation was less outspoken among the male newcomers. They counted on support and solidarity on the part of their community in Belgium, but this expectation was rarely fulfilled.

Both male and female newcomers had a positive attitude towards the official reception policy of the centers visited. Most said they were pleasantly surprised when they were told that such facilities existed. Moreover, the courses more than fulfilled their expectations, so that they found it difficult to formulate any points of criticism. Most respondents did however indicate they had intended to start a course in "Dutch as a foreign language" sooner, but that they had lost time because of the existing waiting list. This feeling was even more pronounced among the men, who were for that matter slightly more critical of such courses, as they interfered with their urgent desire to find a job. Many men indicated that they had left their homeland in the hope of finding immediate employment. They therefore felt frustrated first to have to attend "school," especially without any guarantee of subsequent employment. More highly skilled men were also more critical: they felt the courses were not always adapted to their abilities. It was unclear to them what value a social orientation program might have for them.[68]

In our sample,[69] especially women said explicitly that "integration programs" should be made compulsory, as this was a way to break the authoritarian power of their husbands and in-laws.[70] At present, "integration programs" are compulsory for newly arrived partners of Belgian residents who do not have Belgian nationality. However, as mentioned above, the majority of Turks living in Belgium acquired Belgian citizenship, which means that their partners are not obliged to take these courses. Nonetheless it is clear that it would also be beneficial for them. As stated before, we have to take into account that especially Turkish female newcomers belong to a precarious socio-economic category due to their young age and low educational background. These "integration courses" could inform them—besides providing them with language and professional skills—of their rights and duties, and how to call on outside assistance whenever required.

Conclusion

Gender is a known divide in all societies, also in Turkish society. Although from a Kemalist perspective men and women are equal in public life, for the Islamic-based frames of reference gender is a very decisive criterion for the organization of society. Within the Turkish migrant communities in Western Europe a new divide is emerging: between newcomers and settled immigrants.

"Opposed expectations" run as a thread through this story. Many prospective emigrants have unrealistic expectations about life in Belgium or Western Europe in general. They believe that they will be moving to an idyllic place where they will be liberated from all restrictions and injustices that exist in their home country. Their future home will be more modern, freer and wealthier. They see their migration as a step towards "the new." In contrast, Turks residing in Belgium choose marriage partners from their land of origin often because of a nostalgic longing for "the familiar" or "the authentic" culture. What the newcomer is trying to escape from is often precisely what the partner (and his/her family) living in Western Europe is trying to regain. After arrival, the disappointment is often great for both parties. Yet here too perceptions differ. While the newcomer is often shocked by his or her new social environment, the one already living in Belgium often looks down on the underdeveloped material situation from which the newcomer has "escaped." The newcomer expects respect for what he/she brings, while the Turkish resident expects gratitude for what he/she has to offer.

These two divides—gender and newcomer/established resident—intervene in a particular way, in which marriage migration plays a crucial role. A large proportion of marriages within the Turkish diaspora in Western Europe are still contracted with partners from the region of origin. Marriage being generally framed within the traditional cultural framework undergoes crucial modifications in the context of migration that in turn influence gender roles. In this context, traditional gender roles are often accentuated but prove to be rather inadequate for adjusting to Western society. Female newcomers in particular find themselves completely dependent on their husband and/or his family since their traditionally dependent role is further enhanced by their lack of knowledge of the host society. Nonetheless, often these women came to Western Europe with emancipation ambitions. They hoped to become part of Western society, an ambition that is often frustrated by their own environment. On the other hand, traditional patterns are sometimes rearranged for emancipating reasons. Among other reasons, young Turkish women in Western Europe opt for a partner who is raised in Turkey because they expect that this will give them more freedom: the parents-in-law will stay behind in Turkey and the husband will depend on the woman for orienting himself in society. Indeed, male newcomers do not fit traditional marriage arrangements—instead of the bride doing so, they had to leave their family—on top of that they often find themselves in a precarious economic situation. Moreover, they must often come to terms with the fact that the image of the "rich migrant" is a myth.

Marriage migration accentuates the inadequacy of traditional gender roles in meeting the demands of Western European society. The dependent role of female newcomers—which explains why brides from Turkey are often preferred over (Turkish) brides from Western Europe—is often cherished by the in-laws. On the other hand, male newcomers, whose patriarchal attitudes and ambitions are often dramatically frustrated because of their inadequacy to take efficient control of family life and because of the unexpected hard socio-economic situation, feel themselves often ignored or even threatened by (Western) society.

It is clear that this situation does not provide the best conditions for adequate participation in society, or for the socialization of future generations. For the newcomer, acquiring sufficient skills is a difficult task, also for his/her environment it is a demanding situation. In order to minimize problems in adjusting to their new society newcomers should be prepared for their new way of life.

First of all they should have a realistic picture of their new homeland before emigrating. Local governments and non-governmental organization of emigration areas in Turkey could play a role in providing their citizens who are interested in emigration with better and more accurate information about life in Western Europe. They should especially target those prospective emigrants who are most vulnerable: uneducated women. For this task Turkish organizations could rely on the assistance of West European organizations dealing with "integration courses" to provide adequate introductions about specific Western European countries. As the decision to emigrate is a very important one with a lot of consequences for the families involved it should not be taken lightly. In order to enhance the chances for a mature decision, people emigrating on the basis of marriage should not be too young: a minimum age of 21 years makes it more likely that they make a relatively independent and informed choice.

On the European side we see that Turkish communities and especially Turkish young people should be better equipped to face the challenges of living in a West European country. First of all education has to play a major role. This tremendous task should be the shared responsibility of the Belgian education system, civil society and the Turkish communities. They have to join forces in order to socialize young citizens towards becoming sufficiently equipped to make their living in a West European society. The existing "integration programs" prove to be a good instrument for making newcomers more capable of managing their life in a West European country. However, in order to be more effective, they should especially target those who need it most: women with a low educational background. The obligatory nature of the program should be extended towards the entire population of newcomers, including those who are married to a Belgian citizen and are therefore currently exempt.

In order to understand gender dynamics related to marriage migration, both the impact of Turkish emigration areas and of Western Europe have to be taken into account. At the same time, problems associated with marriage migration can only be solved if Western Europe and Turkey join forces in dealing wisely with the migration issue.

Notes

1. C. Timmerman, K. Van der Heyden, Y. Ben Abdeljelil and J. Geets, *Marokkaanse en Turkse Nieuwkomers in Vlaanderen. Onderzoeksgroep Armoede, Sociale Uitsluiting en Stad* [Moroccan and Turkish Newcomers in Flanders. Research Unit on Poverty, Social Exclusion and the City] (Antwerp: OASeS—UFSIA, 2000), pp.34–6.
2. Belgian National Institute of Statistics.
3. S. Gsir, M. Martiniello and J. Wets, "Belgium Country Report on Immigration Management," in J. Niessen, Y. Schibel and R. Magoni (eds.), *EU and US Approaches to the Management of Immigration* (Brussel: Migration Policy Group, 2003). Available online: http://www.migpolgroup.com/upload-store/Belgium.pdf.
4. First there is the special marriage visa and second there is the possibility of family reunification. Non-EEA partners who plan to marry in Belgium can apply for a Type C visa (known as the "visa with view to marriage") from the Belgian authorities, if the sponsor living in Belgium has a residence permit for more than 3 months. In general, all persons entering Belgium for family reunification have to apply for a Type D visa from the diplomatic or consular authorities competent for the district where they reside. The conditions for the application and the stay depend on whether a women is married to a Belgian, EEA citizen or a non-EEA national. For more detail see: C. Nahr, K. Mahnkopf and M. Gulicova, "Protection and Aid Measures for Female Marriage Migrants from Third Countries in the EU Member States" (DAPHNE Programme—European Commission, 2005).
5. L. Deschamps, "De Internationalisering van de 'Vlaamse' Huwelijksmarkt, een Oriënterende Schets" [The Internationalization of the 'Flemish' Marriage Market, an Exploratory Sketch], in F. Caestecker (ed.), *Huwelijksmigratie: een Zaak voor de Overheid? Reeks Minderheden in de Samenleving* [Marriage Migration: A Matter for the Government? Series Minorities in Society] (Leuven: Acco, 2005, in press).
6. Deschamps (2005).
7. Timmerman *et al.* (2000), pp.57–65.
8. J. Lievens, "Family-Forming Migration from Turkey and Morocco to Belgium. The Demand for Marriage Partners from the Countries of Origin," *International Migration Review*, Vol.33, No.3 (Fall 1999), pp.717–44.
9. J.Geets and R. Marynissen, "Morroccan Marriage Migration in Flanders: Facts and Figures," *Onderzoeksgroep Armoede, Sociale Uitsluiting en Stad/Steunpunt Gelijke Kansenbeleid* [Research Unit on Poverty, Social Exclusion and the City/Policy Centre of Equal Opportunities] (Antwerpen: UA, in press).
10. E. Hooghiemstra, "Trouwen over de Grens. Achtergronden van Partnerkeuze van Turken en Marokkanen in Nederland" [Cross-border Marriage. Background to the Partner Choice of Turks and Moroccans in the Netherlands] (Den Haag: Sociaal en Cultureel Planbureau. SCP-publicatie 2003/4, 2003).
11. C. Timmerman, *Onderwijs maakt het Verschil. Socio-Culturele Praxis en Etniciteitsbeleving bij jonge Turkse Vrouwen* [Education makes the Difference. Socio-Cultural Praxis and Ethinicity Experience of Young Turkish Women] (Leuven: Acco, Minderheden in de samenleving, 1999), p.279.
12. M. Meeker, "The New Muslim Intellectuals in the Republic of Turkey," in R. Tapper (ed.), *Islam in Modern Turkey. Religion, Politics and Literature in a Secular State* (London: I.B. Tauris & Co Ltd, 1991), pp.189–222; M. Meeker, "Oral Culture, Media Culture and the Islamic Resurgence in Turkey," in E. Archetti (ed.), *Exploring the Written in Anthropology* (Oslo: Scandinavian University Press, 1994), pp.31–63; R. Tapper, "Introduction," in R. Tapper (ed.), *Islam in Modern Turkey. Religion, Politics and Literature in a Secular State* (London and New York: I.B. Tauris & Co Ltd,

1991), pp.1–30; D. Kandiyoti, "End of Empire: Islam, Nationalism and Women in Turkey," in D. Kandiyoti (ed.), *Women, Islam and the State* (London: Macmillan, 1991), pp.22–47; D. Kandiyoti, "Patterns of Patriarchy: Notes for an Analysis of Male Dominance in Turkish Society," in S. Tekeli (ed.), *Women in Turkish Society: A Reader* (London: Zed Books Ltd, 1995), pp.306–18.

13. For more concrete information see: Timmerman (1999).
14. L. Soysal, "Labor to Culture: Writing Turkish Migration to Europe," *South Atlantic Quarterly*, Vol.102, No.2/3 (Spring/Summer 2003), p.491–507.
15. Timmerman (1999).
16. A. Akbar, "'Ethnic Cleansing': A Methaphor for our Time?" *Ethnic and Racial Studies*, Vol.18, No.1 (1995), pp.26–45.
17. F. Barth, *Ethnic Groups and Boundaries: The Social Organization of Cultural Difference* (London: George Allen & Unwin, 1969).
18. C. Timmerman, "Secular and Religious Nationalism Among Young Turkish Women in Belgium: Education May Make the Difference," *Anthropology and Education Quarterly*, Vol.31, No.3 (2000), pp.333–54.
19. E. Roosens, *Creating Ethnicity. The Process of Ethnogenesis* (Newbury Park, London, New Delhi: Sage Publications, 1989); E. Roosens, "The Primordial Nature of Origins in Migrant Ethnicity," in H. Vermeulen and C. Govers (eds.), *The Anthropology of Ethnicity. Beyond 'Ethnic Groups and Boundaries'* (Amsterdam: Het Spinhuis, 1994), pp.81–104; Timmerman (1999); Timmerman (2000).
20. Timmerman and Van der Heyden (1995).
21. See also E. Zürcher, *Turkey. A Modern History* (London and New York: I.B. Tauris & Co Ltd., 1993).
22. D. Barchard, *Turkey and the West* (London: Routledge & Kegan Paul, 1985); J Ross, "Politics, Religion, and Ethnic Identity in Turkey," in M. Curtis (ed.), *Religion and Politics in the Middle East* (Boulder, CO: Westview Press, 1981); Kandiyoti (1995), pp.306–18.
23. Zürcher (1993).
24. Barchard (1985).
25. S. Tekeli, "The Meaning and Limits of Feminist Ideology in Turkey," in F. Ozbay (ed.), *Women, Family and Social Change in Turkey* (Bangkok: UNESCO, 1990), pp.145–65.
26. G. Okman-Fişek, "Turkey," in L. Adler (ed.), *International Handbook on Gender Roles* (Westport: Greenwood Press, 1993), pp.438–51; S. Tekeli, "Introduction: Women in Turkey in the 1980s," in S. Tekeli (ed.), *Women in Turkish Society: A Reader* (London: Zed Books Ltd, 1995), pp.1–22; A. Duben and C. Behar, *Istanbul Households. Marriage, Family and Fertility: 1880–1940* (Cambridge and New York: Cambridge University Press, 1991).
27. This traditional Islamic vision of society is broadly compatible with what Michael Meeker (1994) describes as the world picture of "local and oral Islam."
28. For more information see Timmerman (2000).
29. R. Çakır, "La Mobilisation Islamique en Turquie" [The Islamic Mobilization in Turkey], *Esprit* (August–September 1992), pp.130–42; O. Roy, "L'Échec de l'Islam Politique" [The Setback of the Political Islam], *Esprit* (August–September 1992), pp.106–29.
30. For a very recent and comprehensive assessment of the role of Islam in Turkey see special issue on Religion and Politics in Turkey: *Turkish Studies*, Vol.6, No.2 (June 2005).
31. A. Martens, N. Ouali, M. Van de Maele, S. Vertommen, P. Dryon and H. Verhoeven, "Etnische Discriminatie op de Arbeidsmarkt in het Brussels Hoofdstedelijk Gewest" [Ethnic Discrimination on the Labor Market in Brussels-Capital Region] (Brussel/Leuven: ULB/K.U.Leuven, Institut de Sociologie/Departement Sociologie, Centre de sociologie du Travail, de l'emploi et de la formation/ Afdeling Arbeids-en Organisatiesociologie, 2005).
32. C. Timmerman, E. Vanderwaeren and M. Crul, "The Second Generation in Belgium," *International Migration Review*, Vol.37, No.4 (Winter 2003), pp.1065–90.
33. T. Koçtürk, A Matter of Honour. Experiences of Turkish Women Immigrants (London and New Jersey: Zed Books, 1992).
34. C. Timmerman, "Jeunes Filles de Turquie: Vie Familiale et Instruction Scolaire" [Turkish Girls: Family Life and School Instruction], in: N. Bensalah (ed.), Familles Turques et Maghrébines

Aujourd'hui. Evolution dans les Espace d'Origine et d'Immigration [Turkish Families and Maghrébines Today. Evolution in the Space of Origin and of Immigration] (Paris: Maisonneuve et Larose, 1994), pp.175–88.

35. Yeşim Arat, "Feminism and Islam: Considerations on the Journal 'Kadın ve Aile'," in S. Tekeli (ed.), Women in Modern Turkish Society (London: Zed Books Ltd, 1995), pp.66–78.

36. K. Van der Heyden et al., Marokkaanse Huwelijksmigratie, Onderzoeksrapport Steunpunt Gelijke Kansenbeleid [Moroccan Marriage Migration, Research Report Policy Centre of Equal Opportunities] (Universiteit Antwerpen, 2005, in press).

37. E. Vanderwaeren, "Moslima's aan de Horizon. Islamitische Interpretaties als Hefbomen bij de Emancipatie van Moslima's" [Muslimas on the Horizon. Islamic Interpretations as Levers for the Emancipation of Muslimas], Ethiek en Maatschappij, Vol.7, No.4 (2005), pp.94–111.

38. For more information, see Van der Heyden et al. (2005).

39. Timmerman (1999); Timmerman et al.(2000); C. Timmerman and K. Van der Heyden, "Turkish and Moroccan Newcomers in Flanders," in H. De Smedt, L. Goossens and C. Timmerman (eds.), Unexpected Approaches to the Global Society. OASeS—monograph (Leuven and Apeldoorn: Garant, 2005); ongoing research on Turkish marriage migration (2005–06) and on family reunion (2005–06).

40. Timmerman et al. (2000).

41. Timmerman (1999); Timmerman and Van der Heyden (1995).

42. Timmerman et al. (2000), pp.263–5.

43. P. Stirling, A Turkish Village (London: Weidenfeld & Nicoloon, 1965); C. Delaney, The Seed and the Soil. Gender and Cosmology in Turkish Village Society (Berkeley and Los Angeles: University of California Press, 1991); Timmerman (1999), p.279; Meeker (1994).

44. Timmerman (1999); Timmerman et al.(2000); Timmerman and Van der Heyden (2005).

45. C. Timmerman, "Creativiteit binnen Conformisme: Huwelijksregelingen van Turkse Migranten-meisjes" [Creativity within Conformism: Marriage Arrangements of Turkish Migrant Girls], in K. Luyckx (ed.), Liefst een Gewoon Huwelijk? Creatie en Conflict in Levensverhalen van Jonge Migrantenvrouwen [Rather a Normal Marriage? Creation and Conflict in Life Stories of Young Migrant Women] (Leuven: Acco, 2000), pp.117–38.

46. T. Erman, "The Meaning of City Living for Rural Migrant Women and their Role in Migration: the Case of Turkey," Women's Studies International Forum, Vol.20, No.2 (1997), pp.263–73.

47. Timmerman et al. (2000), pp.263–5.

48. Ibid.

49. K. Luyckx (ed.), Liefst een Gewoon Huwelijk? Creatie en Conflict in Levensverhalen van Jonge Migrantenvrouwen [Rather a Normal Marriage? Creation and Conflict in Life Stories of Young Migrant Women] (Leuven: Acco, Minderheden in de Samenleving, 2000); Van der Heyden et al. (2005).

50. Timmerman (1999); Timmerman et al. (2000); Van der Heyden et al. (2005); Timmerman and Van der Heyden (2005).

51. Hooghiemstra (2003).

52. Roosens (1998); Timmerman (2000).

53. Hooghiemstra (2003).

54. Timmerman (1999); Timmerman (2000); Timmerman and Van der Heyden (2005).

55. Hooghiemstra (2003); Timmerman and Van der Heyden (2005)

56. Lievens (1999).

57. Timmerman et al. (2000), pp.233–57.

58. M. Tribalat, Faire France: une Enquête sur les Immigrés et leurs Enfants [To Make France: A Survey of the Immigrants and their Children] (Paris: La Découverte, 1995).

59. Timmerman and Van der Heyden (2005), pp.97–8.

60. Ibid.

61. Van der Heyden et al. (2005).

62. Ibid.

63. Timmerman and Van der Heyden (2005), pp.96–8.
64. Timmerman et al. (2000), pp.252–7.
65. Ibid., pp.247–9.
66. Ibid. This research was conducted in 1999–2000: 72 persons were interviewed of which 40 Turks, 19 men and 21 women.
67. Timmerman et al. (2000), pp.265–9.
68. Ibid., p.262.
69. See n. 68 above.
70. Timmerman et al. (2000), pp.252–6.

Political Participation and Associational Life of Turkish Residents in the Capital of Europe

DIRK JACOBS*, KAREN PHALET** & MARC SWYNGEDOUW†
*Free University of Brussels (ULB) and KUBrussel, Belgium, **Utrecht University, The Netherlands,
†Catholic Universities of Leuven and Brussels, Belgium

Notwithstanding the fact that the Brussels-Capital region government nowadays has a deputy-minister of Turkish origin, judging from an overall perspective, the Turkish community is in relative terms still underrepresented in the political sphere in Belgium. Data from several Western European cities shows that Turkish immigrants in the European Union tend to have a strong associational life, dense social networks and a strong sense of community. In addition, for Turks living in major Western European cities like Amsterdam, Berlin and Brussels, a pattern emerges showing that those people who are active in local Turkish associational life tend to be also involved in cross-ethnic associations of the host society. Nevertheless, while it is often claimed that a strong associational life has a spillover effect into increased political trust and political involvement in Amsterdam, this seems to be less the case in the Belgian Brussels-Capital region.

Integration in civil society seems to be an empirical fact among the Turks in Belgium. Integration in the host society at large is, however, not a question of all or

Correspondence Address: Dirk Jacobs, Institut de Sociologie, GERME, ULB, CP124, 44 Avenue Jeanne, 1050 Brussels, Belgium. Email: dijacobs@ulb.ac.be

nothing. Integration has different dimensions: social-cultural, economical and political. We define integration as participation in these different spheres.[1] However, regardless of the level of associational organization, immigrant-origin minorities in Belgium—as in almost all other Western European countries—are, on the group level, often only marginally integrated into important spheres of societal life. This is particularly the case with regard to the economic and political spheres. Turks are often integrated into the socio-cultural sphere, especially through associational inclusion organized on an ethnic basis while inclusion in other areas is more problematic. This is partly related to a lack of "bridging capital" such as educational achievement. In schooling, the Turkish-origin minority's second generation fails in large numbers (up to four times as often as the Belgian majority-group children).

This contribution wishes to shed further light on the integration of Turkish immigrants in the political and civic fields. Political scientists like Fennema and Tillie[2] claim that there is an important link between associational participation on the one hand and political participation on the other. In the Brussels-Capital region, however, a different pattern can be observed: Turks have an active associational participation but do not perform well in the elected political arena, in contradiction to the postulation by Fennema and Tillie, who based their argument on their research in Amsterdam. Taking the situation of the Moroccan immigrant community in Brussels as a point of reference, we have to conclude that Turks are not so successful in the political sphere although they have remarkable patterns of associational involvement. This contribution argues that this discrepancy might very well be linked to the fact that Turkish immigrants tend to opt for more collective forms of interest representation, while the Belgian political establishment prefers more individual trajectories of political inclusion. Another key for solving the puzzle has to do with the sub-optimal levels of linguistic command of the languages of the host country by the Turkish immigrants. The second generation of the Turkish minority has considerable difficulty in overcoming its arrears in education and, as a consequence, language skills tend to suffer. This equally has some consequences for political involvement.

In this contribution, we will discuss the structure of Turkish associational life in Brussels and address the issue of political involvement of the Turkish community in the Belgian and European capital. In doing so, we will make use of a threefold set of data sources: survey data among a representative sample of Turkish residents, a network analysis of Turkish association life, and data generated through questionnaire research among Turkish organizations.

Political Participation of Turkish Immigrants in Brussels

The gradual introduction of *jus soli*[3] in the nationality legislation and the growing demographic importance of immigrant-origin residents resulted in the increasing importance of the immigrant-origin electorate and politicians in the Belgian political landscape. This is especially the case in the Brussels-Capital region, where approximately 38 percent of all inhabitants are either non-national (nearly 25 percent) or are

Belgian citizens from immigrant descent. About half of the foreign-origin population is of EU descent, the other half originates from countries outside of the
(current) European Union. Only Belgian nationals have voting rights for the
regional and the national level, but EU citizens have held local voting rights since
2000 and non-EU citizens will be able to participate in local elections in 2006. The
largest immigrant group of non-EU origin consists of the Moroccans, with approximately 90,000 residents in Brussels. The second largest group of (current) non-EU
origin consists of the Turks, with approximately 35,000 residents in Brussels. Exact
figures are unavailable due to the lack of official statistics with regard to ethnicity—
only with regard to nationality—in Belgium.[4]

The striking importance of the foreign population in the total population of
Brussels is due to a number of factors: On the one hand, over the last few decades a
substantial number of middle- and upper-class Belgians have been leaving the city
due to the process of suburbanization.[5] On the other hand, due to a shortage in
manual laborers, low-skilled foreign workers were attracted to the city in the 1960s
and early 1970s. In addition, due to its international political role (as capital of the
European Union and host of NATO) and its position in the global economy,
Brussels has attracted (and still attracts) substantial numbers of highly educated
foreign professionals, originating from OECD countries.

Judged by its Gross Regional Product, Brussels is the third richest region of
Europe. Nevertheless, considerable numbers of its inhabitants are socio-economically disadvantaged. In a services-oriented economy, which is increasingly demanding high education levels, those who are low-skilled have considerable difficulty in
finding and maintaining jobs. Although there is a well-developed welfare program
in Belgium, this has not been able to prevent the social exclusion of considerable
segments of the population. To some extent there has been a socio-geographical
"translation" of social exclusion, leading to the existence of disadvantaged neighborhoods with derelict housing, high unemployment and little hope for short-term
socio-economic revival. In these poor neighborhoods, which are mainly inhabited
by low-skilled workers, there is a considerable residential concentration of
Moroccan and Turkish immigrants, who are in the majority low-skilled. In some
neighborhoods, specific groups of immigrants dominate the area and are even more
numerous than the indigenous Belgian inhabitants, the majority of whom are
equally low-skilled.

Figure 1 presents the geographical distribution of Turkish citizens who do not
hold Belgian nationality in the Brussels-Capital region. The data, taken from the
2001 Census, shows that Turkish non-nationals tend to live in a clustered set of
neighborhoods, situated near the north train station of Brussels, in the municipalities
of Schaerbeek and Sint-Joost. To a lesser degree, Turks also tend to live in a number
of neighborhoods in the west of Brussels, in the municipalities of Anderlecht and
Molenbeek and in the borough Laeken of the city of Brussels.

As can be seen when one compares Figure 1 with Figure 2, the clustered set of
neighborhoods, near the northern train station, where a significant concentration of
Turkish immigrants is to be found, is part of a larger group of poor neighborhoods in

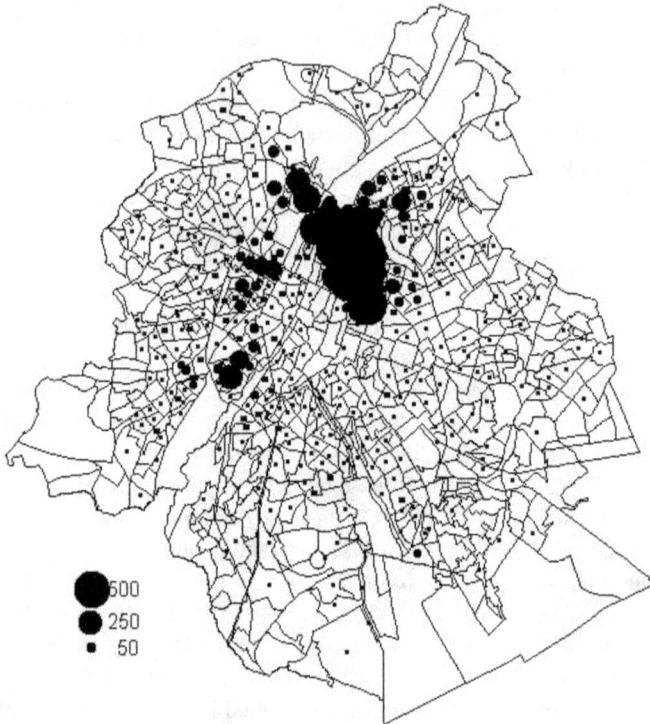

geographical distributions of Turks (not
holding Belgian nationality) in the Brussels
Capital Region, 2001

data source: FPS Economy - Statistics Division
General Socio-Economic Survey 2001 (Census)

cartography: Jacobs - ULB

Figure 1.   Geographical distribution (in 2001) of Turkish citizens who do not hold Belgian
nationality in the Brussels-Capital region. Information is taken from the most recent Census,
2001. The map displays the different neighborhoods of Brussels.

the Brussels-Capital region. In this area, to the north and west of the historical city
center, a predominance of nineteenth century housing infrastructure is to be found,
originally built to accommodate the Belgian—mainly Flemish—working class.
Apart from the Turkish group, there is a very strong concentration of Moroccan residents in these areas. While the Turks dominate Schaerbeek and Saint-Josse (to the
north), the Moroccan population dominates Anderlecht and Molenbeek (to the west).

Since the mid-1990s, the immigrant-origin electorate (migrating from countries
outside the current European Union), predominantly living in these poor neighborhoods and increasingly acquiring Belgian state citizenship (and thus voting rights
on all levels), has been given increasing attention by political parties. In the neighborhoods with high concentrations of immigrants—which, as we have said, tend to
largely overlap with the poor areas of the city—there have been very lively and

cartography: Jacobs - ULB

disfavoured neighbourhoods in the Brussels Capital Region
(based on calculations by Jacobs & Swyngedouw (2002)
using the 1991 Census data)

Figure 2.   Disadvantaged neighborhoods in the Brussels Capital Region. For the methodology concerning the identification of disfavored neighborhoods, see Dirk Jacobs and Marc Swyngedouw, "Een nieuwe blik op achtergestelde buurten in het Brussels Hoofdstedelijk Gewest" [A New Look at Disfavoured Neighbourhoods in the Brussels Capital Region], *Tijdschrift voor Sociologie*, Vol.21, No.3 (2000), pp.197–228.

intense campaigns of all parties. Indeed, since 1999 it is really only in the immigrant neighborhoods of Brussels that one cannot help noticing when elections are being held. It is worth noting that many shops in these areas displayed posters of immigrant-origin candidates from different political parties in the same window, predominantly of candidates of the same ethnic background, but also candidates of different ethnic backgrounds (and parties). Indeed, street-level campaigning in immigrant neighborhoods seemed to be both relying on ethnic and anti-racist discourses.

Immigrant-origin politicians have become steadily more and more successful in Brussels.[6] A number of reasons can be highlighted for this development. First of all, there is the increased demographic weight of immigrants among the electorate. Secondly, there is increased attention of political parties for this immigrant-origin electorate. Finally, the preferential and proportional voting system in Belgian elections allows for effective mobilization of minority candidates.

In the local elections of 1994, out of a total of 651 elected councilors, 14 were of non-EU origin (2.1 percent). The next year, in the regional elections of 1995, out of a total of 75 members of the Brussels Regional Parliament, four candidates of foreign origin (three Moroccan and one Tunisian) were elected into Parliament (5.3 percent). After the 1999 regional elections, no less than eight members of the Brussels Parliament (or 10.6 percent) were of foreign origin. All were actually Belgian-Maghrebians (7 of Moroccan and one of Tunisian origin) origin. In the 2000 local elections, a striking number of 90 (or 13.8 percent) of the 652 elected councilors were of non-EU immigrant, mainly Maghrebian, origin.[7] Not surprisingly, in the 2004 regional elections, Belgians of non-EU immigrant background once again played a prominent role in electoral campaigns and had quite some electoral success. Of the 72 Francophone members of the Brussels regional parliament, 17 were of non-EU origin. Among them, 12 were of Moroccan origin, 2 of Turkish origin, 1 of Tunisian origin, 1 of Congolese origin and 1 of Guinean origin. Of the 17 Flemish members of the Brussels regional parliament, one was of Moroccan origin. In total, 20.2 percent of the 89 regional MPs were of non-EU immigrant origin. In addition, the growing success of politicians of immigrant origin was translated into executive power. On the local level, following the 2000 local elections, 12 politicians of immigrant (Moroccan, Turkish and Congolese) origin have become aldermen.[8] In 2004, a Francophone politician of Turkish origin (Mr. Emir Kır) was appointed secretary of state in the Brussels government.[9] At the same time, a person of Moroccan origin (Mrs. Fadila Laanan) was appointed as Minister of French Culture, Youth and Public Broadcasting in the government of the French Community of Belgium, while a Brussels politician of Congolese origin was appointed as secretary of state for Family Affairs at the federal level (Mrs. Gisèle Mandaila).

Notwithstanding that Brussels in 2005 does have a deputy-minister of Turkish descent, judging from an overall perspective and comparison with the Moroccan group, the Turkish community is in relative terms still underrepresented in the political sphere in the Brussels-Capital region. How can this be explained? One potential explanation might be the level of associational involvement of the Turkish community, as suggested by the Dutch political scientists Fennema and Tillie.[10] Before we look into this hypothesis, we will first discuss the characteristics of Turkish associational life in Brussels.

Turkish Associational Life in Brussels

In her study of Turkish associational and political life in Germany, political scientist Betigül Ercan Argun suggests that diaspora associations are better organized, more vocal and more visible when they are grounded in more permissive political environments in host countries than in the country of origin.[11] In this sense, discursive practices and political activities in diasporas "may be treated as accentuated extensions of the civil society of origin and its public sphere."[12] Argun even argues that it makes sense to investigate Turkish civil society outside of Turkish national boundaries to gain a better understanding of civil society and politics in Turkey proper. She therefore opted for a seemingly twisted research strategy of studying "Deutschkei"—an inventive amalgam of the German words "Deutschland" and "Türkei"—to learn more about Turkish politics. Argun convincingly points to one very striking and important example of the importance of the transnational flow of ideas, strategies, information and money for Turkish politics: in the 1990s, the privatization and commercialization of the Turkish media was triggered by a "pirate" (Germany-based) satellite TV station broadcast into Turkey. Argun equally shows that diaspora associations have played an important role in reinvigorating several Turkish political movements and parties. For instance, during the military coup in the early 1980s, all banned political parties could continue their activities in Western Europe relatively freely and have afterwards rearticulated themselves in the Turkish context. Studying the entire political spectrum is easier in the diaspora, Betigül Ercan Argun furthermore argues, since in the diaspora access and interaction between groups is facilitated by a higher density of networks. The relatively smaller size of diaspora communities would lead to the increased frequency of inter-group contacts, resulting both in integration and in visible societal polarization.

We do not believe that a study of Turkish associational life in Brussels is the best way to study Turkish civil society and Turkish politics—at least we have no intentions in that direction. We can, however, confirm that major political cleavages and ideological fault-lines of Turkish politics are equally reflected in Turkish associational life in the Belgian capital. At least, this seems to be the result of a network analysis among Turkish organizations in Brussels. Similar patterns have been observed in other European cities such as Vienna.[13]

Voluntary organizations are expected to register themselves in Belgium if they are to be recognized by law, by sending their mission statement, mentioning their organizational structure, to the Ministry of Justice for publication in the *Belgisch Staatsblad/Moniteur Belge*, the official state publication. We surveyed the Ministry of Justice online database of registered non-profit associations. In doing so, we used a number of search strings and combined them with a procedure of name recognition. We were able to trace 159 Turkish associations in the Brussels-Capital region for the period of 1998–2003. The bulk were situated in Schaerbeek (49 percent), Saint-Josse (13 percent), Brussels (12 percent) and Anderlecht (10 percent). The most important limitation to our tracing method, which is inspired by Dutch research into the registers of the Chamber of Commerce,[14] is that it is limited to registered associations. Unfortunately, there is no alternative method available which would allow us to equally trace all non-registered organizations systematically. One could argue that such organizations are of lesser importance, precisely because they have not (yet) adopted a formal legal structure. Mosques will be an important exception to this rule. Although a number of mosques have registered themselves and/or are linked to registered organizations, this is clearly not the case for all mosques in Brussels. Apart from this bias, we should equally acknowledge that registration is no guarantee for actual (ongoing) existence. There can be quite a number of "paper" or "dormant" associations in the list, since not all organizations bother to remove themselves when they cease to exist. Last but not least, it is possible that organizations which we have classified as being "Turkish" on the basis of the nationality of the board members and/or other criteria, might not be willing to label themselves as such.

Taking these caveats into account, we can say that there are relatively more Turkish than Maghrebian associations in the Brussels-Capital region. During the same period, we counted 351 Maghrebian associations in the above mentioned database. If we take the population figures of 1998 as our point of reference, this means that there was one Maghrebian association for every 196 Moroccan non-nationals, while there was one Turkish organization for every 122 Turkish non-nationals living in Brussels. For all these associations, a dataset was constructed in which the names of all members of the board were registered. Using this data, it is possible to show the existence of interlocking directorates between different associations.[15] One might assume that these interlocking directorates testify to the existence of shared interests between the interconnected organizations.[16] In Figure 3 only those Turkish associations which interlock on the board level with other associations are shown. Of all 159 organizations, 64 (or 40 percent) interlock. On the basis of our field research, the most important and most active organizations are to be found among these "interlocked" associations.

The largest chain of relations is constituted by ten organizations among which we find the Schaerbeek-based association EYAD (*Fondation internationale belgo-turque d'Entraide*). EYAD aims to associate all Turks originating from the region of Emirdağ in Turkey. As a remarkable example of transnational political activity, it can be noted that the president of EYAD, who resides in the Brussels' municipality of Schaerbeek and has a business there, has also been alderman in Emirdağ since mid-2004. He figured as a candidate for the extreme right-wing Nationalist Action Party (MHP) on an AK party-dominated local list.[17] The AK party (Justice and Development Party) has been in power in Turkey since November 2002. In Belgium, EYAD has endorsed both socialist (left-wing) and liberal (right-wing) candidates at local and regional elections. In the largest chain we equally find the *Centre d'Information et de Dialogue Islamique* (CIDI), which has ties to PRIZMA (Prizma Egitim Merkezi), an association linked to the *Nurcular* fraternity of Fetullah Gülen. The people of PRIZMA have in 2003 successfully opened up a Turkish–Flemish school in Schaerbeek (and the Flemish cities of Antwerp, Ghent and Genk). The Turkish business association BETIAD[18] is, through a link with an organization focusing on immigrants for the Bayat area, equally linked to this largest chain of interlocked organizations.

Next to this large chain, we find a number of "cliques" (mini-networks of mutually interrelated associations), as for instance around the left-leaning association

Accueil, Orientation et Aide (AOA)
Fédération turco-héllénique
ISPAT
SIMA / Turk-Danis
CCS Jeunesse Araméenne
Centre culturel et sportif d'Urhoy
Fédération des Araméens (Syriaques) de Belgique
FC Suryoyés Bruxellois
Centre culturel et sportif du Tour-Abdin
Mohammed Ali
Ehli Beyit Dayanasma Der Negi
Gestion Halal (Gestion de l'EMB)
Islam Vlaanderen
Moslimexecutieve
Federatie van de Islamitische Kultuurverenigingen in België (BIF)
Communauté musulmane de Belgique, "CMB"
Association de l'Union de l'Islam de Bruxelles
Association sociale et culturelle des Travailleurs turcs résidant en Belgique
Fondation religieuse islamique turque en Belgique (DIYANET)
Vereniging van de Turkse Islamitische Godsdienstleerkrachten van België

Association Internationale Belgo-Turque d'Entraide, et de Solidarité de Bayat et de sa Région
Betiad, Association d'Entrepreneurs belges et turcs
PRISMA (Prizma Egitim Merkezi)
Centre d'Information et de Dialogue islamique — Samanyolu
Centre de Recherche de la Communauté turque de Belgique
Fondation internationale belgo-turque d'Entraide (EYAD) — Papatya
Groupe d'assistance culturelle et sociale des Travailleurs turcs résidant en Belgique
Sportif SK — Groupe des Jeunes, en abrégé "Gözde"
Brussels UTD
Association culturelle belgo-turque (ACBT) — Yuvam — Amitié belgo-turc
Le Bridge Club
Top Musique
Firikli Genclik
Vereniging van de Atatürkgedachte Hoofdstad-Brussel
Association de la Pensée d'Atatürk de Belgique (APAB)
Le Tekilla
European Association of Turkish Academics (EATA)
Association féminine belgo-turque "A.F.B.T."
Dostlar Kosesi Saz Grubu
Belgika Turk Dostluk Dernegi (BTDD - voorheen FSTB)
L'Association culturelle turque
Het Verbond der Turkse Verenigingen in Belgie (Belçika Türk Federasyonu - BTF)
Fondation islamique d'Education culturelle turque et de Sécurité sociale

SILA
F.C. Molenbeek-Turk
Club Nur — Uluday (Aksany)
Sivrihisar — F.C. Mizizah
FC Kaldirim — Aydin
Antalya Club
F.C. Azeri
Anadolu
Deniz — Cukurova
Ozgur — Akdeniz
FC Kayseri

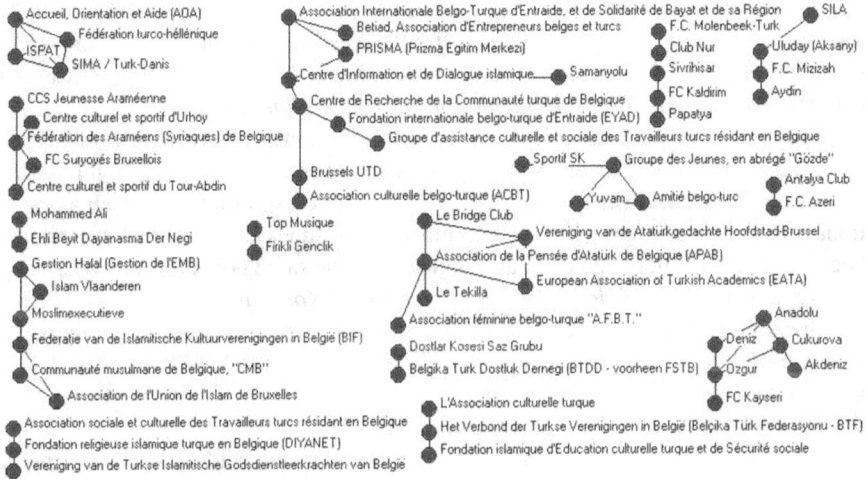

Figure 3. Interlocking directorates between Turkish associations in the Brussels-Capital Region (1998–2003). Formal associational links between Turkish associations in the Brussels Capital region (1998–2003). *Data source:* Moniteur Belge/Belgisch Staatsblad. Data collection by Eric Cillessen, Fran Vandenberghe and Dirk Jacobs. Network analysis by Dirk Jacobs.

SIMA/Türk Danis in Saint-Josse or around the secular-nationalist *Association of Ataturkist Thought*. We equally notice a small chain of ultranationalist organizations in Brussels around the central organization Belçika Türk Federasyonu (BTF), the Gray Wolves associated with the ultranationalist party MHP.[19] DIYANET (*Fondation religieuse islamique turque en Belgique*), the Turkish Directorate of Religious Affairs, is interconnected with the association of Turkish-Islamic teachers of religion and is officially designated to be the mother organization of the socially active *Association sociale et culturelle des Travailleurs turcs*. We further notice that the Islamists of the Islamic Federation of Belgium (BIF), *Milli Görüş*, had a firm presence in the pre-2005 representative body for Muslim affairs in Belgium. There are also a number of dyads (pair relations) between a number of Turkish football clubs and other associations. There is equally a small network of *Arameic* organizations. Ninety-five Turkish associations are isolated—at least when using the criterion of formal interlocking directorates. This does not mean that these internally unconnected organizations are all unimportant organizations. There are a number of social democratic organizations, Alevi associations and extreme left-wing organizations which are isolated in our network analysis but do have visible activities. Kurdish organizations, for example, are also not present in Figure 3, although they can at times be quite active in Brussels. The *Kurdish Institute*, which is equally very active with regard to the issue of immigrant integration and language acquisition, has for instance been able to attract considerable Belgian and European attention to the Kurdish issue.[20]

It is clear that the formal interlocking directorates only give an indication—albeit a strong one—with regard to patterns of collaboration between Turkish organizations. They do not tell us the entire story. Judging by the network figure, it might perhaps seem as if DIYANET (*Fondation religieuse islamique turque en Belgique*) does not have a very central role in the Turkish community in Brussels, while it is in fact quite an influential actor. Neither can the formal network analysis highlight the discrete influence the Turkish consular services try to exert on the Turkish associational fabric. As we have noted, a number of mosques do not enter our picture because they have not been officially registered. The same holds for an ultranationalist organization like *Belçika Türk Federasyonları Koordinasyon Kurulu* (BTKK), which claims to federate 93 organizations, which has refrained from officially registering itself during our research period. This organization has in the past had a number of joint activities with diverse kinds of associations such as the *Association of Ataturkist Thought*, EYAD or DIYANET. We, for instance, equally know of documented joint activities against the Armenian genocide monument in the Brussels municipality of Ixelles by left-leaning *Ataturkists* connected to the student organization EATA[21] and ultranationalist MHP members, which are not reflected in the network figure.

Explaining Political Participation by Looking at Associational Involvement?

Dutch political scientists Fennema and Tillie[22] maintain that differences in the political participation of ethnic minorities are related to differences in "civic community," interpreted as the amount of "ethnic" social capital (participation in ethnic associational life) of the particular group. In their research on Amsterdam, Fennema and Tillie have found an interesting correlation at the *aggregate (group) level* between political participation and political trust of ethnic minorities, on the one hand, and the network of ethnic associations on the other. For instance, Turks in Amsterdam have a denser network of associations than Moroccans. Turks at the same time have been documented to have more political trust and a larger participation in the political field (e.g. voting behavior in local elections) than Moroccans. Similar aggregate-level results, linking associational networks and political participation, have been found for Surinamese and Antilleans. Fennema and Tillie claim—but do not prove—that there is a causal link underlying this correlation. Inspired by Putnam,[23] they argue that voluntary associations create social trust, which spills over into political trust and higher political participation. In addition, they claim that a network of organizations further increases political trust through interlocking directorates. In this context, they speak about the degree of civic community within ethnic groups—or "ethnic civic community"—as a basis for political trust and political participation.[24]

Data from several Western European cities show that Turkish immigrants in the European Union tend to have a strong associational life, dense social networks and a strong sense of community. It has been documented that ethnic membership levels are high for Turks in Belgium (35 percent),[25] Germany (31 percent)[26] and Denmark

(32 percent).[27] Although the membership level is lower in the Netherlands (11 percent), the Turks score highest on other indicators of "ethnic civic community"[28] in Amsterdam. In line with these observations and the Fennema and Tillie argument, one would expect to find high levels of political involvement of Turks in Europe.

A number of general critical remarks have been raised with regard to the limitations of the argument and research of Fennema and Tillie.[29] First of all, attention remains limited to "ethnic" social capital (embedded in ethnic associations) without taking into account forms of cross-cultural social capital (embedded in mixed and more mainstream organizations) and the relationship between these two types of social capital.[30] In addition, there is a disregard of potential differential effects according to the type of organization—participation in a sports club is different to participation in a cultural association.[31] Furthermore, there is no acknowledgement of the importance of forms of social and cultural capital which one could designate as stimulating the formation of "bridging" capital. One should think of forms of social and cultural capital which are differentially distributed amongst (ethnic) groups and are influential for integration in the "host society" (i.e. language proficiency, entrepreneurship, educational participation, etc.). Furthermore, the issue should be addressed as to why—if this is the case—there is a link between social capital (participation in associational life), political trust and political participation and whether this link is always univocal. It has to be discovered what exactly in associations is responsible for this effect. In doing this, not only do the types of organization and their activities have to be taken into account, but attention should equally be paid to different kinds of networks in which associations are potentially embedded. One can add that Fennema and Tillie have never advanced convincing data for the supposed causal argument at the individual level. Last but not least, one should look at the national and city-related processes—political opportunity structures[32]—which can lead to differential effects of associations for different groups. For instance, one cannot rule out that a typical national political opportunity structure is responsible for the phenomena which have been observed in the Netherlands.

In earlier work,[33] making use of data of the *Brussels Minorities Survey 1995* (short: BMS survey) among Moroccans, Turks and less educated Belgians, we have shown that the argument of Fennema and Tillie does not hold in a straightforward way for Brussels. In the Belgian context, it makes sense to think of the Turks (leaving the Kurds, Assyrians and Armenians aside) as constituting a genuine community. Due to chain migration from a limited number of Anatolian villages and towns, one can indeed think in terms of the existence of a Turkish community in Brussels.[34] Moreover, when we posed the question to Turks themselves in the BMS survey, 80 percent of the Turks confirmed that they see themselves as a genuine community. As another proxy for the strength of the civic community among Turks, we can take a look in the BMS data at the percentage of people who are members of (ethnic) voluntary associations. Participants reported their active membership of a list of organizations. Active membership was defined as "having participated in one or more activities of an organization over the last year." In both ethnic minority samples, a distinction was made between perceived ethnic minority and Belgian (or mixed) types of organization. A comparison of overall participation rates reveals striking ethnic differences between a very active Turkish community, somewhat less active working-class Belgians, and a much less active Moroccan community in Brussels. Over two-thirds of the Turks (68 percent) are found to participate in one or more organizations, compared to half of the Belgians (52 percent) and one-fifth of the Moroccans (19 percent). Of the Turks, 35 percent are members of a Turkish organization, while 10 percent of the Moroccans are members of a Moroccan organization. It is also interesting to note that Turks who are active in Turkish organizations tend to be active also in Belgian associational life.[35] Participation in ethnic associational life is thus not at all a zero-sum game to the detriment of cross-ethnic involvement, but is indeed often compatible with intercultural contacts. Interestingly, similar results are to be found in Berlin and Amsterdam.

Although we see a high score of Turks on a number of indicators of an "ethnic civic community," it is the Moroccans who—hitherto—have had a higher success rate of electoral involvement in Brussels.[36] With regard to general political involvement and political interest, we furthermore did not find any significant differences between Turks and Moroccans in the BMS survey.[37] Moreover, on the individual level, we did not find proof of a strong positive link between membership participation in ethnic associations as such and political involvement. Multiple linear regressions we reported on in earlier work[38] showed that the level of informal political participation among Turks is primarily explained by gender, knowledge of French, unemployment and union membership. Ethnic membership had only a minimal positive effect on informal political participation. With political interest as a dependent variable, knowledge of French appeared to be the most important explanatory factor, followed by gender. There were minor effects of unemployment and educational level but none of membership. An alternative way of putting it is that ethnic membership does at least not hinder political involvement. In any event, however, the overall conclusion can only be that further arguments show that the Fennema and Tillie hypothesis does not hold entirely, and certainly not for the Brussels case.

What can then explain the bigger political success of Moroccans compared to Turks? Most probably an important reason has to be found in the better overall knowledge of French (the dominant political language in Brussels) among the Moroccans—for whom French is equally an official language in the country of origin. As Table 1 shows, the self-reported level of knowledge is much higher among Moroccan residents than among Turkish residents in Brussels. Earlier multivariate analyses[39] have shown that proficiency in French is an important explanatory factor for political involvement. It is also quite plausible that political parties will prefer candidates who master the language of the dominant group well.

Furthermore, the Moroccans have a numerical advantage in the electoral competition in which, in the end, not the relative volume but the absolute volume of preferential voting scores is important. Belgium has a two-tier proportional electoral system (Imperiali for local elections and d'Hondt for regional and national

Table 1. Self-reported Knowledge of French (passive knowledge: understanding) of Turks and Moroccans in BMS Survey 1995 (5)

	Understands a Bit of French	Understands French Fairly Well	Understands French Well	Understands French Very Well
Turks	24.2	23.7	18.0	24.9
Moroccans	12.5	13.3	17.3	53.1

elections) in which voters can cast preferential votes for individual candidates on the list of their choice. Due to the scope of this current study, we refrain from going into the technical details, but let us stress that the system of preferential voting functions as an additional incentive for parties to offer some diversity in candidate profiles—including minority group members—to the voters. At the same time, however, it pushes political parties into privileging candidates who have a profile which is considered able to appeal to and attract the largest possible number of ethnic voters. As a result, there is some openness to minority group candidates but at the same time there will be a tendency to privilege the largest minority groups as a reservoir for candidates.

We are, however, equally inclined to stress the potential importance of the political opportunity structure in the Brussels-Capital region as far as ethnic associational life is concerned. Ethnic civic community might be neutral or detrimental for political involvement of ethnic minority groups in Brussels and the quality of ethnic associational life might have different effects for different groups, while it might be a much clearer incentive in Amsterdam. Indeed, in the Netherlands it was the official policy to integrate ethnic minority groups *as groups* and encourage self-organization as a basis for contact with the host society. Perhaps this indeed results in the fact that the degree of ethnic civic community (or ethnic associational life) is an important factor for political involvement of all ethnic minority groups. In Brussels, however, there is a much more complex policy situation to be found due to multi-leveled governance.[40] There is an important difference in the approach of the Flemish authorities and the Francophone authorities vis-à-vis immigrants and ethnic minorities. The Flemish encourage collective mobilization—as do the Dutch—and they support the self-organization of ethnic minorities. The Francophones, however, opt for an individual assimilationist approach and want to insert immigrants—and their (political) mobilization—into existing structures, organizations and networks. Overall, the (seemingly) contradictory policy schemes of the Flemish and Francophone authorities create all kinds of obstacles as well as possibilities for immigrant mobilization. Since the Francophones are, however, dominant in the Brussels-Capital region, political involvement of people from ethnic minorities is still to be seen above all as a matter of individual insertion into the Belgian Francophone system. In such a case, ethnic social capital does not necessarily enhance political involvement but could be neutral or even detrimental to it, if not combined with cross-ethnic social capital. The strong sense of community of the Turks might be a disadvantage when Belgian political parties prefer to negotiate with isolated individuals rather than with entire organizations or a strong community.

An alternative (and competing) explanation would be another variant of the social capital thesis, stressing differences of network structures of interconnected Turkish and Moroccan organizations. In trying to save the ethnic civic community argument when faced with seemingly falsifying data, Tillie suggests that there might be an interaction effect between the impact of individual membership of an ethnic association, on the one hand, and the position of this ethnic association in a wider network of organizations, on the other.[41] Membership of an isolated organization or a less-interconnected organization might be less of an incentive towards successful political involvement than membership of an organization which is part of a dense network. This hypothesis could function as a last resort to explain why a relatively larger number of Turkish organizations in Brussels leads to less successful political participation, while still holding on to the Fennema and Tillie perspective.

Let us look into the plausibility of this kind of alternative explanation by comparing network structures for Turks and Moroccans in Brussels. Figure 4 shows the interlocking directorates for all interconnected Moroccan organizations (39 percent of 351). We notice that there is one large network of which 14 percent of all Moroccan associations are members. The older left-leaning organizations *Avicenne*

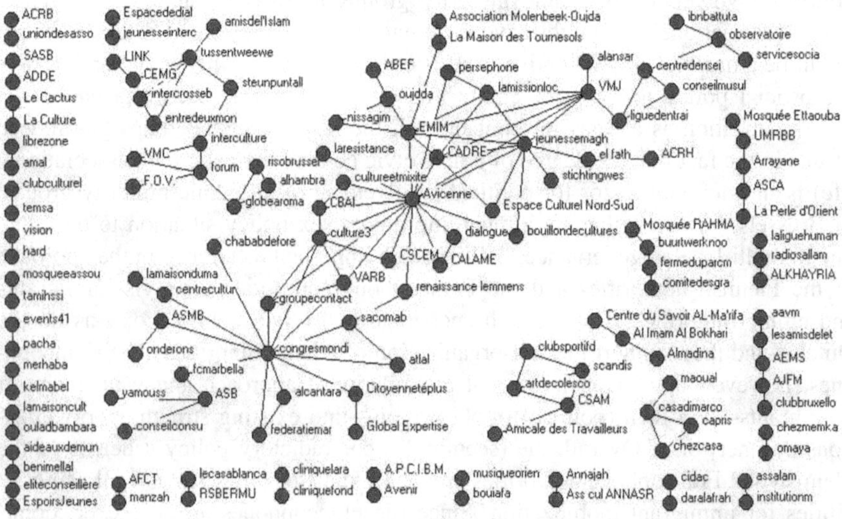

Figure 4.   Interlocking directorates between Maghrebian associations in the Brussels-Capital region (1998–2003). *Data source:* Moniteur Belge/Belgisch Staatsblad. Data collection by Tomas Debroyer, Mieke Beckers, Julie Brant and Eric Cillessen. Network analysis by Dirk Jacobs.

and *Jeunesse Maghrébinne* have pivotal positions, just as the young association *EMIM* (*Espace Mémorial de l'Immigration Marocaine*), which was set up in 2001 in order to prepare the commemoration of the 40th anniversary of the Belgian–Moroccan bilateral agreement on foreign labor. Organizations such as *Vereniging van Marokkaanse jongeren* (VMJ-AJM) and *Congrès mondial des Marocains de l'étranger* also fulfill important bridge functions.

One might now hypothesize that the more densely interconnected part of Moroccan associational life (Figure 4) is more effective in resorting to political involvement than the more fragmented Turkish associational life (Figure 3). Ethnic civic community—and more particularly the network structure within ethnic communities—would then, after all, still be able to explain observed patterns of political involvement in Brussels. This explanation seems to be fairly far-fetched, especially if we keep in mind that only 10 percent of all Moroccans are members of Moroccan associations while 35 percent of the Turks are members of a Turkish association. At the moment, however, it cannot be ruled out completely either since we do not (yet) have qualified data—survey material in which we know the exact names of associations of which they are members—to refute the hypothesis.

Conclusion and Debate

Judging on the basis of results from existing studies, there does not seem to be a strong empirical link between levels of social capital—operationalized as associational involvement and network density of associations—on the one hand and political participation of immigrant-origin groups on the other. Until now, Amsterdam is the only place where such a link has been noted—and then only on the aggregate level. Perhaps this is not so surprising. Social capital is merely one of the factors contributing to integration and participation of immigrant-origin groups. Educational level seems to be a much more important element of integration and participation—equally comprising political participation. It is education which leads to sufficient "bridging" capital such as language skills and general knowledgeability on how to live in a place like Belgium.

In Belgium, social mobility is increasingly embedded in individual models of achievement and less and less linked to group models. The Turkish model of collective interest representation might have become less effective and more poorly adapted in the Brussels context with regard to political influence. The Brussels Minorities Survey showed that Moroccans opt more for individual strategies for social mobility than Turks do. Perhaps this strategic difference explains the large(r) success of individual Moroccan candidates. Turkish immigrants tend to do more poorly with regard to the linguistic command of French, which gives the group an additional disadvantage. If Turkish immigrants wish to improve their integration in the political field in Brussels, they probably should not merely rely on their strong associational life and group strength. They should equally invest more in individual success. Undoubtedly, better language acquisition and better performance in the educational arena are key elements to achieve this.

Notes

1. K. Phalet and M. Swyngedouw, "Measuring Immigrant Integration: The case of Belgium," in C. Bonifazi and S. Strozza (eds.), *Integration of Migrants in Europe: Data Sources and Measurement in Old and New Receiving Countries*. Special issue of *Migration Studies—Studi Emigrazione*, Vol.XL, No.152 (2003), pp.773–803.
2. Meindert Fennema and Jean Tillie, "Political Participation and Political Trust in Amsterdam. Civic Communities and Ethnic Networks," *Journal of Ethnic and Migration Studies*, Vol.25, No.4 (1999), pp.703–26.
3. *Jus soli* is the Latin concept for rights which are acquired as a result of one's place of birth and/or residence.
4. In 2002, there were 47,657 Moroccan residents not holding Belgian nationality and 13,577 Turkish residents not holding Belgian nationality in Brussels. In 1999, there were 63,809 Moroccan non-nationals and 18,678 Turkish non-nationals in the Belgian capital. The striking difference between the figures is not due to emigration but to nationality acquisition.
5. Chris Kesteloot, Katrien Peleman and Trees Roesems, "Terres d'exil en Belgique" [Territories of Exile in Belgium], in M.T. Coenen and R. Lewin (eds.), *La Belgique et ses immigrés—Les politiques manquées* [Belgium and its Immigrants—Missed Policies] (Bruxelles: De Boeck-Université, 1997), pp.25–43.
6. Hassan Bousetta, Sonja Gsir and Dirk Jacobs, *Active Civic Participation of Immigrants in Belgium*, Country Report prepared for the European research project POLITIS, Oldenburg, 2005, available online at: http://www.uni-oldenburg.de/politis-europe.
7. Dirk Jacobs, Marco Martiniello and Andrea Rea, "Changing Patterns of Political Participation of Citizens of Immigrant Origin in the Brussels Capital Region: The October 2000 Elections," *Journal of International Migration and Integration/Revue de l'intégration et de la migration internationale*, Vol.3, No.2 (2002), pp.201–21.
8. On the municipal level, the mayor and a number of aldermen—each of whom have their own specific policy field—hold executive power. Their policy has to be endorsed by the municipal councilors.
9. D. Jacobs and M. Swyngedouw, "Territorial and Non-territorial Federalism: Reform of the Brussels Capital Region, 2001," *Regional and Federal Studies*, Vol.13, No.2 (2003), pp.127–39.
10. Meindert Fennema and Jean Tillie, "Civic Community, Political Participation and Political Trust of Ethnic Groups," *Connections*, Vol.24, No.1 (2001), pp.26–41.
11. Betigül Ercan Argun, *Turkey in Germany: The Transnational Sphere of Deutschkei* (New York and London: Routledge, 2003), p.199.
12. Ibid., p.5.
13. Karin Sohler, "Turkish and Kurdish Migrants' Associations in the Austrian and Viennese Context: Development, Structure and Relevance for Civic and Political Participation," Paper for the Conference on "Integration of Immigrants from Turkey in Austria, Germany and the Netherlands," Boğaziçi University, Istanbul, February 27–28, 2004.
14. Anja Van Heelsum, *Marokkaanse Organisaties in Nederland, een netwerkanalyse* [Moroccan Organizations in the Netherlands: A Network Analysis] (Amsterdam: Het Spinhuis, 2001); Anja Van Heelsum, *Turkse Organisaties in Amsterdam, een netwerkanalyse* [Turkish Organizations in the Netherlands: A Network Analysis] (Amsterdam: Het Spinhuis, 2001).
15. Network analysis was performed using S. Borgatti, M. Everett and L. Freeman, *UCINET 6 for Windows* (Harvard: Analytic Technologies, 2002).
16. D. Knoke and J. Kuklinski, *Network Analysis. Quantitative Applications in the Social Sciences* (London: Sage, 1982).
17. Dirk Jacobs, Eric Cillessen and Mehmet Koksal, "Une communauté interconnectée" [An Interconnected Community], *Politique*, Vol.36 (2004), pp.22–5.
18. Belçika Türk İşadamları Derneği [Belgian Turkish Business Association].
19. It may be noted that the Islamist-nationalists sympathizers of the Big Unity Party (BBP), organized in Europe through the European Turkish-Islamic Union of Cultural Associations (ATIB), seem to be more active in Antwerp and Limburg than in Brussels.

20. http://www.kurdishinstitute.be.
21. European Association of Turkish Academics (Avrupa Türk Akademisyenler Birliǒi Belçika).
22. Fennema and Tillie (1999 and 2001).
23. Robert Putnam, *Making Democracy Work. Civic Traditions in Modern Italy* (Princeton, NJ: Princeton University Press, 1993).
24. Fennema and Tillie (1999 and 2001).
25. Jacobs *et al.* (2004), p.546.
26. Maria Berger, Christian Galonska and Ruud Koopmans, "Political Integration by a Detour? Ethnic Communities and Social Capital of Migrants in Berlin," *Journal of Ethnic and Migration Studies*, Vol.30, No.3 (2004), pp.491–508.
27. Lise Togeby, "It Depends … How Organizational Participation affects Political Participation and Social Trust among Second-generation Immigrants in Denmark," *Journal of Ethnic and Migration Studies*, Vol.30, No.3 (2004), pp.509–28.
28. Jean Tillie, "Social Capital of Organizations and their Members: Explaining the Political Integration of Immigrants in Amsterdam," *Journal of Ethnic and Migration Studies*, Vol.30, No.3 (2004), pp.529–42.
29. Dirk Jacobs and Jean Tillie, "Introduction: Social Capital and Political Integration of Migrants," *Journal of Ethnic and Migration Studies*, Vol.30, No.3 (2004), pp.419–27.
30. Karen Phalet and Marc Swyngedouw, "National Identities and Representations of Citizenship: A Comparison of Turks, Moroccans and Working-Class Belgians in Brussels," *Ethnicities*, Vol.2, No.1 (2002), pp.5–30.
31. Marc Hooghe, "Waardencongruentie binnen vrijwillige verenigingen: een sociaal-psychologisch verklaringsmodel voor de interactie van zelfselectie en socialisering" [Congruence of values in associations: a socio-psychological explanatory model for the interaction of self selection and socialization], *Mens en maatschappij*, Vol.76, No.2 (2001), pp.102–20.
32. Ruud Koopmans and Paul Statham, "Migration and Ethnic Relations as a Field of Political Contention: An Opportunity Structure Approach," in R. Koopmans and P. Statham (eds.), *Challenging Immigration and Ethnic Relations Politics. Comparative European Perspectives* (Oxford: Oxford University Press, 2000), pp.14–56.
33. Dirk Jacobs, Karen Phalet and Marc Swyngedouw, "Associational Membership and Political Involvement among Ethnic Minority Groups in Brussels," *Journal of Ethnic and Migration Studies*, Vol.30, No.3 (2004), pp.543–59.
34. A. Manco and U. Manco, *Turcs de Belgique. Identités et trajectoires d'une minorité* [Turks of Belgium. Identities and Trajectories of a Minority] (Brussels: Info-Türk, 1992).
35. Correlation between cross-ethnic and ethnic participation: r=0.52, p-value < 0.0001.
36. An exception is, however, constituted by the 2005 election of the representative council of Belgian Muslims, in which the Turks were much more successful than the Moroccans, of whom many faithful Muslims decided to boycott the elections.
37. See Jacobs *et al.* (2004).
38. Ibid.
39. Ibid.
40. Dirk Jacobs, "Multinational and Polyethnic Politics Entwined: Minority Representation in the Region of Brussels-Capital," *Journal of Ethnic and Migration Studies*, Vol.26, No.2 (2000), pp.289–304.
41. Tillie (2004).

Conclusion

REFİK ERZAN* & KEMAL KİRİŞCİ**

*Department of Economics, Boğaziçi University, Istanbul, Turkey, **Department of Political Science, Boğaziçi University, Istanbul, Turkey

Determinants of Immigration

In a historical perspective, demographic differentials, if not the most important causes of migration, are certainly counted among them. However, Cem Behar challenged the idea of a "complementarity" between a "young" Turkey and an "older" Europe. This, he demonstrated, was due to two simple facts: young immigrants required to prevent ageing and population decline would have to make up an unrealistically large flow—and the immigrant population itself would be ageing in the host country. Nevertheless, studying the demographic trends Behar argued that managing migration would soon become a European priority—rather than trying to prevent it. Europe will have to consider these temporary demographic differentials an advantage and make migration a socially and politically acceptable issue. In fact, many EU countries are embarking upon a revision of their immigration policies in the face of acute labor shortages in areas such as health care and IT services.

In light of the demographic imbalances, Refik Erzan, Umut Kuzubaş and Nilüfer Yıldız attempted to estimate the magnitude of eventual Turkish immigration that would actually take place when Turkey becomes a full EU member. Essentially,

Correspondence Address: Refik Erzan, Department of Economics, Center for Economics and Econometrics, Boğaziçi University, 34342 Bebek, Istanbul, Turkey. Email: erzan@boun.edu.tr; Kemal Kirişci, Department of Political Science, Director of the Center for European Studies, Boğaziçi University, 34342 Bebek, Istanbul, Turkey. Email: kirisci@boun.edu.tr

they relied on the experience of countries that joined the EU. Their estimates for net migration from Turkey to the EU15 in the period 2004–30 was between 1 and 2 million, foreseeing a successful accession period with high growth and free labor mobility starting 2015—a rather optimistic assumption to explore the upper bound of the immigration potential.

Erzan *et al.* argued that any slowdown or suspension in Turkey's accession process would likely lead to lower growth and higher unemployment in Turkey. Moreover, the reform process might slow down or be partially reversed. They demonstrated that the consequence of such a combination would be a drastically higher number of potential migrants. It is thus possible that if Turkey loses the prospect of membership, the EU may end up having more immigrants than under a free movement of labor regime with a prosperous EU member Turkey. Moreover, the composition of this migration would be less conducive for the EU labor markets—and for integration in the host societies. The experiences of Greece, Portugal and Spain indicated that a successful accession period with high growth and effective implementation of the reforms reduced and gradually eliminated the migration pressures. Erzan *et al.* conclude that there is no *a priori* reason why Turkey would not go through a similar experience.

While the Erzan *et al.* study pursued the econometric route, Hubert Krieger and Bertrand Maître analyzed migration trends in "an enlarging European Union" based on *Eurobarometer* survey data collected for the European Commission. They analyzed potential migration towards the old EU15 from three regions: the ten new members, the two accession countries entering in 2007—Romania and Bulgaria—and Turkey.

Krieger and Maître found that the Turkish respondents topped the list of all 13 countries as far as "the general intention" to migrate was concerned and were nearly at the bottom of the list concerning a "firm intention." In terms of the Turkish migration potential, over five years under the condition of free mobility this would imply a migration potential between 3.03 million for the general intention and 0.15 million for the firm intention. Using a "more realistic" third indicator, the "basic intention to migrate," they predicted a migration potential of around 0.4 million Turkish migrants over five years in the EU15. This result is compatible with the estimates of Erzan *et al.* predicting a total of 1 to 2 million migrants over a longer horizon—with a front loaded flow.

As to the socio-economic structure of potential migrants compared to the Central and Eastern Europeans, Krieger and Maître found a stronger rural background among the Turks, more often in the lowest income quartile and a higher mobility among the unemployed. On the positive side concerning labor market integration in the receiving countries, potential Turkish migrants had the highest proportion with university degrees and a significant segment was still studying. They concluded that all in all the structural patterns in Poland and Turkey were quite similar.

Determinants of Integration

As Wets and Avcı amply highlight in their contributions, what constitutes "integration" is highly contested and the term itself is difficult to define. Nevertheless, the ability and the level of participation in the host society's labor market are considered as one of the important measures of integration. Similarly, the level and form of participation by the immigrants in the local and national political systems is considered as another measure of integration. Yet as important as these two areas of integration, if not more so, is the educational performance of immigrants and their children. This is critical because it is the level of education that strongly determines linguistic capabilities and general development. An immigrant's prospect of employment and participation in social and political life of the host society is very closely related to the immigrant's command of the local language and the quality of the education the immigrant attains.

The picture in respect of Turkish immigrants is a complex as well as dynamic one. One distinguishing aspect of this complexity is that an important proportion of Turkish immigrants experience serious problems of integration. As all the authors of the second part of this volume have pointed out, unemployment, with the exception of Austria, is very high and endemic among Turkish immigrants compared to the locals of the host society and other comparable immigrant communities. Regarding education, with the exception of some, most children of Turkish immigrants do not perform well at school and lack proficiency in local languages. This complicates their ability to perform well on the job market as well as hindering their better participation in social and political aspects of life in their host societies. Furthermore, with the exception of Austria, generous social welfare arrangements lead to an "unemployment trap." This provokes alienation and exacerbates the integration problems they already face, leading to allegations that immigrant youth and their parents withdraw into parallel, ghetto-like societies. This fuels anti-immigrant feelings and prejudice in host societies, often provoking intolerance and discrimination against Turkish immigrants. This in turn is translated into fears about Turkey and Turks in general and a widely held resistance to Turkish membership.

There are, though, some signs of hope. Avcı as well as Söhn and Özcan report very modest signs of improvement in respect of the educational performance of second and third generation immigrant children. In Germany, for example, compared to their predecessors, second and third generation immigrants are able to make it to better schools and they are also more likely to complete their schooling. Some even make it to university. Looking at employment, Avcı reports a growing level of self-employment and establishment of small businesses that in itself is a sign of a certain level of capital accumulation and economic dynamism. However, it should be noted, some see this development as one that accentuates isolation from the host society rather than as a sign of integration. In respect of political participation Jacobs, Phalet and Swyngedouw together with Avcı note how Turkish immigrants have a very lively associational life, often livelier than locals and other immigrant communities. Yet these authors do suggest that this political participation is often geared toward either the intra-Turkish immigrant community or homeland political activity. They add that at least as far as the Brussels region is concerned, compared to Moroccans Turks lag behind in respect of gaining political office at the local and regional level.

Notwithstanding the "signs of hope" and those Turkish immigrants that do and have integrated, why do many of them fail to integrate? There is now a wide body of literature that documents the "failure" of Turks and Turkish immigrants in integrating themselves into their respective host societies. Most of this literature is, however, of a descriptive nature and often falls short of providing a parsimonious explanation. Undoubtedly, the answer to the question is a complicated one. Yet one common denominator to all the studies in the second part of this volume is the importance they attribute to the role of education. Poor educational performance appears to be one of the leading causes behind the poor integration of Turkish immigrants, at least with regard to labor markets, social life and also participation in local and national politics. Then the inevitable question is to ask why there is a poor educational performance and what is the link between poor education and integration in general.

Söhn and Özcan seek an explanation for the poor educational performance of Turkish children in the structure of the German educational system. They underline the importance of good knowledge of German for successful studies. In that respect they add how important pre-school is for acquiring the German language, especially for children whose parents do not know German and sometimes have not even had any schooling themselves. The absence of proper command of German plays a critical role in the placement of the majority of Turkish children in *Hauptschule* rather than *Realschule*, which provides better prospects for vocational training, or *Gymnasium*, which opens the way to university studies. Many Turkish children fail to complete even *Hauptschule*. Söhn and Özcan also note the parents' lack of knowledge of the German schooling system and often their associated poor socio-economic background plays a critical role in this situation as they fail to manipulate the German schooling system to the advantage of their children. This is aggravated by the fact that the German school system to this day remains ill-prepared to deal with "second language" learners. This is particularly conspicuous in the case of gifted children with language difficulties who fail to receive any special attention. Overall, Söhn and Özcan underline that socio-economic factors play a critical role in the emergence of ethnically segregated schools as middle-class German families knowledgeable of the schooling system send their children to better schools while immigrant children congregate in disadvantaged schools.

Poor educational performance is aggravated by the common practice of arranged marriages. As Timmerman notes, arranged marriages have become one of the sole means for foreigners to settle in Belgium. She argues that such marriages aggravate the integration problem precisely because the bride or groom arriving from Turkey has no or extremely limited knowledge of the local language. The absence of language plays an important role in respect of participation in the life of the host society and integration in general. It also renders the socialization of future generations difficult as absence of language and knowledge about the host society stands as a major obstacle in the way of the parents' ability to ensure a decent level of education for their children. Timmerman also notes that the fact that host societies render Turkish qualifications and work experience irrelevant and worthless aggravates the situation. A further complication, she notes, arises from the strong sense of national identity that Turkish nationalism engenders.

There are clearly multiple reasons for the poor educational performance and language acquisition of Turkish immigrants. The consequence of this poor performance is poor participation in the labor market. Avcı and Wets have highlighted this situation in their respective studies. Jacobs, Phalet and Swyngedouw note the lively associational life of Turkish immigrants compared to the poor performance in local elections in the Brussels region. They attribute this difference, partly, to a lack of linguistic capabilities that makes it more difficult for Turks to operate beyond the Turkish-based associational political life and mobilize non-Turks, be they other immigrants or locals. It is interesting to note that those Turkish immigrants who have done well in local, national and EU-level politics are Turks with a good command of the local language and higher levels of education. Undoubtedly, education is not the sole parameter for explaining the poor performance of the integration of Turkish immigrants. Yet it can be argued that education is an important and necessary but not sufficient condition for better integration and participation in the host society.

Integration as a Three Way Process

In the course of a decade or so there has been a growing recognition that for integration to occur both the immigrants and the host society have to make an effort. This has been reflected in the notion that integration is a "two way process" and has also been acknowledged and stressed at the EU level. Avcı provides a survey of how German and Dutch immigration policies have evolved and have increasingly come to stress governmental policies to encourage and in some cases even "coerce" integration. Attendance at "integration courses" and signing of "integration contracts" have been two methods with which some EU governments have tried to contribute to the idea of integration being a "two way" process. In the case of Austria, Wets shows how the government there has tried to promote integration by "coercive measures." This has involved the threat not to renew work and residence permits in case of persistent unemployment and the denial of naturalization in the event that one fails language and culture tests. Wets notes that compared to the Netherlands these "coercive measures" have ensured lower levels of unemployment. However, Wets adds that these measures have forced immigrants to be stuck in low paid and low skill jobs rather than encourage their integration.

Implicit in the idea of integration being a "two way process" is that the host society would play a welcoming or at least facilitating role in the integration of immigrants. Yet Timmerman and Wets note that the intolerance and racism expressed towards immigrants aggravates the problem of integration. This is exacerbated by the growth of a politics that emphasizes anti-immigrant discourses, especially in the Netherlands and France. The violence that erupted in France in November 2005 has generally been attributed to the French government and French public's discriminatory treatment of particularly North African immigrant youth.

Many of the immigrants that rioted in France were actually French nationals and generally had a good command of French and a reasonably decent level of education. Hence the notion of extending citizenship has not necessarily been a panacea. Instead, as Avcı and Wets point out, locals have tended to employ derogatory terms towards naturalized immigrants by referring to them as "pass Belgians" or "pass Germans." Such terms do reflect locals' questioning of the immigrants' entitlement to citizenship as well as emphasizing their "otherness." Such attitudes undoubtedly complicate the problem of integration and seriously undermine the notion of integration being a "two way process."[1] Naturally, for the "two way process" to really be a two way process in the positive sense of the word such racism and intolerance would need to weaken.

On the other hand, the "two way process" approach on its own may not necessarily be adequate. Such an approach completely ignores the positive role that sending countries with their governments and civil societies could play. Actually, implicit in the "two way" approach is the idea that both sending governments and civil societies only aggravate the integration problem. This need not be the case.

Traditionally, the Turkish government has been seen in Europe as part of the problem. The Turkish teachers and religious leaders that were sent by the Turkish government on the basis of bilateral agreements lacked knowledge about their host societies and the local language. Many host governments also felt that by accentuating the cultural elements of the homeland these officials were actually undermining, if not complicating, integration. On the other hand, the authoritative nature of Turkish politics was also leading to the organization in Europe of fringe and radical groups from both the Right and the Left. This not only encouraged cleavages within the Turkish community but also often prevented Turkish immigrants from becoming engaged in local civil society. Furthermore, non-governmental organizations supported by the Turkish government tried to control the public space of Turkish immigrants not covered by radical and fringe groups.

This situation is changing. The current government in Turkey has on a number of occasions highlighted the importance of the integration of Turkish immigrants in Europe. The Turkish Prime Minister, Tayyip Erdoğan, during his visit to Germany, underlined the importance of taking up local citizenship, learning the local language and participating in local politics. He argued that it is possible to integrate into host societies without compromising one's cultural identity.[2] Similarly, in a very eloquent speech the Minister of State responsible for religious affairs and Turks living abroad, Mehmet Aydın, also stressed the importance of integration of Turks into their respective host societies and stressed that in a multicultural framework this was perfectly possible.[3] In an unprecedented manner the Turkish parliament adopted in December 2003 an extensive report investigating the problems of Turkish nationals living abroad. The report emphasized the importance of language skills and education. It elaborated on a list of recommendations to encourage and facilitate the integration of Turkish nationals into their host societies.[4]

During a series of conferences held at Boğaziçi University focusing on the problems of Turkish immigrants in EU countries, numerous participants, including government officials representing the Ministry of Education, Ministry of Labor and Social Security and the General Directorate of Religious Affairs acknowledged that for a long time government policy was problematic.[5] These participants cited at least two reasons for the negative role of the government. Firstly, they argued that Turkish government policy for a very long time was based on the premises that the "guest workers" would one day return. Ironically, just like many of their counterparts in Europe, they assumed that these "guest workers" were not immigrants and that they would not settle in their host countries permanently. Therefore, the education and socialization programs were very much based on the assumption that the children of the "guest workers" would one day actually return to Turkey. Hence, the concern was not so much their integration into host societies but their reintegration into Turkish society. Secondly, it was noted that the government personnel sent to cater for the needs of the immigrant communities were often ill-prepared. They rarely knew much about the countries they were sent to, not to mention lack of knowledge of the local language. They themselves suffered from difficulties in integrating into the societies where they would operate and were in no way equipped to assist the integration of immigrants and their children.

Both the Ministry of Education and the Directorate of Religious Affairs are much more conscious of these problems and have instituted, with the cooperation of a number of universities, training programs for their personnel. These programs are still of a very modest nature. However, the transformation of Turkey as a result of reforms adopted to meet the requirements for EU membership has had two important consequences in terms of addressing the integration problems of Turkish immigrants. Firstly, the Turkish state is becoming much more liberal. Hence, the tendency of the Turkish state to want to "control" Turkish immigrant communities is diminishing. This urge to "control" is gradually being replaced by a growing preparedness to cooperate in addressing common problems. This should open the possibility of closer cooperation with EU governments. Secondly, the reform process in Turkey and the EU's engagement of Turkey has helped Turkish civil society to blossom and acquire some clout. Today it is generally recognized that civil society plays a much more central role in Turkish politics and policy making compared to the past. In this civil society there are a number of non-governmental organizations that deal with problems in Turkish society resembling the ones that the Turkish immigrant communities suffer from.

"Honor killings," arranged marriages, domestic violence against women and especially the education of young girls are endemic problems in certain parts of Turkey. These problems overlap with those among Turkish immigrant communities in Europe. Non-governmental organizations such as Women for Women's Human Rights, Women's Center, Purple Roof Women's Shelter Foundation, Association for the Promotion of Contemporary Life, have been very active and very visible in addressing these problems. They also organized themselves into a "Women's Platform" and successfully lobbied the government to incorporate terms favorable to the protection of women's rights into legislation adopted as part of Turkey's reform process.[6] These organizations have also worked closely with a governmental body called Directorate General on the Status and Problems of Women. Hence, they are organizations with ample experience in lobbying, in coordinating campaigns and cooperating over field projects. This experience could be channeled to address the problems of Turkish immigrants in Europe. Cooperation between Turkish civil society and their counterparts in Europe as well as in Turkish immigrant communities could generate synergies with widespread consequences.

Unfortunately, the right attitude does not seem to be in place. The Hague Programme of the European Union adopted in November 2004 to assist the development of a "common" immigration problem does acknowledge that integration has to be a "two way process."[7] The European Commission's *Handbook on Integration* encourages member states to take more proactive measures toward ensuring greater inclusion of immigrants into the host society.[8] However, the idea that the sending country may have something to contribute to the better integration of their immigrants into their host societies has been completely ignored. At a time when Turkish state and civil society is changing and at a time when transnationalism remains a major challenge for host countries a better dialogue between Turkey and member states could help. Furthermore, considering that Turkey is supposed to become a member one day makes the need for this dialogue more urgent. Lastly, there is a growing recognition that European demographics will require some form of immigration. Involving Turkey in efforts to develop legal immigration into the EU could help to bring about the kind of immigration from Turkey that may help to change the stock of Turkish migrants in Europe and also facilitate the integration of the existing stock.

The EU, European governments and European civil society must make a greater effort to recognize the potential that a three way process approach to addressing integration problems offers. It seems a pity to see the EU playing such a critical role in Turkey's transformation and then fail to benefit from the fruits of this transformation in addressing its own problems. Adopting a three way process approach to addressing the integration problem of Turkish immigrants would have added advantages. It would contribute to the weakening of the perception and treatment in Europe of Turkey and Turks as the "other." The synergy that this approach would create would inject a lot of confidence into the Turkish immigrant community in overcoming its sense of alienation and isolation from the larger society. Similarly, it would also show that Turkey and Turks can actually be partners in addressing and solving European problems. This would make an enormous contribution to Turkey's image and membership prospects. It would also help to transform a divisive problem into one that helps to bring Turkey and the EU closer to each other.

Turkish Accession to the EU and Integration of Turkish Immigrants

Turkish accession to the EU is likely to have a positive effect on the integration of Turkish immigrants into their host societies. Turkish accession is going to be a process that will challenge established patterns of thinking about Turkey and Turks as the "other." Slowly and surely many among those in Europe that have regarded Turkey as culturally, socially and politically different will revise their perceptions, prejudices and images of Turkey and Turks. This in turn is likely to help to alleviate some of the alienation that Turkish immigrants experience. As the day-to-day discrimination is gradually replaced by a more balanced and less hostile environment the so-called "ghetto effect" on the immigrants will diminish. A Turkish immigrant observing this change and the gradual integration of Turkey itself into Europe will be more forthcoming in terms of integration. The two processes are likely to feed on each other and transform gradually the current vicious circle of mutual alienation to a virtuous circle of mutual integration. Even if these processes may not be all-encompassing, a good portion of the host society and the immigrant community would be absorbed in it.

In a similar vein, the EU anchor will enable higher growth and lower unemployment in Turkey, drastically reducing the number of potential immigrants. Under such a scenario immigration from Turkey, its magnitude and composition, will be more demand driven. Furthermore, a smooth accession period will enable policy coordination for enhancing integration, especially in the "three way process" sense. On top of these, a successful accession and a prosperous Turkey will improve the status of the Turkish immigrants in the host societies, as the Italians, Greeks, Portuguese and Spaniards have experienced. Education and language skills of the migrants are certainly crucial for their integration. However, discrimination often prevails if their country of origin is despised in the host communities. Lastly, parallel to the increase in foreign direct investment to Turkey from the EU, outward investment from Turkey to the EU is expanding. There is a new class of permanent and temporary immigration associated with these flows. A wealthier and more dynamic Turkey in the EU opens other avenues for better integration of the Turkish immigrants as well. An increase in cross-border investments and the single market will provide job opportunities for Turkish immigrants whose language and local skills will be a major advantage.

One final point concerns an almost inevitable improvement in the status of immigrants in the EU because of demographic trends. The most important single impediment to economic integration of the immigrants in the host countries is high rates of unemployment. Indeed, unemployment among the immigrants exceeds 40 percent in some communities, largely due to the impact of the general labor market conditions in the host countries. The overall unemployment rate has been near 10 percent for a generation in major EU countries. Among the youth, this rate has been double the overall average. However, the labor force in the EU is shrinking and the pension funds in most countries would go bankrupt if the current trends are projected. The good news is that the EU countries will have to revitalize their economies by reforming their labor markets. This will not only reduce unemployment rates but will also call for more liberal immigration policies. As a consequence, discriminatory practices in the labor market will decline. Also, the immigrants who will for a while be shouldering a more than fair share of the national pension bills will be treated with greater understanding by their host communities.

Notes

1. Cem Özdemir, a current member of the European Parliament, recounted his personal experience with persons who questioned his "German" citizenship and identity to the participants at the workshop on "Integration of Turkish Immigrants in Austria, Germany and the Netherlands," Boğaziçi University, Istanbul, February 27–28, 2004. He noted that he is frequently characterized as a "Turk with a German passport," which he believes questions his "Germanness."

2. The Prime Minister's remarks were reported in *Radikal*, November 8 and 9, 2005.

3. Speech delivered by Mehmet Aydın on December 9, 2005 at the *International Migration Symposium*, December 8–11, 2005, Istanbul.

4. *Yurtdışında Yaşayan Vatandaşlarımızın Sorunlarının Araştırılarak Alınması Gereken Önlemlerin Belirlenmesi Amacıyla Kurulan Meclis Araştırma Komisyonu Raporu* (Report prepared by the Parliamentary Commission set up to study the problems of Turkish nationals living abroad and to determine the measures to be adopted), Turkish Grand National Assembly, Legislative Session: 22, Legislative Year: 2, December 17, 2003.

5. These conferences were "Integration of Immigrants from Turkey in Austria, Germany and the Netherlands," Boğaziçi University, Istanbul, February 27–28, 2004; "Integration of Immigrants from Turkey in Belgium, Denmark, France and Sweden," Boğaziçi University, Istanbul, March 26–27, 2004; "Immigration Issues in EU–Turkish Relations: Determinants of Immigration and Integration," Boğaziçi University, Istanbul, October 8–9, 2004. The programs and some of the papers presented at these conferences can be found at http://www.ces.boun.edu.tr.

6. For the activism of these organizations and their place in Turkish politics see Yeşim Arat, "Contestation and Collaboration: Women's Struggles for Empowerment in Turkey," in Resat Kasaba (ed.), *Cambridge History of Turkey* (Cambridge: Cambridge University Press: forthcoming).

7. See *European Council Presidency Conclusions*, Hague Programme, November 4–5, 2004 and Communication from the Commission, *The Hague Programme: Ten Priorities for the Next Five Years*, COM (2005) 184 Final, 10.5.2005.

8. *Handbook on Integration for Policy Makers and Practitioners* (Brussels: European Commission, Directorate General for Justice, Freedom and Security, November 2004).

Index

For Product Safety Concerns and Information please contact our EU
representative GPSR@taylorandfrancis.com
Taylor & Francis Verlag GmbH, Kaufingerstraße 24, 80331 München, Germany